WESTBURY-ON-TRYM TO AVONMOUTH

THROUGH TIME

Anthony Beeson

AMBERLEY PUBLISHING

Acknowledgements

Thanks must go to Dawn Dyer, Jane Bradley and my ex-colleagues at Bristol Reference Library, Rosemary Scott, Jacqueline Claridge, Keith Powell, Mia Hale and Eric White, Tim Wallis, Jenny Birnie, Keith Yeandel, Bill Blackmore Andrew Townsend, Mr and Mrs Trayhurn, Revd Christopher Penn, Antony and Ruth Keyworth Berridge, Bristol Museum and Andrew Brozyna for the photograph on page 72 from his book *Longshore Soldiers*.

Christopher Mark Beeson and Sarah Elizabeth Beeson
With love from Uncle Anthony

First published 2013

Amberley Publishing
The Hill, Stroud, Gloucestershire, GL5 4EP
www.amberley-books.com

Copyright © Anthony Beeson, 2013

The right of Anthony Beeson to be identified as the
Author of this work has been asserted in accordance with
the Copyrights, Designs and Patents Act 1988.

ISBN 978 1 4456 1536 3 (print)
ISBN 978 1 4456 1559 2 (ebook)

British Library Cataloguing in Publication Data.
A catalogue record for this book is available from the
British Library.

Typesetting by Amberley Publishing.
Printed in Great Britain.

Introduction

Westbury-on-Trym (sometimes Westbury-super-Trym) was already old when its upstart neighbour Bristol was founded in the tenth century. Once in the territory of the Hwicce and, subsequently, the kingdom of Mercia, Saxon Uuestburg or Westbyrig is said to have gained its first church by 757. By the ninth century, this was described as 'Westmynster', or an establishment served by a commune of clergy, and probably stood near the later college site. Originally the property of the family of Eanwulf, in 824 the church passed to Worcester Cathedral by bequest of Æthelric. By 1194 it was a collegiate church and was rebuilt on the hill. Westbury College rose on the site of earlier buildings in the 1450s. Attempts to raise Westbury church to cathedral status in the thirteenth and fifteenth centuries ultimately failed and, with the Dissolution, Bristol's former abbey of St Augustine gained the bishop's throne. Westbury played only a minor role in the Nation's history but was unfortunate enough to have suffered the partial destruction of its college during the Civil War. By the eighteenth century its rustic charms and proximity to Bristol saw an influx of wealthy merchants and the building of country seats within its boundaries. Indeed, by the 1830s, the prosperity of the parish would lead house advertisements to entice with 'being in Westbury the poor rates are remarkably low'.

North-west Bristol has provided the greatest evidence for early settlement in the city, ranging from its oldest architectural monument, the cromlech at Stoke Bishop, to the Bronze Age hoard from Coombe Dingle and the large concentration of Roman antiquities from Sea Mills and the Lawrence Weston areas.

The medieval parish of Westbury-on-Trym encompassed fourteen modern parishes. Neighbouring Henbury (anciently Heanburu) had a Roman settlement and was even older than Westbury. Henbury parish itself was vast, stretching from Aust to Sea Mills. Possibly from 699 it was gifted to the Bishops of Worcester, who had an episcopal manor house there that survived until the sixteenth century. Henbury's history is intertwined with that of Westbury. Its subsequent development into the 'opulent parish' of the Georgian era eclipsed even that of its neighbour in the splendour of the establishments. Both Henbury and Westbury parishes were divided for secular purposes into tithings; some had chapels. Weston St Laurence (Lawrence Weston) had one by 1274 dedicated to St Laurence, and King's Weston by 1345 dedicated to St Thomas. More existed at Shirehampton and on Blaise Castle Hill. Tithe maps show a complicated intermingling of parish land ownership. Land at Coombe Dingle was divided between Westbury and Henbury. The Celtic 'Coombe' (Combe) and Middle English 'Dingle' both mean 'wooded valley'. The similarity with *The Pickwick Papers*' Dingley Dell, which was written soon after Dicken's brief visit to Bristol, is striking. His fictitious Kentish name Dingley Dell also means wooded valley (twice!). Might not Dickens have heard of Coombe Dingle while here and found it the perfect bosky inspiration for his hospitable creation's name?

Shirehampton was originally a detached tithing of Westbury and had a chapel before 1510. Its original prosperity no doubt originated from its proximity to the mooring stations Hungroad and Kingroad, where ships with cargoes bound for Bristol or departing would temporarily moor to wait for suitable tides and winds. The eighteenth century was the greatest period of prosperity for Shirehampton. Its proximity to the Southwell's seat, King's Weston, then one of England's most popular tourist sights, together with the beauty of the neighbourhood made it a highly desirable place to reside. Shirehampton's future would be largely determined by the owners of the house.

Squire Philip William Skinner Miles had envisaged Avonmouth as a pleasure resort, but its potential as a dock development to avoid the inconvenience of the river approach to Bristol soon outweighed this. New York is said to be the inspiration for Avonmouth's gridded street plan. Philip Napier Miles oversaw its development with care, employing Frederick Bligh Bond as architect. If tidied, preserved and promoted, Avonmouth village's buildings might yet be a lifeline to its economy through tourism. Is it too fanciful to imagine Avonmouth as Bristol's arts and crafts village?

The British love of the countryside and the wish to live amongst it has been a curse to many lauded landscapes, and though north-west Bristol remains beautiful, an inhabitant of 1913 would no doubt be horrified to see the results of a century of private and council enterprise. Notwithstanding the presence of conservation areas, infilling still continues apace by those more intent on making a profit and moving on than having concern for the damage done to the area. Wartime requisition of large properties between 1939 and 1945 often allowed them to be bought up cheaply by the Corporation later when the family link had been broken. This, together with Bristol's ruthless serving of compulsory purchase orders after 1946, destroyed the area's former social structure. Certainly the post-war need for housing was great, but developing new estates in the country rather than rebuilding within the city resulted in many problems ranging from traffic congestion to isolation.

This volume is a textual peregrination around Westbury and its surrounding villages, stopping to point out interesting features and facts, many of which have not previously been published. There are five walks commencing from Westbury Road, Canford Park, The Dingle, Henbury Hill and King's Weston Road. The areas covered include Westbury village, Canford and Coombe Lanes, Coombe Dingle and Bowden's Fields, Henbury and Blaise, King's Weston, Lawrence Weston, Shirehampton and Avonmouth. Historically, area boundaries within Westbury parish have been fluid, and thus the author has partially included Coombe Lane in Coombe Dingle as its early inhabitants once firmly believed it to be. A forthcoming volume will include Sea Mills, Stoke Bishop, Sneyd Park and Henleaze.

The illustrations have been chosen for their rarity and come from the author's own collection, those of the Bristol Reference Library and from private albums. The latter include those of the Sargent family of Ashburnham and provide a wonderful record of the area between 1909 and 1931.

Walk 1

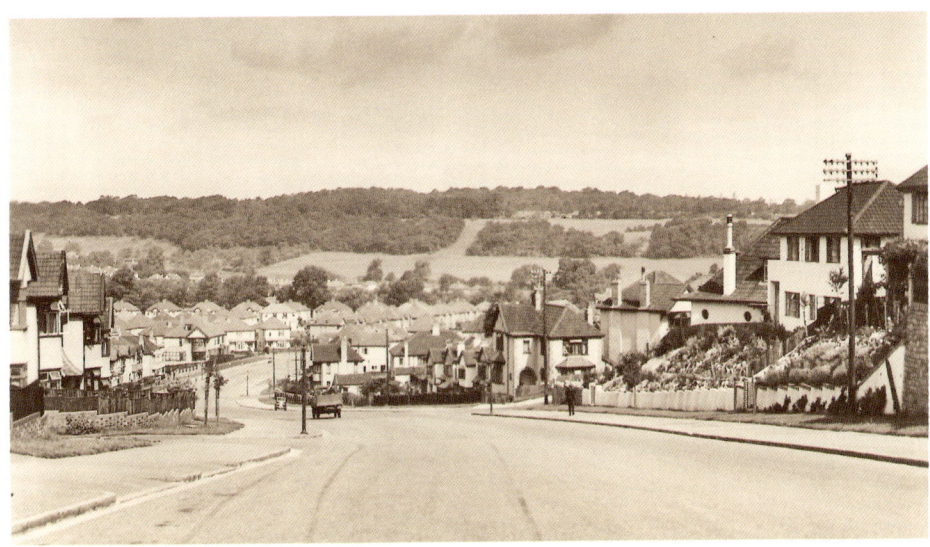

Falcondale Road, Highway to the North

A 1930s view, taken from the junction with Westbury Road, looking down Bristol's grand interwar suburban bypass for Westbury after housing developers had been at work. The road and houses were built on the grounds of the demolished mansion, Cotebank. Many of the houses on the right of the photograph now bear little comparison with their original appearance. In the valley, the line of new houses in Canford Lane stretches away to the left where, below the woods crowning Coombe Hill, the spaced trees of Cherry Orchard appear above them. To their right, the links of Henbury Golf Course appear and cover the rest of the hillside. Falcondale was the name of the house near Lampeter that passed to John Scandrett Harford of Blaise Castle in 1819 and remained in the family until 1951. The road first appears in the directories in 1932, when there were nine houses listed.

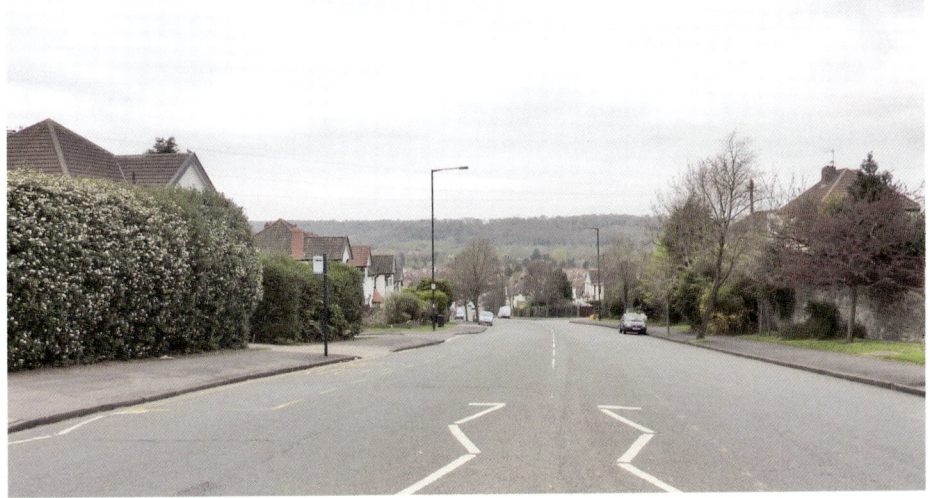

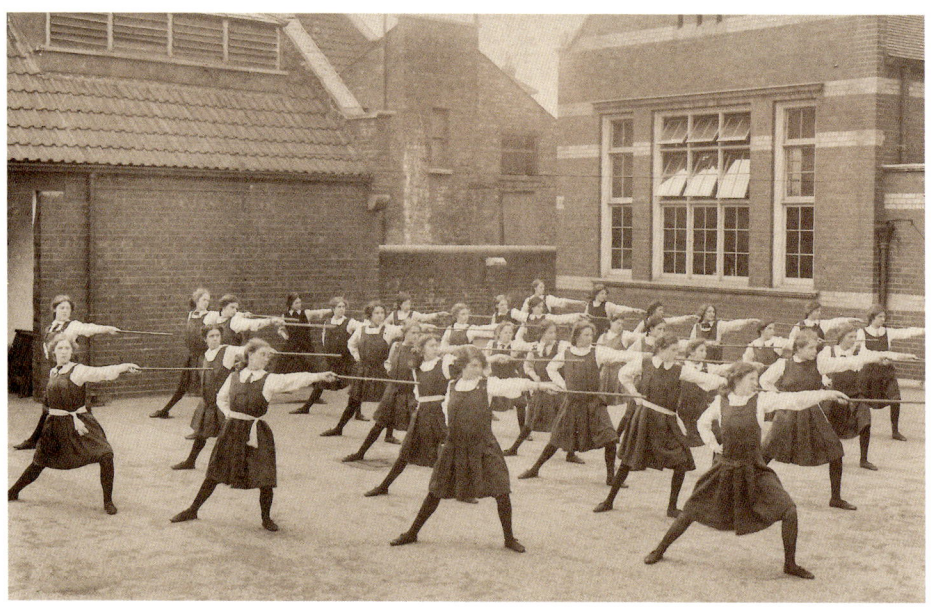

Red Maids En Garde!

As the Empire moved towards war in 1913, pupils of Westbury's Red Maids School practised fencing moves. The gymslip was then *de rigueur* for female athletics, offering modesty and yet freedom of movement. In 1911 the school had moved from Denmark Street to take over the early nineteenth-century Burfield House, previously the residence of Sir Robert Symes. Burfield's grounds adjoined those of The Priory and its lodges still survive on Westbury Road. Additional buildings were added by F. W. Wills & Sons. The school's tenure was short lived, as in 1916 the building became a Red Cross hospital and the girls were transferred to Manor Place, Clifton, not returning until 1920. New classrooms, again by Wills, arose in front of Burfield in the early 1930s, and additional structures have arisen since then. The school remains a vibrant Westbury institution. The 1930s postcard shows the new classroom block with Burfield beyond.

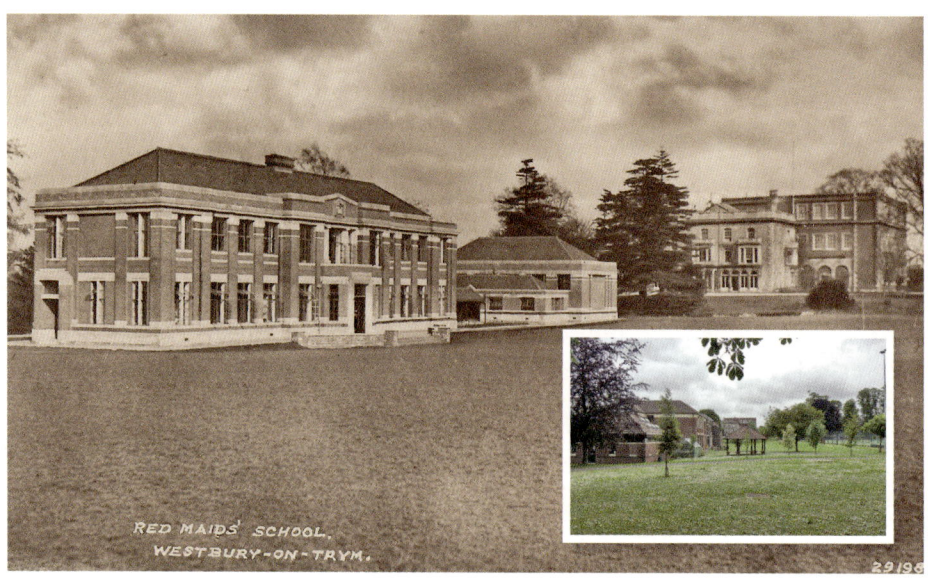

RED MAIDS' SCHOOL.
WESTBURY-ON-TRYM.

29195

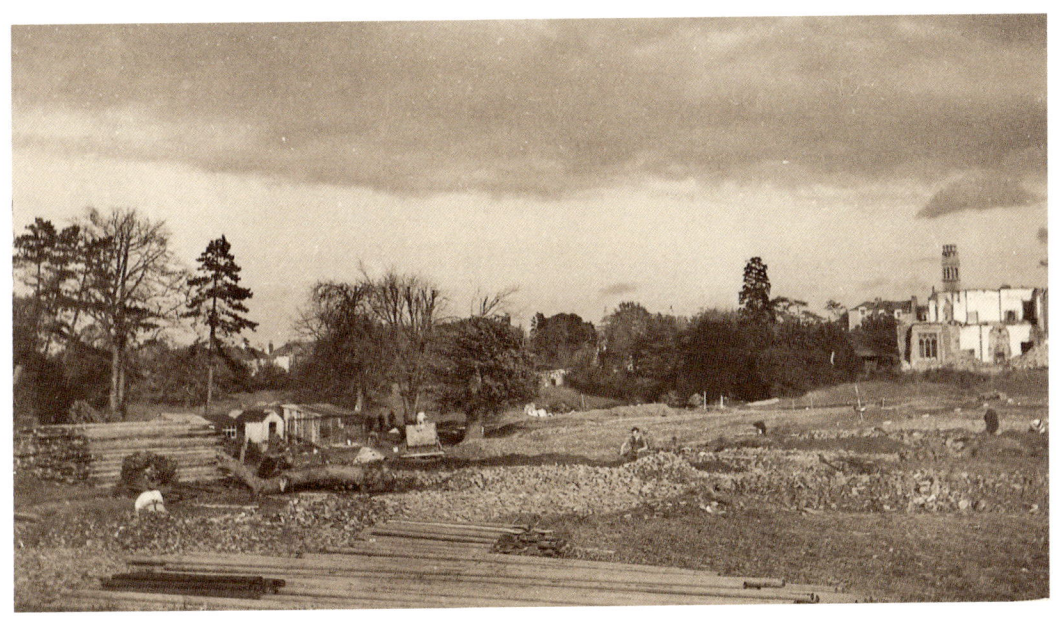

The Last Days of The Priory

One of the great houses of Westbury was The Priory (sometimes Burfield Priory). This was a remarkable 1830s Gothic Revival building that in distant silhouette rather resembled a pyramid with its chimneys and observation tower. Natural polychromy was achieved on the façade by the use of different stones. An L-shaped house, with a square block and attached service wing had, by 1880, sprouted a spectacular apsidal conservatory. Its grounds stretched from neighbouring Burfield House (now the Red Maids School) and were bounded by East Hill, Eastfield and Eastfield Road. The garden parties enjoyed in the 1920s have now become legendary but, following the death of its last owner, William Henry Butler, the estate was sold at auction in 1938 and the buildings demolished apart from the Westbury Road lodge. Priory Avenue was built before the war and Priory Court Road after it. The photographs chronicle the demolition.

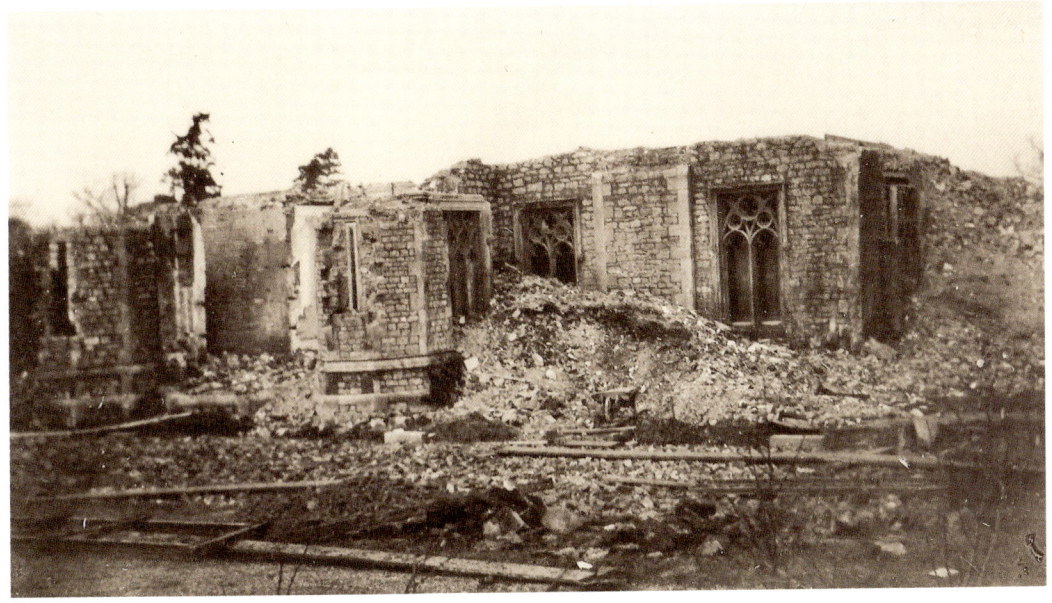

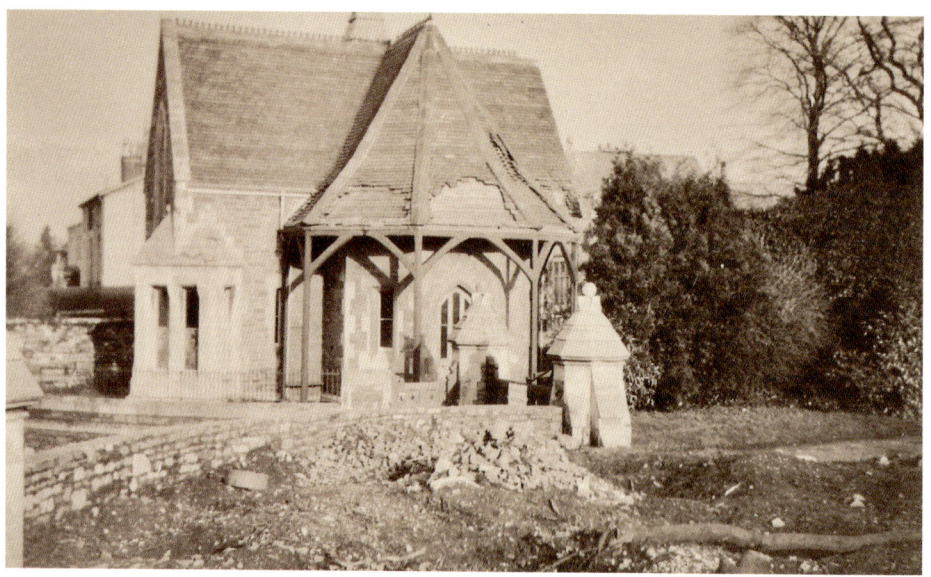

The Entrance to The Priory

The earliest lodge to The Priory still survives on Westbury Road, but by the 1880s the main entrance to the house was via a suitably impressive Gothic building in Eastfield Road, on the site now occupied by numbers 15 to 17. Some time before this date, a new drive had been laid across a newly acquired extension to the grounds close to the boys' school in Eastfield Road. Photographs taken in 1938 show the main drive curving up towards the house, thickly bordered by large clipped rhododendron bushes and mature specimen trees such as araucaria. South of the house, where Grange Close now stands, was the Priory Paddock where horses grazed. The main lodge gate displays a board advertising Stone Hill Builders, who were presumably both demolishing The Priory and building the new estate.

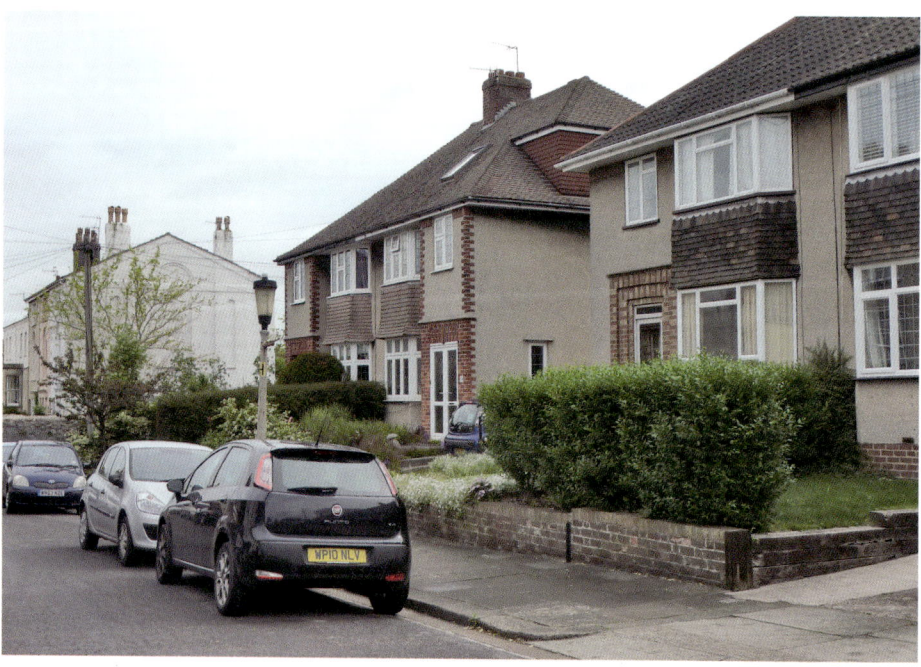

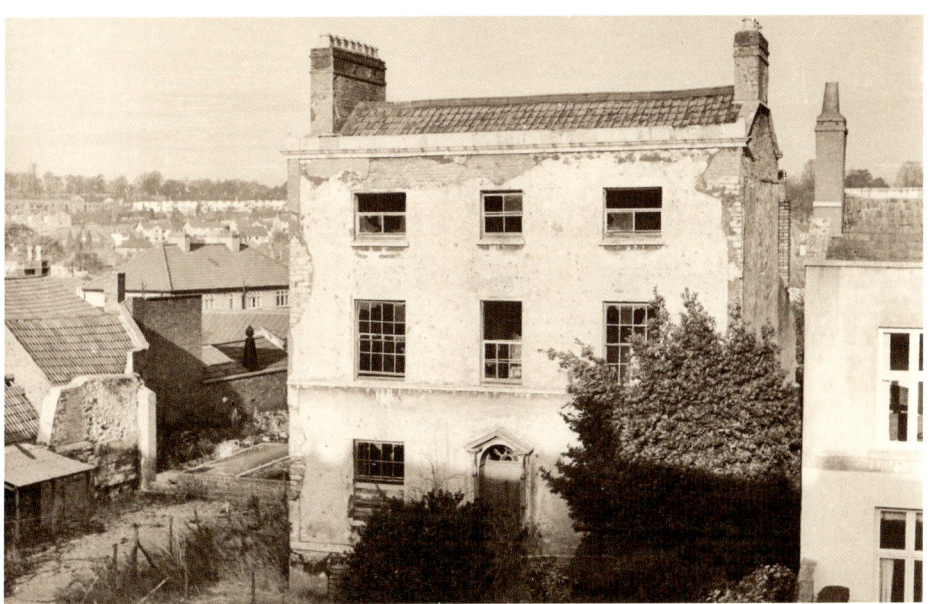

The Lost Houses of Westbury Hill

Bedford House, a once fine Georgian residence, awaits its inglorious fate of replacement by car park in this 1959 photograph by Jim Hale. This house and Melrose House – its then still inhabited neighbour – stood on the lower slopes of Westbury Hill until their demolition in the 1960s. The Ferns, an adjoining and similar residence to Bedford House, was demolished in the 1940s. Fairfield House, a more architecturally countrified residence, still survives lower down the hill, although shorn of its original architectural details and given modern tacked-on bay windows. In its 'restoration' it appears to have inherited a simplified idea of Bedford House's pedimented over-door and fanlight, although unfortunately not the original ones. Before the 1890s, Bedford House and its neighbouring residences faced the extensive gardens of the reputedly haunted Cambridge House, until that mansion was likewise demolished and replaced by shops and the crescent that now bears its name.

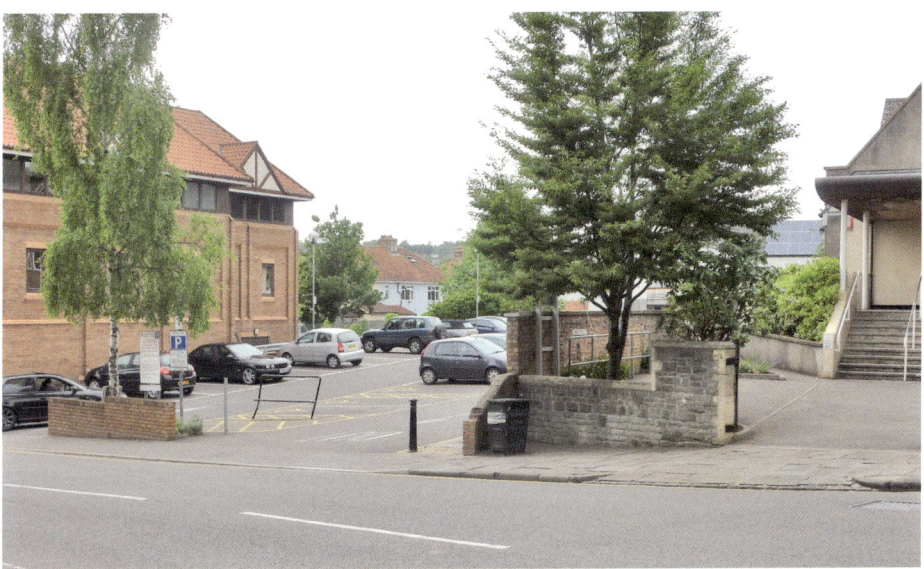

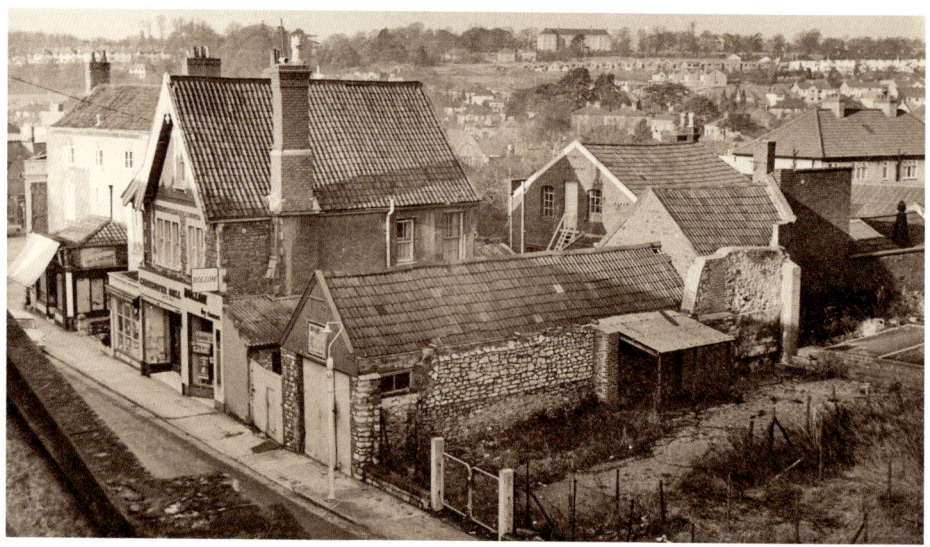

The Lost Shops of Westbury Hill

Here we have another photograph by Jim Hale from 1959, showing the varied collection of shops and outbuildings that were then at the bottom of Westbury Hill. On the right, the devastated site of The Ferns is juxtaposed against some old stables and yards called The Shades, once owned by a fly proprietor who ran a fleet of horse cabs. Mogford's, the village ironmonger's, later used it for storage. Edwardian photographs show both The Ferns and The Shades neatly smothered in Virginia creeper. The attractive gabled Victorian building at numbers 60–62 housed Bollom's the dry cleaner and Christopher Bell the baker. Originally this had been Clake's Westbury Bakery, where ladies took tea amongst the palms. Beyond this in 1959 at numbers 64–68 were the fruiterers, Fruitshop & Co., Trymvision Ltd and the Westbury Stores, which was attached to the façade of Fairfield House and whose sunblind may be seen. All were demolished in 1985 for a new building.

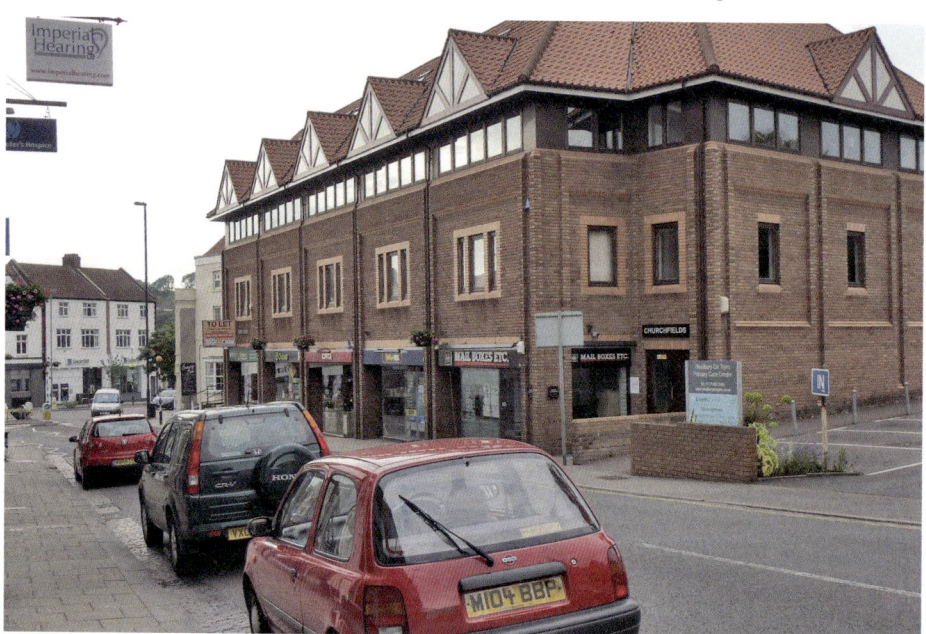

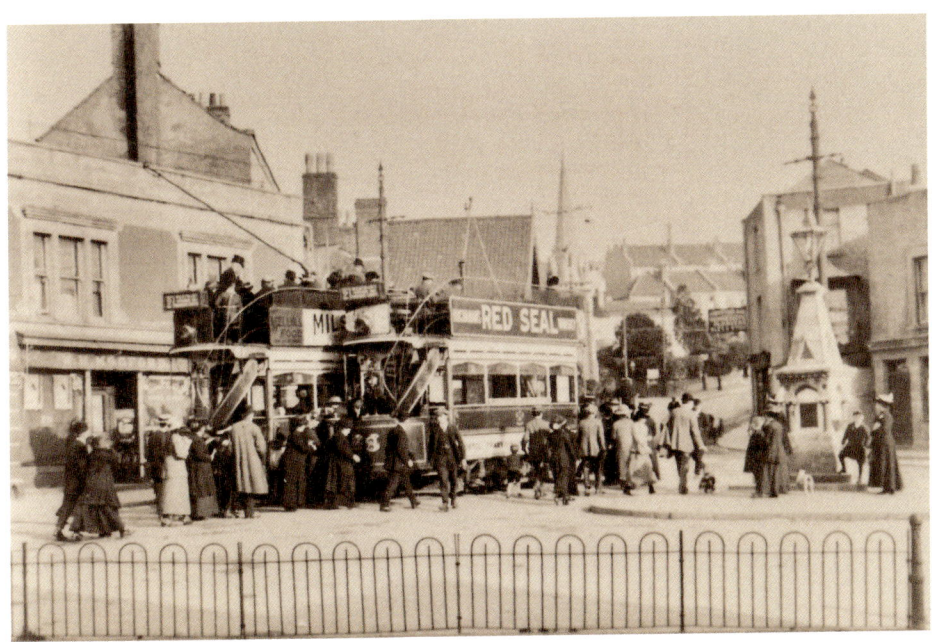

At the Terminus

A bustling scene in Westbury around 1913 as passengers alight and board Bristol trams. The extension of the tram service to Westbury had opened on 23 October 1908, and provided city dwellers with an easy, inexpensive excursion into the countryside. A motorbus service to New Passage later connected with the trams and provided a further link for travellers. Private horse buses also gave a very limited service to the city. The lamp-topped Diamond Jubilee fountain would be moved to Canford Park to make way for the war memorial that was unveiled on 11 July 1920. Behind it is the Foresters' Arms Inn with its fine, canopied side window. The new railings in the foreground surround The Batch, the last remaining scrap of the village green. In earlier times, it was a place where agricultural labourers loitered in hope of employment or tips for minding the mounts of the Foresters' clientele.

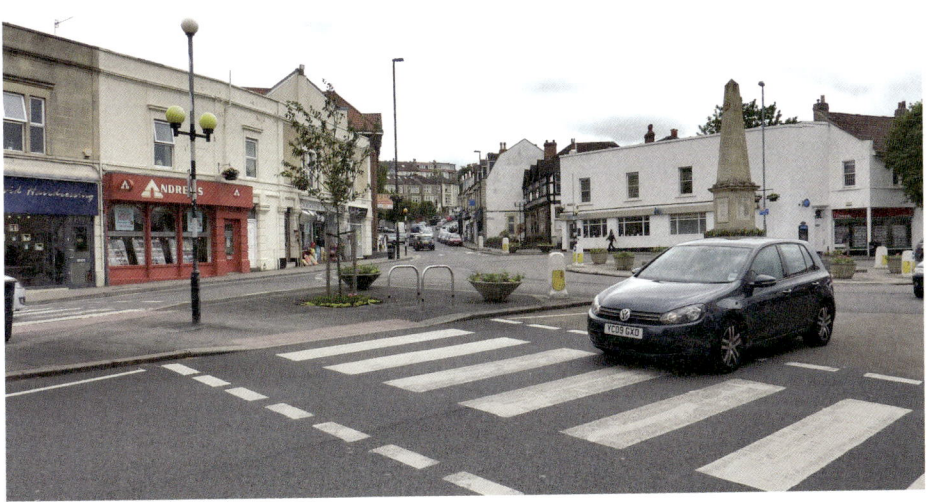

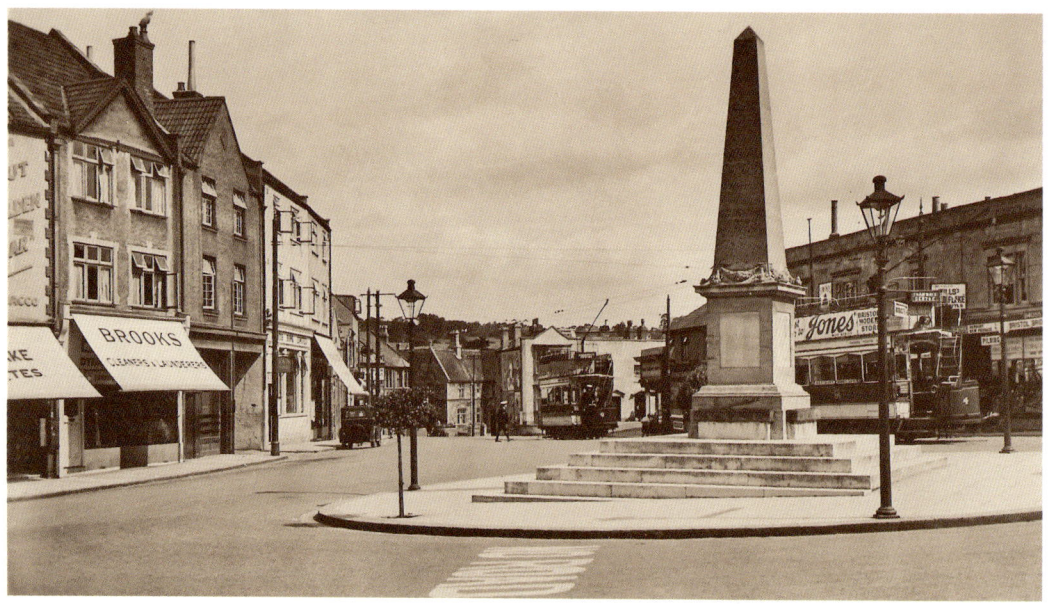

High Noon, Westbury Style

Mid-morning on a hot summer's day in the 1930s, windows are wide open and, crossing the road, the booted driver of the number 2 tram wears a white summer top to his cap, and has his jacket unbuttoned, hinting at the heat. Small bay trees corner the island holding the 1920 war memorial. A large and now-demolished house ends the terrace of Church Road cottages, later replaced by the bland offices of Westbury Court. Otherwise the scene bears comparison with the present day, beyond the absence of road traffic, people and street furniture. The curve of shops on the left-hand side replaced the elms and wall of Westbury Court Farm, and The Batch, which once stretched in front of it, is now gone forever. The lower photograph shows these and the Jubilee Fountain around 1906. Bristol's tram service lasted until 1941 when a bomb severed its power supply.

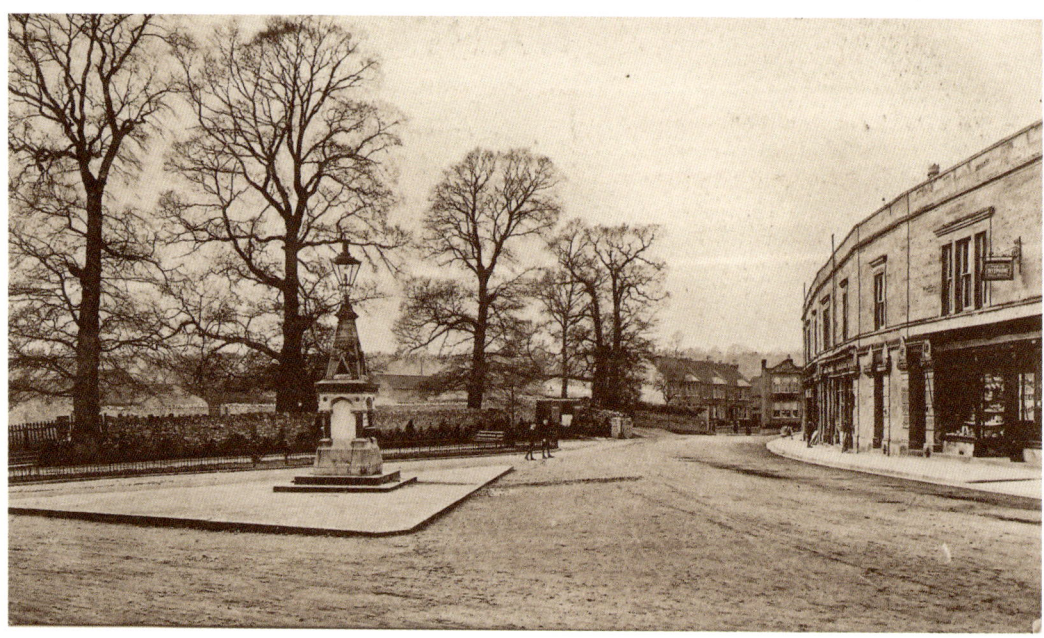

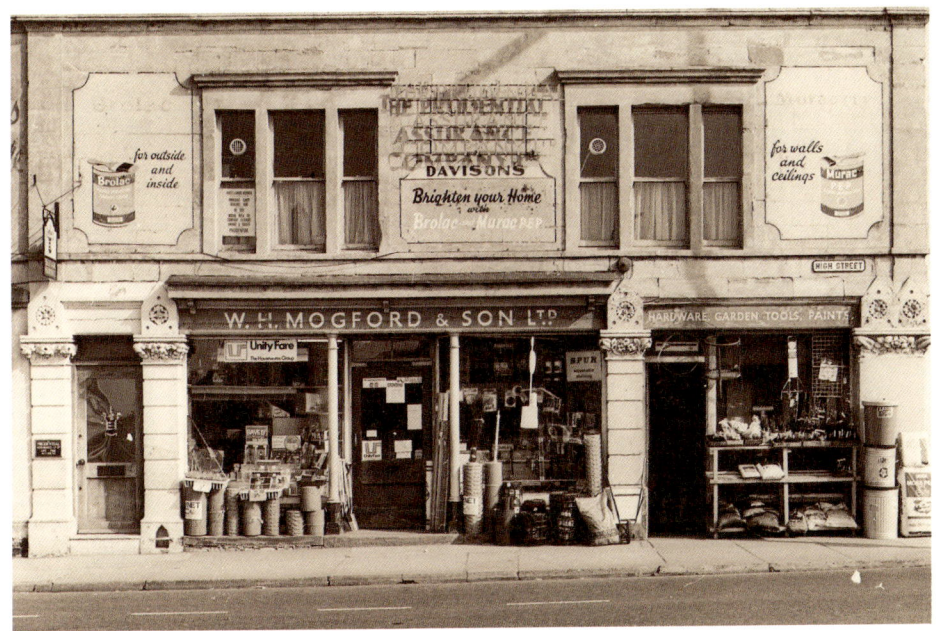

A Westbury Institution

Mogford's ironmonger's in the centre of Westbury village, as photographed by Jim Hale around 1960, was founded by William Henry Mogford in the 1850s in smart new premises on the High Street. First described as a 'plumber, glazier', William gradually developed the firm into a builder and decorator's as well. Mrs Mogford started the ironmongery side of the business, which prospered and was inherited by Ernest Henry Mogford, his daughter Renee, and subsequently her son, John. The smaller section on the right of the building was originally a yard entrance. Westbury's first telephone exchange was housed in the shop. In 1953 the building and decorating side of the business separated from the ironmongery section. The shop retains the family name, although they sold the business in 2004 to Paul Gillam, a long-term employee. It has become one of Westbury's best-loved institutions, with an amazing stock and unfailingly good service.

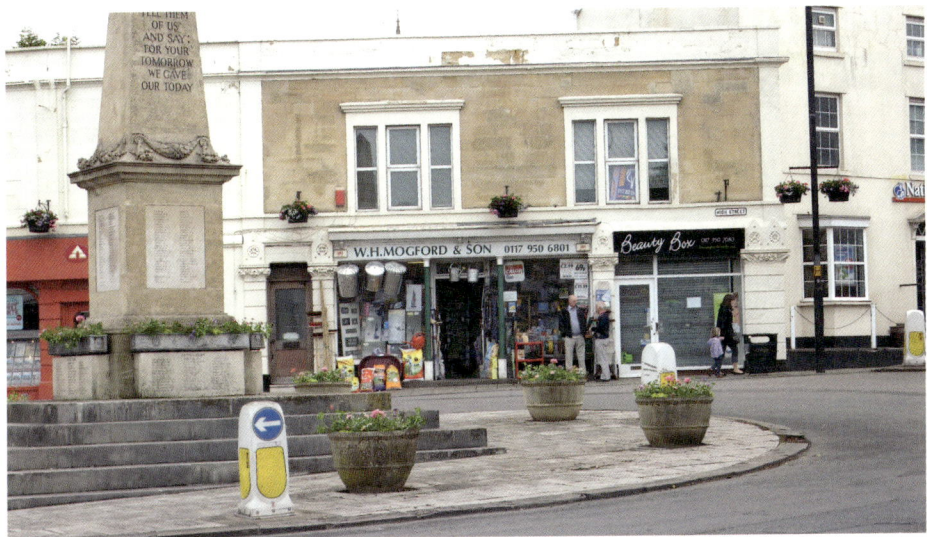

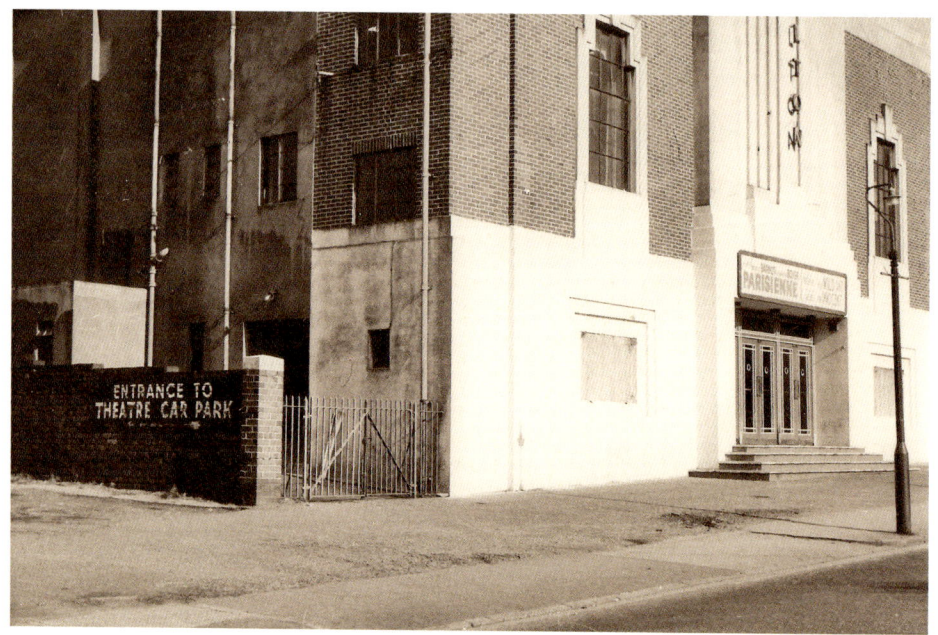

The Last Picture Show at the Carlton

In the early 1960s, the Carlton cinema in Canford Lane awaits demolition and replacement by Carlton Court, the shopping precinct that now enshrines its name. Its façade bears a poster advertising a double bill of Brigitte Bardot's *Parisienne* (1958) and Audie Murphy's *The Wild and the Innocent* (1959). Scars show where the glass cases holding film stills once filled the recesses either side of the entrance. Designed by the prolific Bristol cinema architect W. H. Watkins, it seated 820 and originally included a café amongst its attractions. Its Art Deco façade in brick and stone was both restrained and elegant in conception. It served a wide area of north Bristol, but failed and closed in 1959 at the height of the downturn in cinema attendance. The lane leading to the cinema car park still survives between the precinct and the 1920s parade of shops.

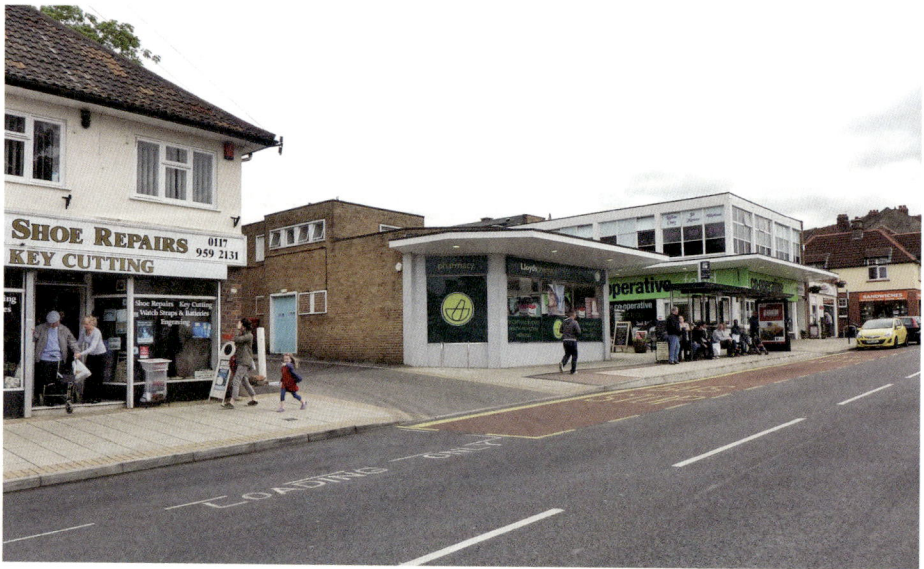

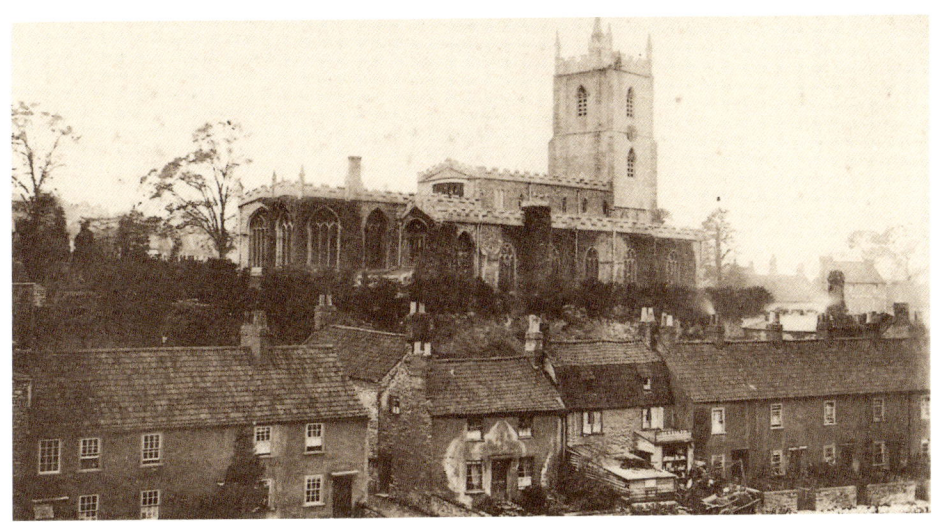

Cathedral of the Trym

Westbury's *monasterium* church was transferred to Worcester Cathedral in 824. Between 962 and 974 it became a Benedictine foundation, re-established in 1093. In 1194 it was established as a collegiate church, but an attempt in 1286 to turn it into a second cathedral for Worcester diocese failed. Under Bishop Carpenter (1444–76) the church entered its golden age and was extended, beautified and raised to cathedral status, if only during his tenure. It still sits magnificently above the surrounding properties. Carpenter also raised fine new collegiate buildings bordering the Trym. Above, the church's south porch is a parvise that for many years was the church museum. Still remaining is a wonderful collection of sculptural and architectural fragments from the pre-Reformation church. The room once connected to a mortuary chapel on the west side that was demolished in 1850. Superb murals discovered in 1852, and subsequently whitewashed, await rediscovery in the crypt.

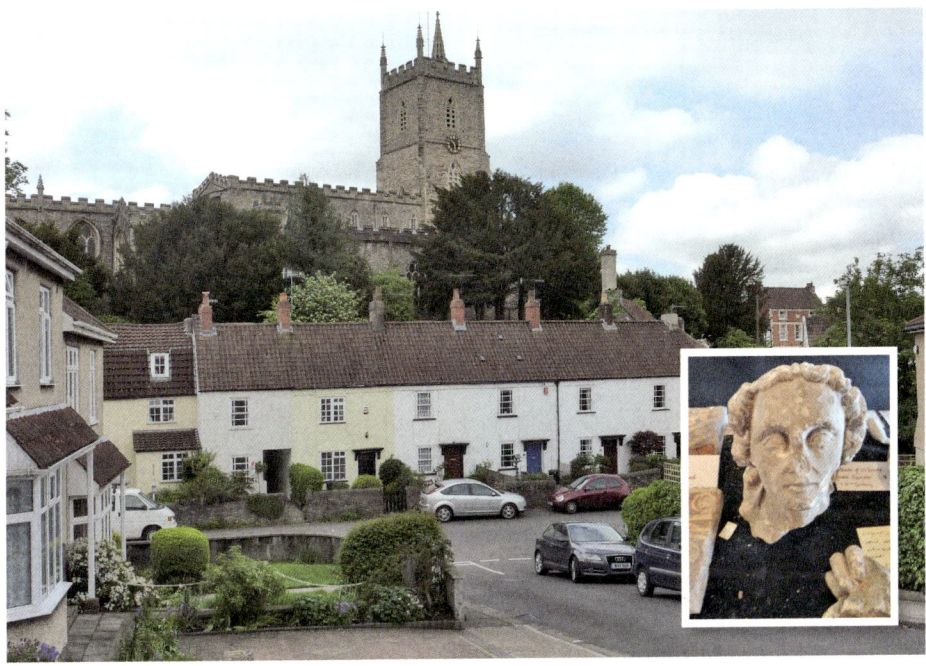

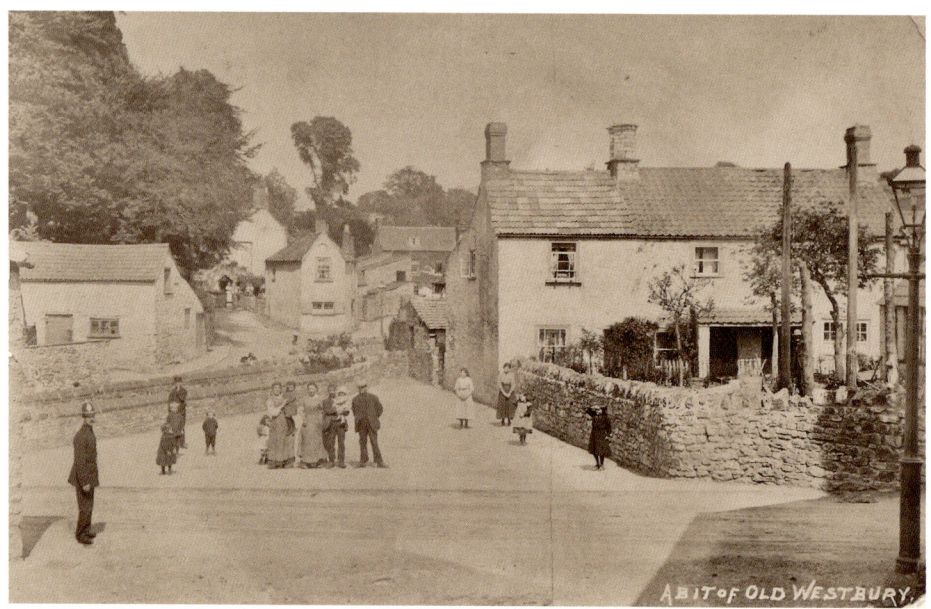

'A Bit of Old Westbury'

A view from around 1910, looking across the bottom of Chock Lane to the triangular space that has now become Bristol's most intimate public park. 'Westburians' gather for posterity; meanwhile, a policeman nervously tries to maintain calm. The parallel walls marked the course of the Trym and kept flooding in check, as waters can rise several feet within minutes following a torrential rainstorm. The river is culverted under the gardens of the houses in Trym Lane from this point until reaching Church Road and has been, to a lesser extent, since before 1845. Local romance spins a story akin to that of Dickens' Miss Havisham for the existence of the clock face on the front of the wedge-shaped Dial House that sits at the confluence of Channell's Hill and Trym Road. A more prosaic explanation may be that, as a former toll house, a clock was deemed a necessary accessory to such structures.

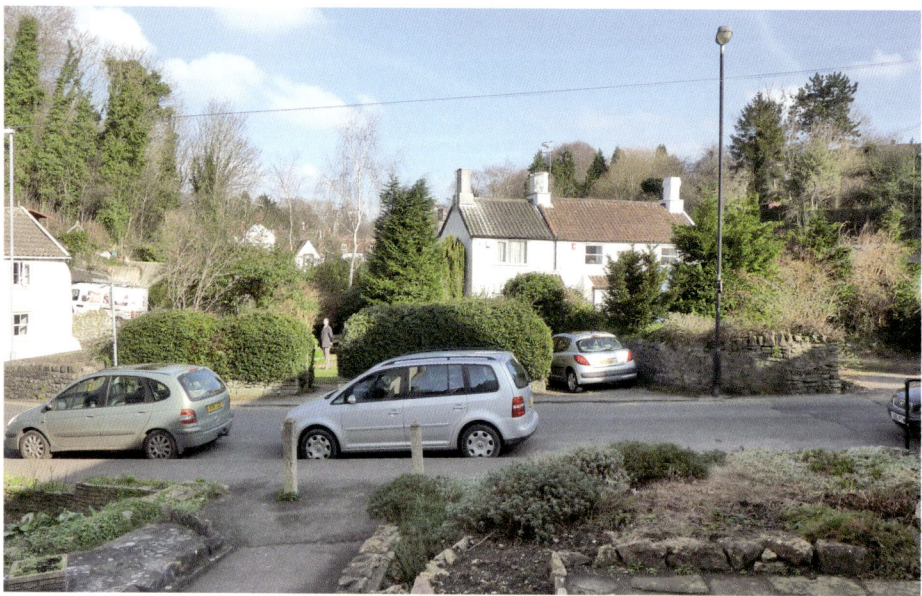

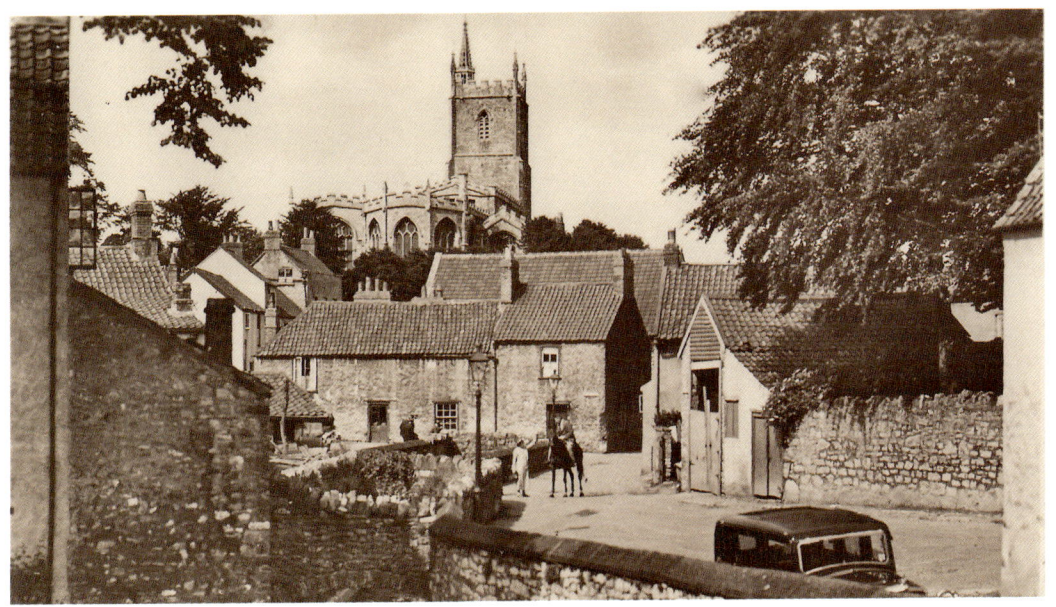

A Morning Chat in Trym Road

An idyll of old England – the village as seen from Trymwood Bridge around 1935. The church sails cathedral-like above the cottages clasping its hill, while the Trym flows beneath its picturesque bridges in the left foreground. A small community park now ornaments the triangular space to its left that was then a work yard. A horseman, possibly identified as Eric Greenslade, Lord Leverhulme's nephew, and a frequent and popular equestrian sight in Westbury, chats to a villager. Beyond them, the two cottages at the bottom of Chock Lane were regrettably replaced in the 1960s by flats. Originally called Chalk Lane, on account of the white pollution of its lime kilns between 1880 and 1900, it was strangely corrupted to the present name. The long roof of the Methodist chapel appears beyond, while a car is parked outside of Dial House. The Malt House, then a shop, is to the right of the rider.

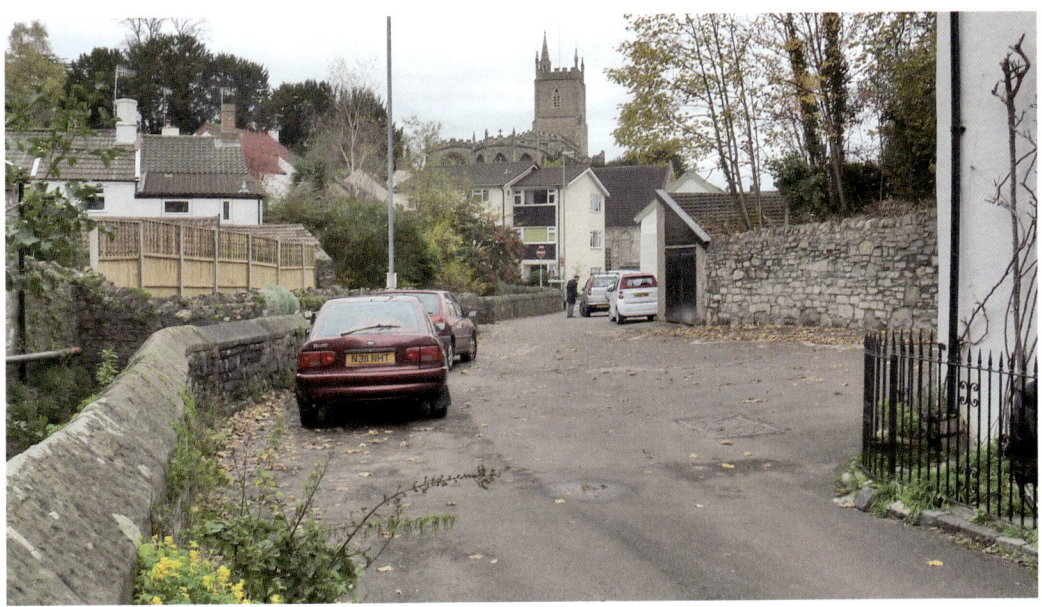

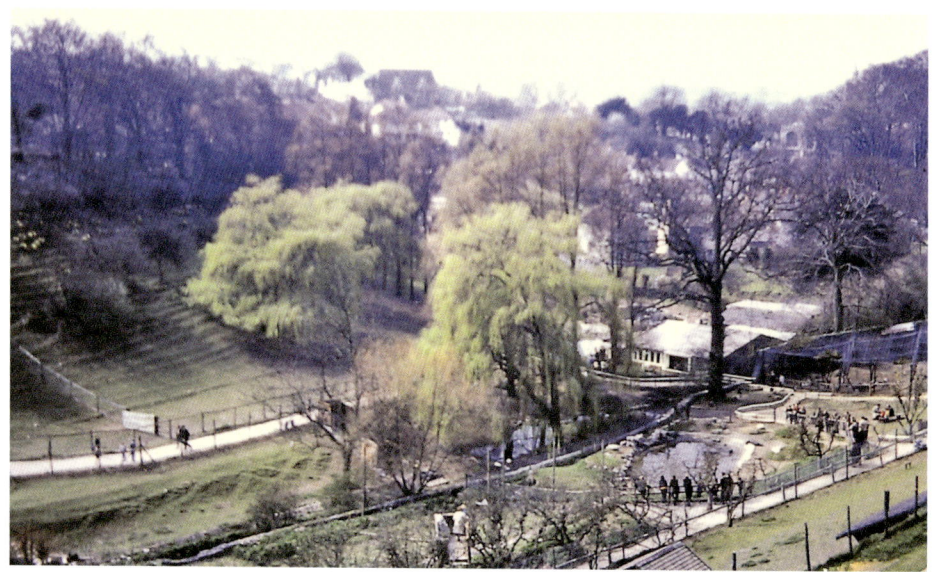

Wild Life, Westbury Style

Westbury Wildlife Park was for many years an unusual attraction of the village. It covered the slopes of the Trym valley beyond Trymwood on 10 acres of land belonging to the Holmwood estate, which included Badock's Wood and the Kitchen Garden. It was acquired in 1964 by the park's creator, David Chaffe, whose self-financed vision was to create a conservation and education centre for British wildlife, where children could view native species. The area, much despoiled by vandalism, was landscaped and the river cleared. In 1967 Sir Peter Scott officially opened the park. The view is taken from the observation tower, formerly a garden building of Holmwood, and saved by Chaffe from council demolition. It appears below in 2013. Alas, the park was beset by disastrous floods, vandalism and attacks on the animals. Vehicular access and parking also proved problematic and, after two decades, it finally closed to the public in 1987.

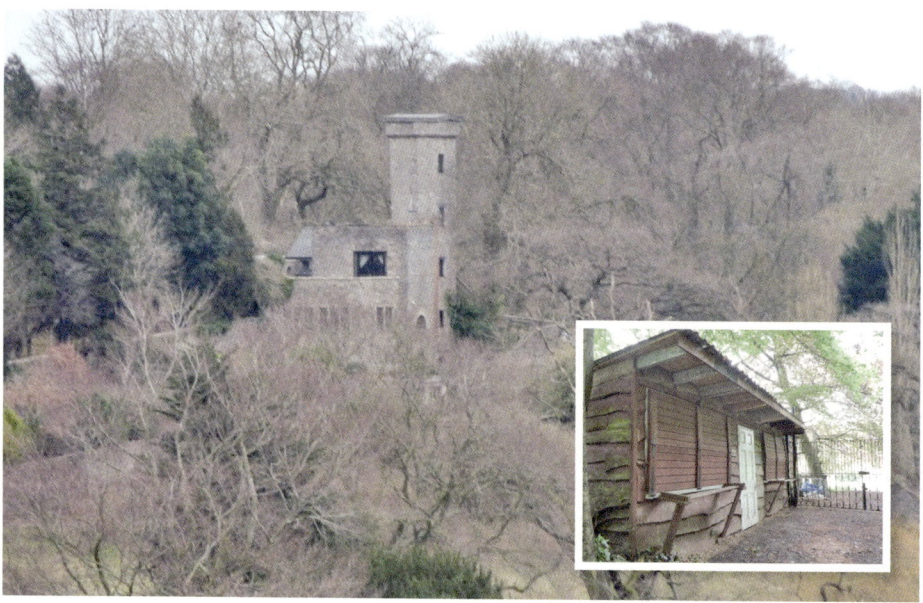

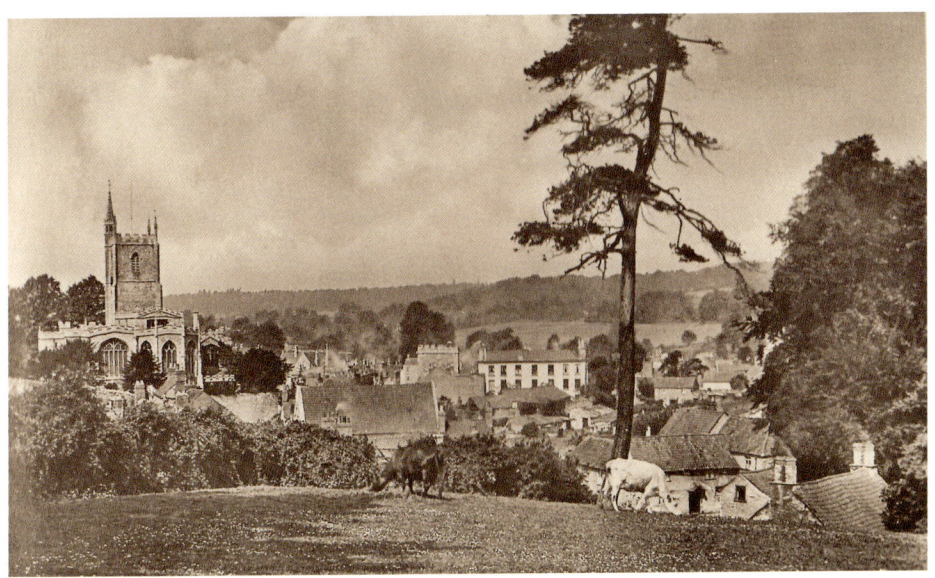

Westbury from East Hill

Cattle graze above Chock Lane on the daisy-covered slopes of East Hill in the mid-1930s in this panoramic view across Westbury. Housebuilding from the 1950s onward, and the present unfortunate tangle of undergrowth occasioned through the cessation of grazing and human neglect, has ensured that the same splendid view is now difficult to achieve. To the right of the church may be seen the long roof of the Methodist chapel, and above that in the distance the impressive Gothic gable and chimneys of the police station on the High Street. Behind the chapel stands the battlemented entrance tower to Westbury College, and the substantial eighteenth-century residence of the Hobhouse family, The College, which was built on its west wing and demolished in 1968. East Hill Farm was the home farm of The Priory.

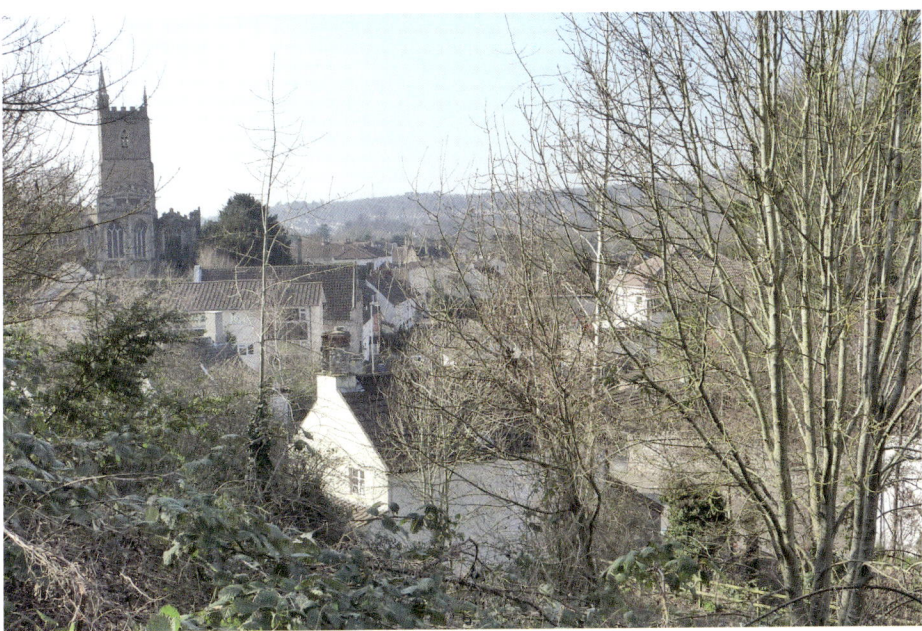

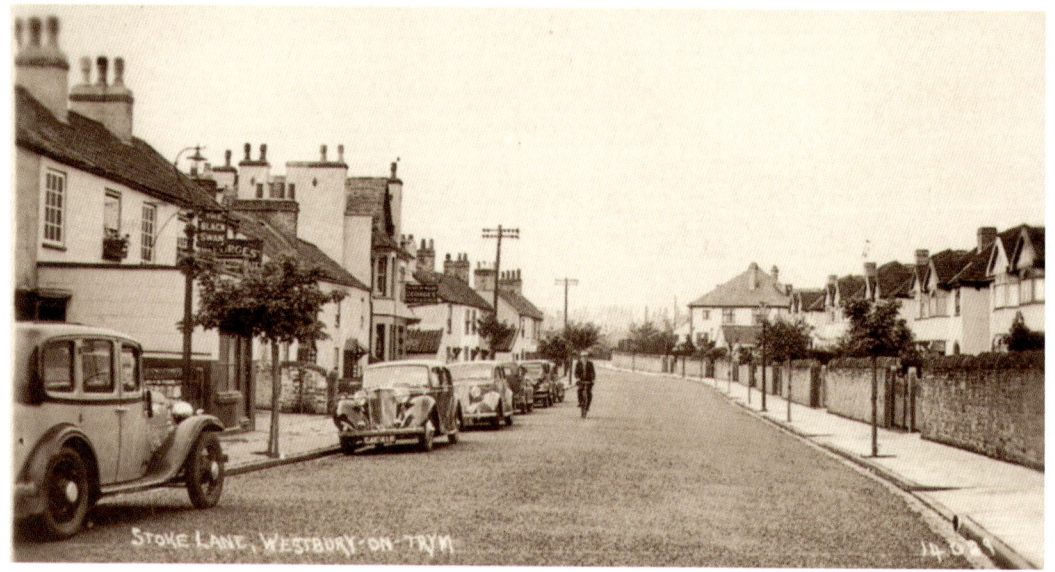

Stoke Lane Refreshment

From 1820, Westbury started to spread in a detached V-shaped development of cottages along Stoke Lane and Back Stoke Lane. Several originally had stone plaques that both named and dated their buildings. Most were semi-detached or in short terraces. The 1930s photograph shows the lane's two public houses on the left, the Black Swan (affectionately known as the Dirty Duck) and beyond it the Prince of Wales. The former was opened by the 1850s and the latter by the 1890s. The picture also shows how the new houses on the right of the photograph utilised as their front garden walls the western boundary wall of Cotebank's Park, which had preceded them. Until the building of Falcondale Road, a substantial pond lay in woodland, approximately where the large house stands in the right distance. The Black Swan was a favourite with US troops billeted on local families in the Second World War.

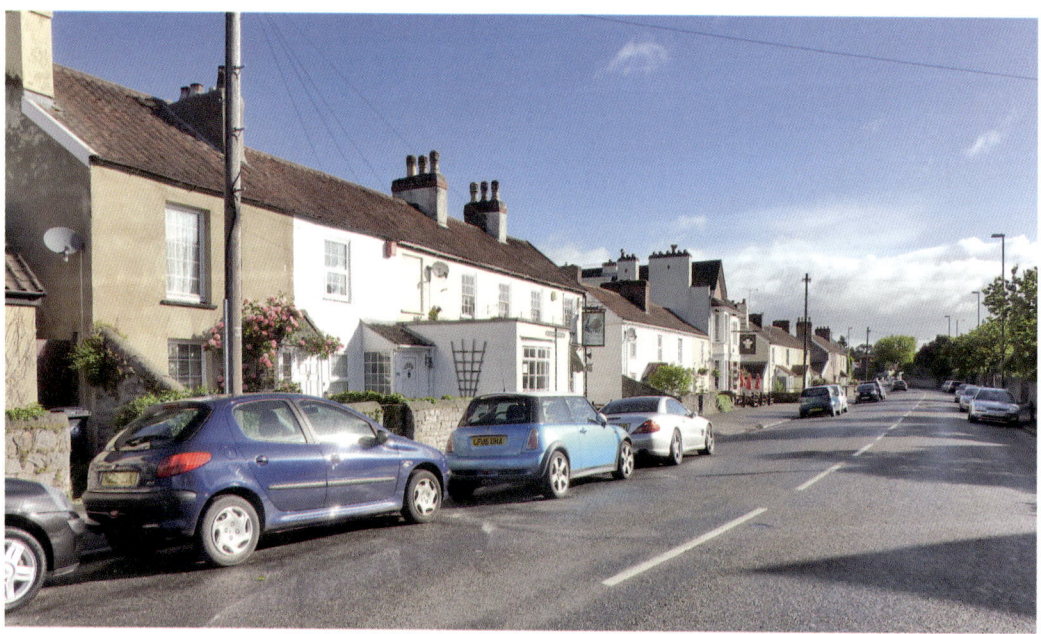

Walk 2

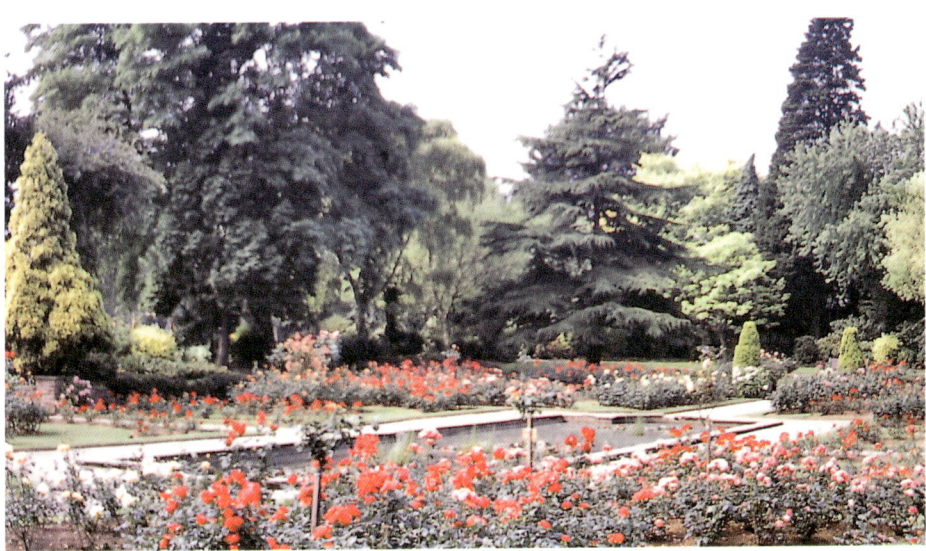

In Canford Park

Originally, Canford Farm occupied the site of the present park and the adjacent cemetery. The name in itself referred to the ford across the Trym that existed to the north, where a branch of the lane ascends to join the Henbury Road near the old quarry on Henbury Hill. The farm was purchased by Revd H. A. Daniel in 1874 for the Clifton Urban Sanitary authority, and a cemetery opened there in 1903. The City Boundary extension of the following year necessitated, via the Bristol Corporation Act of 1904, the opening of a park, and work started in January 1905 on its layout. In 1909 it opened to the public. The rose garden, photographed by Bill Blackmore in 1972, blooms where farm buildings once stood. Blackmore's other photograph shows a display in 1976 by the Avon Mounted Police at the once annual Canford Carnival.

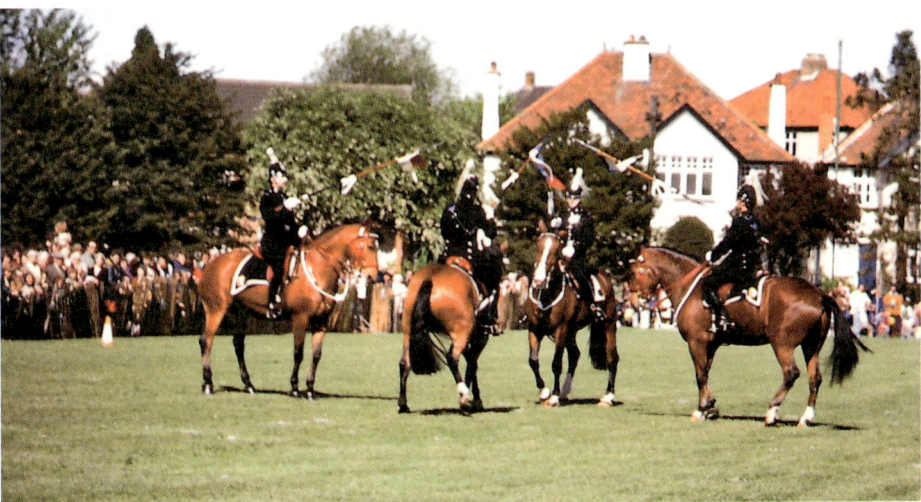

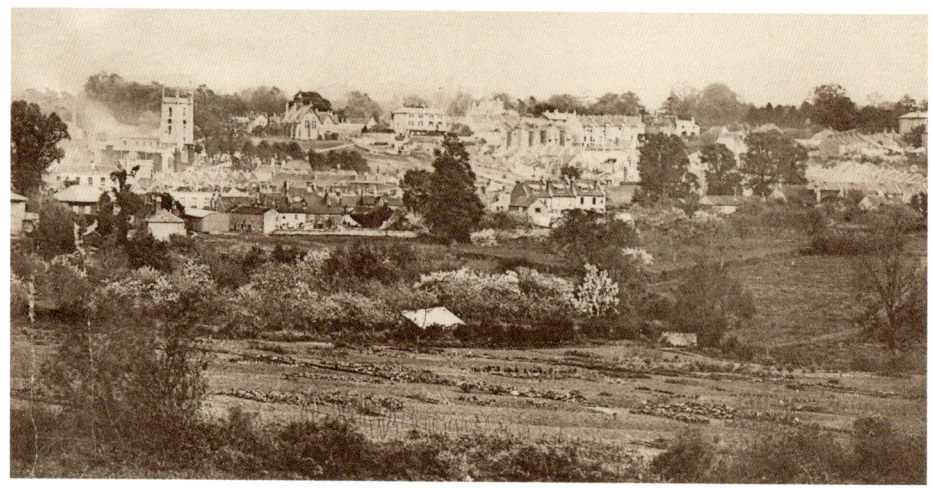

Blossom Time in Westbury, 1901

A springtime photograph, taken from the allotments adjoining the nursery on Henbury Hill. On the left, the nursery's orchard is in full blossom, while beyond it a rectangular, hedged enclosure holds the orchard of Westbury Court Farm. The row of giant elms that overlooked The Batch, now the site of the war memorial, appears beyond the farm buildings that straddled what is now Westbury Court Road. On the far right, the recently built houses of Stoke Lane and those of Cambridge Road appear. On East Hill, Godwin and Crisp's gothic Parish Rooms stand proud and smoke still rises from a limekiln in Chock Lane, behind Westbury church. Eastfield Road shows a clutter of houses. In the foreground, the side walls of a footbridge across the Trym may be seen to the right of a greenhouse in the nursery orchard. The 2013 photograph looks towards the 1901 viewpoint from the church tower.

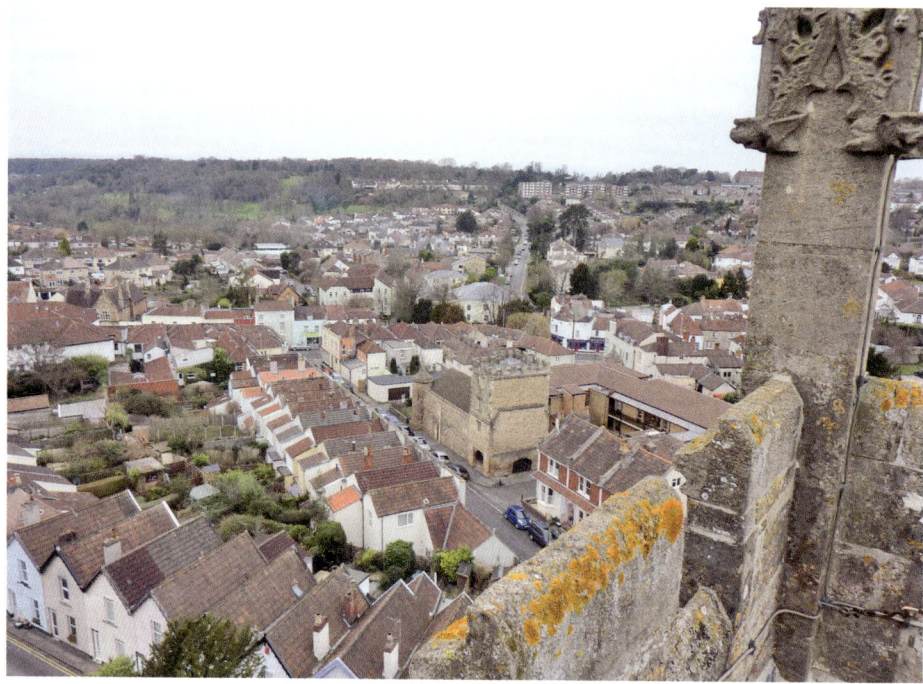

Jassy in Canford Lane, 1865

A young man with a *boutonnière* identified as 'Jassy' sits in a donkey gig in Canford Lane, not far from Canford Farm. The narrow lane was not then the main route linking Westbury to Shirehampton, which was via Henbury and along King's Weston Road. Canford Lane was bordered to the south by allotments, Coombe Nursery and Coombe House's fields, Coombe Paddock and Brookridge. To the north lay the Trym valley and the park of Coombe House. In 1831 Canford Farm's stallions Sailor and Swap were listed in the *Sporting Magazine* as covering at 12½ and 10 sovereigns respectively. From 1874 the farm, despite still having livestock, treated Westbury's sewage. However, 'loud and frequent' protests were made and legal proceedings threatened because of pollution in the Trym at Coombe Dingle. The sewage was henceforth piped to Sea Mills for chemical treatment and the farm eventually made way for Canford Cemetery and Park.

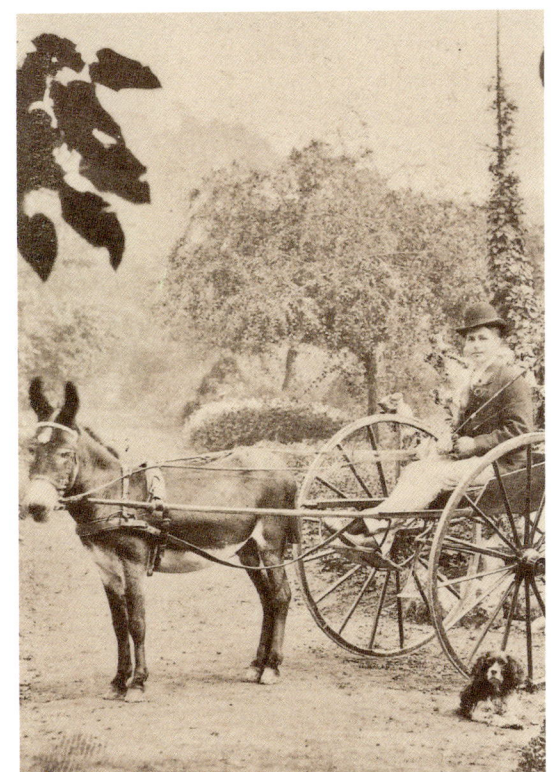

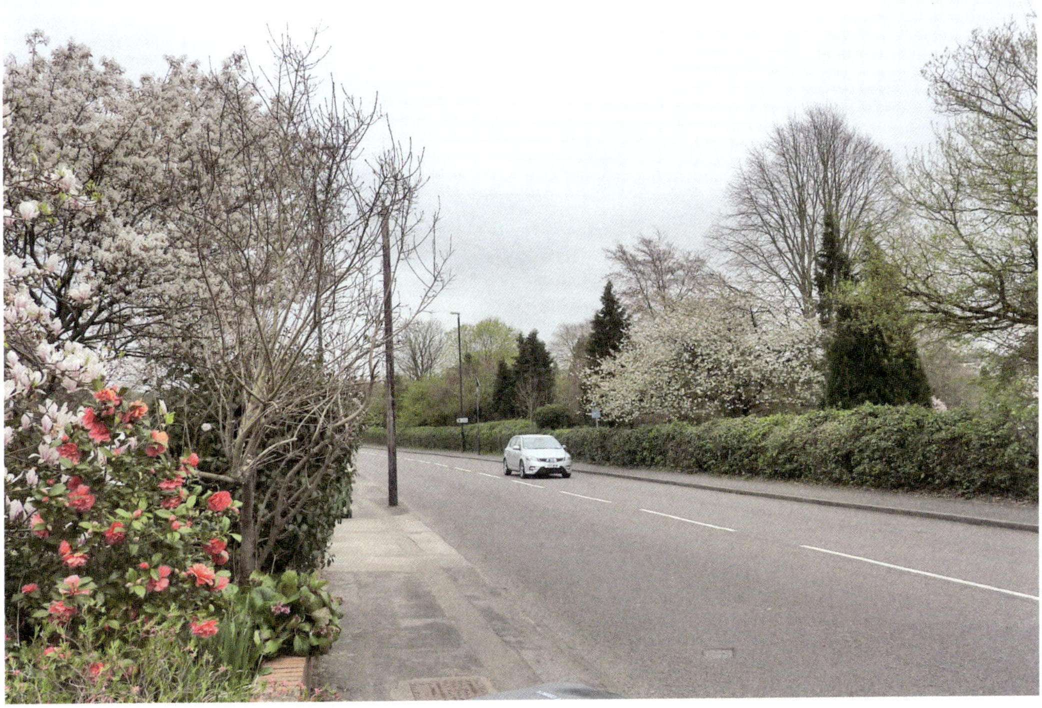

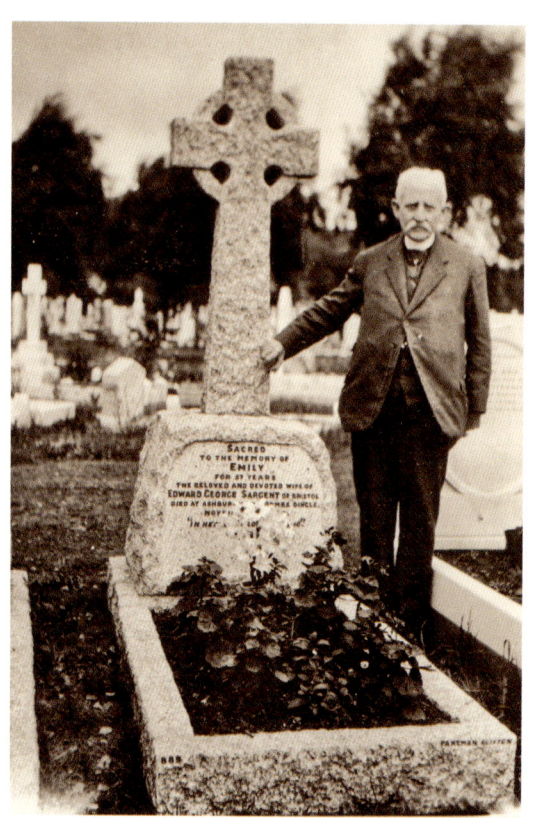

'I Will Come Very Soon', The Diamond Wedding Eve Photograph

Coombe Lane's Edward Sargent wrote the above caption against this photograph of himself taken by the side of his beloved wife Emily's grave in Canford Cemetery. It was the 18 July 1931, the eve of his diamond wedding. Emily, his wife of fifty-seven years, had died on 1 November 1928. He was to join her on 24 October 1934, aged eighty-six. The gravestone, by Pakeman of Whiteladies Gate, survives minus its kerbstones. Canford Cemetery was developed on the site of allotments and had been opened by the Bishop of Bristol on 8 June 1903. A crematorium was added in 1956. Originally, land on the right-hand side of the drive was reserved for members of the Church of England and the left for Nonconformists. The Sargents were leading members of the Tyndale Baptist Church, Whiteladies Road. Together they founded a missionary station on the Congo near Stanley Falls called Sargent Station.

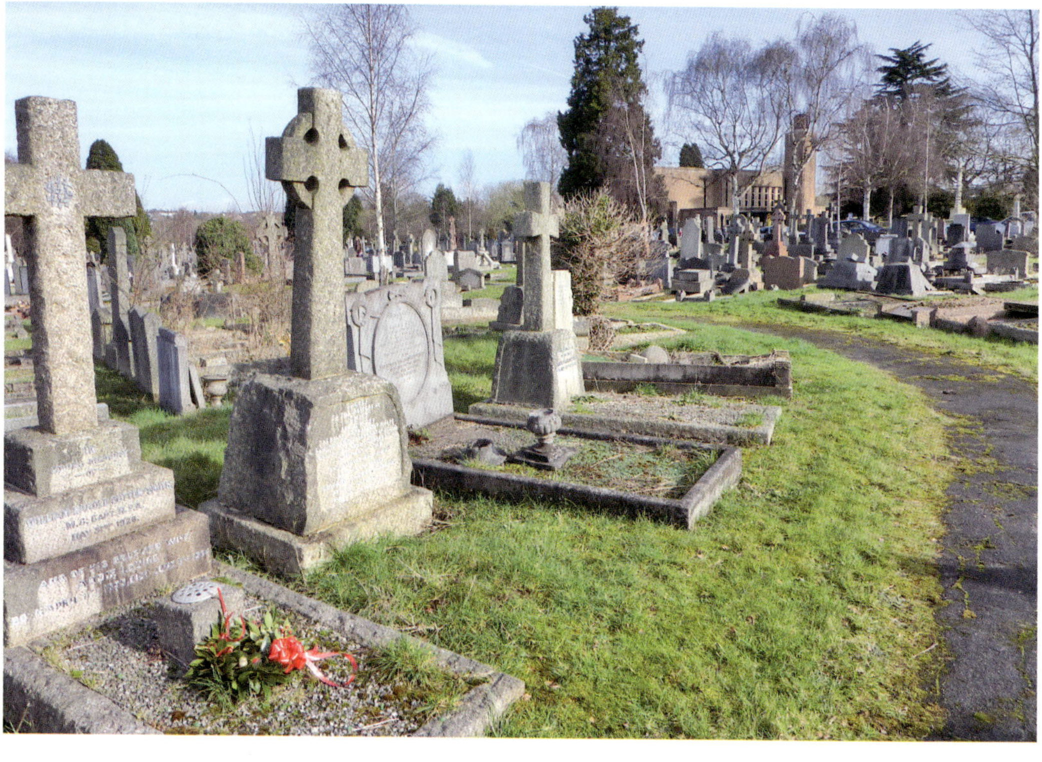

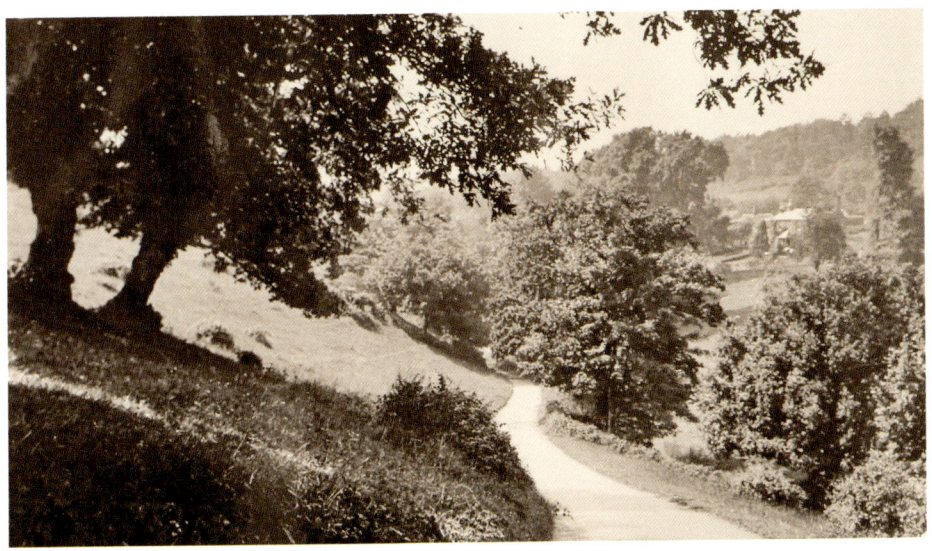

Cherry Orchard, The Secret Valley

The beautiful valley below Canford Lane was accessed as now, either by footpath from Westbury alongside the tree-fringed Trym and through what is now Henbury Golf Course, or down the wooded lane leading from opposite the present cemetery. Its orchards were a seasonal delight. Canford Lane (a popular approach for visitors to the Dingle) overlooked it until housebuilding in the 1930s hid it from view. Today, although pasture has replaced the orchards of the old maps, it remains a little-known country haven within minutes of Westbury village. In Georgian times, limekilns on Coombe Hill burned quarry spoil on the site but the place bore the name Cherry Orchard from at least the beginning of the nineteenth century. The attractive, slightly Germanic-looking Victorian house remodelled a pre-1840s property next door to Coombe Farmhouse. One of the footpaths to the Blaise estate continues up Coombe Hill behind Cherry Orchard.

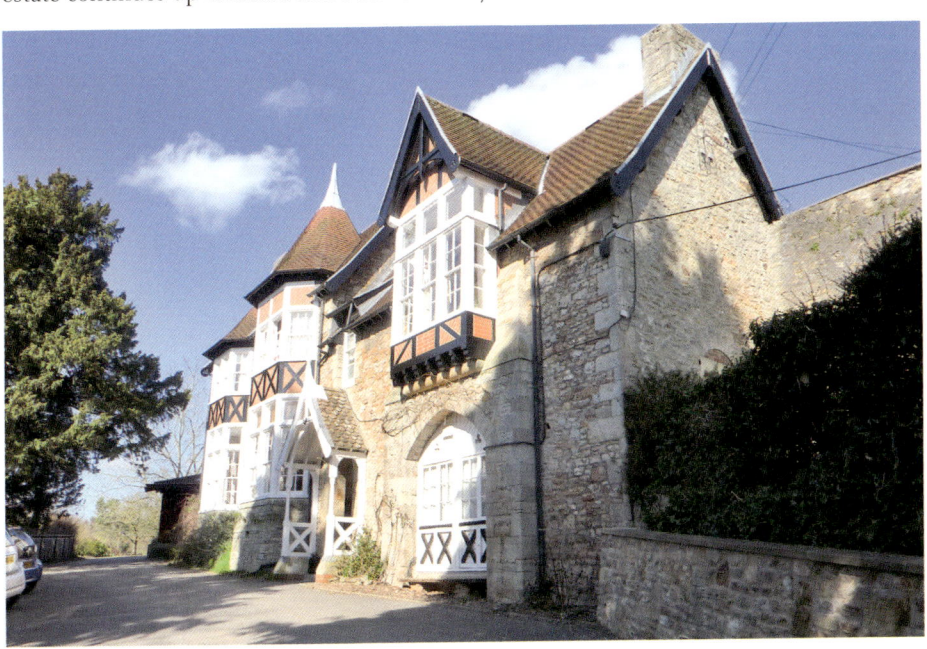

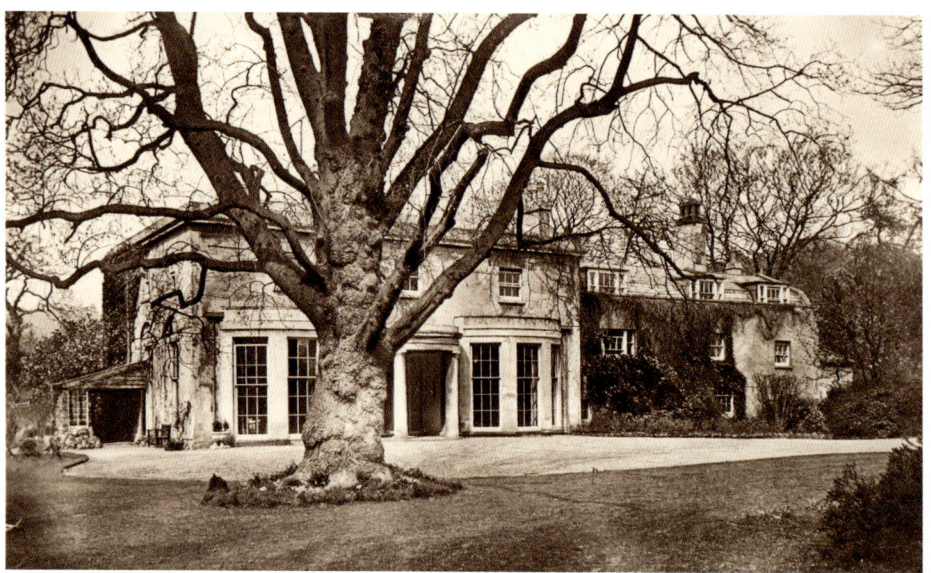

'The Seat of Beauty, Competence and Ease'

A lease proves the existence of Coombe House in 1789, although whether that was this elegant Grecian-style house or an earlier residence that later became the attached eastern wing is uncertain. The Bath stone entrance façade sported a curving Doric porch and shallow bow windows, while the side overlooking the Dingle featured a great apsidal drawing room and enjoyed prospects of Blaise Castle, Coombe Hill and Cherry Orchard. Stables and utilities extended along the eastern scarp together with a large, walled formal garden. Its southern garden wall was bowed and an orangery sat centrally on the northern wall. The Corporation unfortunately acquired Coombe House in 1946 to convert into police flats; houses for married officers were built on its land along Canford Lane. By the 1960s the neglected house was tragically demolished and replaced by a care home, itself now vacated. The sketch, taken from Coombe Lane around 1810, includes a railed Canford Lane.

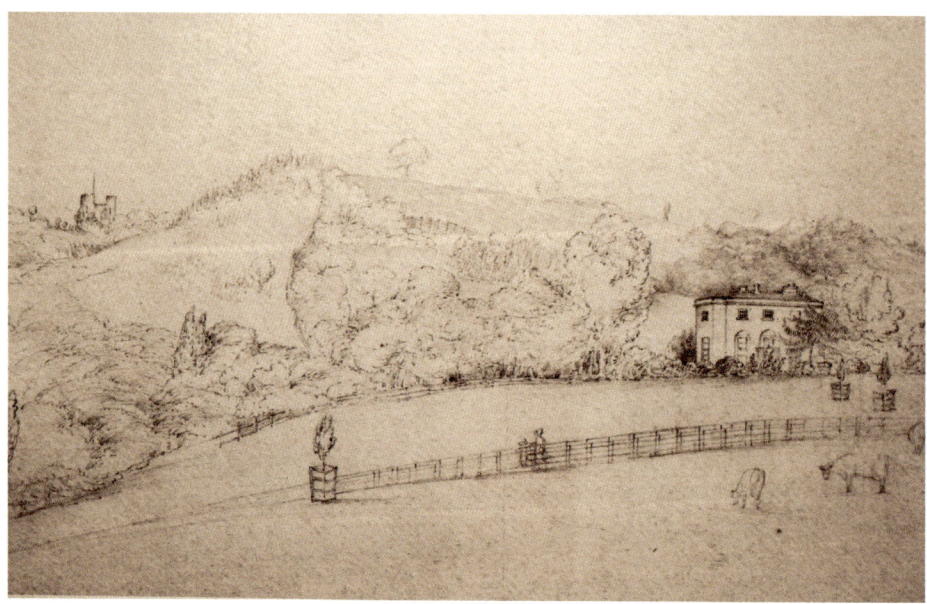

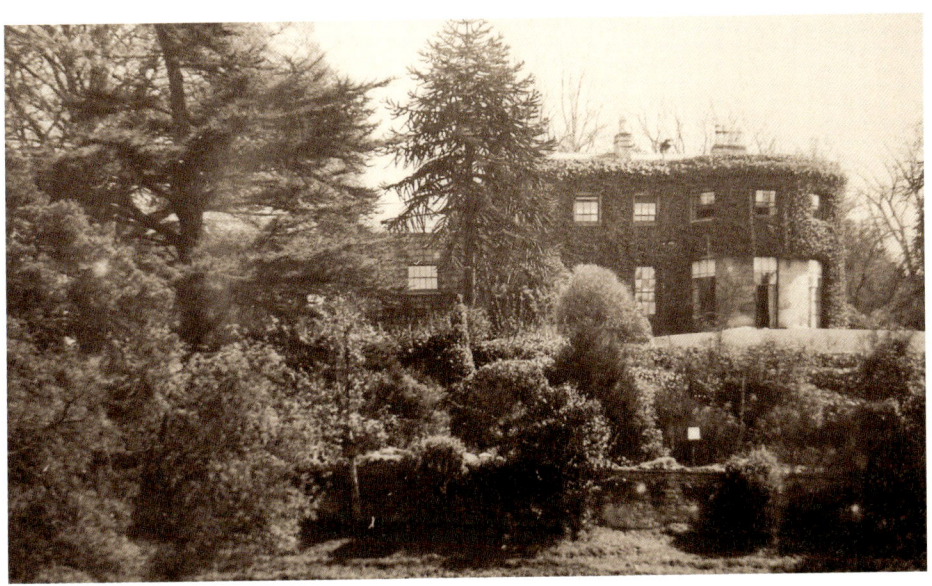

'A Genial Villa Rose Between the Trees'

Coombe House, viewed from Sideland Field, dominated the ridge overlooking the confluence of the Trym and the Hazel Brook. Its sloping northern grounds held simple walks and shrubberies designed not to impede the views from the house. Years of neglect have transformed this aspect, hiding the 1960s replacement. The grounds were 26 acres in extent. The now tangled 'ornamental paddock' next to the surviving lodge on Canford Lane still boasts its specimen trees. During the Second World War a water tank was placed here. It now features the base of a post-medieval corn grinder, presumably removed from the outbuildings. The shipbuilder George Hilhouse was an early owner, and *The Bristol Mercury* of 9 September 1854 includes a useful, detailed advertisement for letting 'Combe House'. In 1899 newspapers reported that, following the cessation of postal deliveries from Westbury, Bristol postmen had been unable to locate the rural Coombe House, to the annoyance of the household.

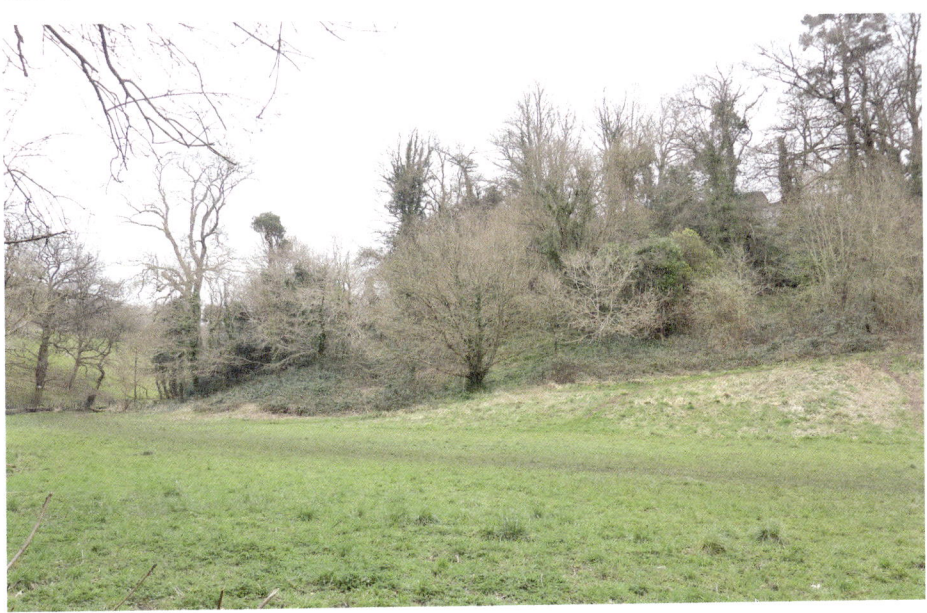

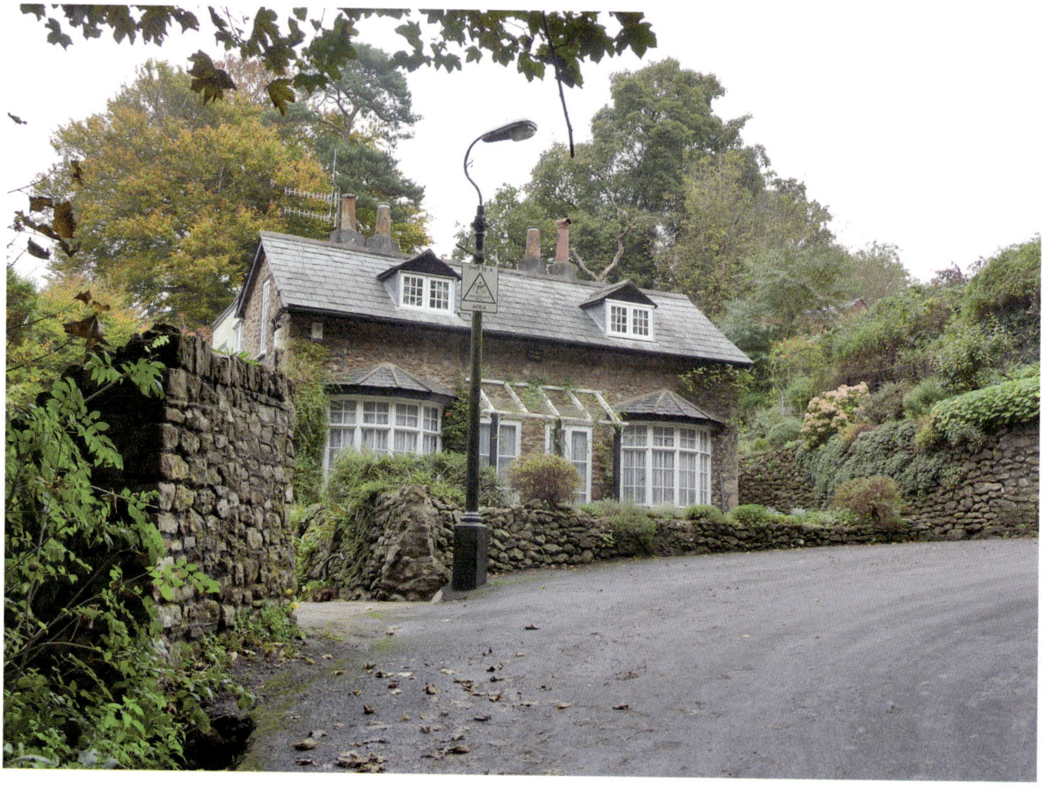

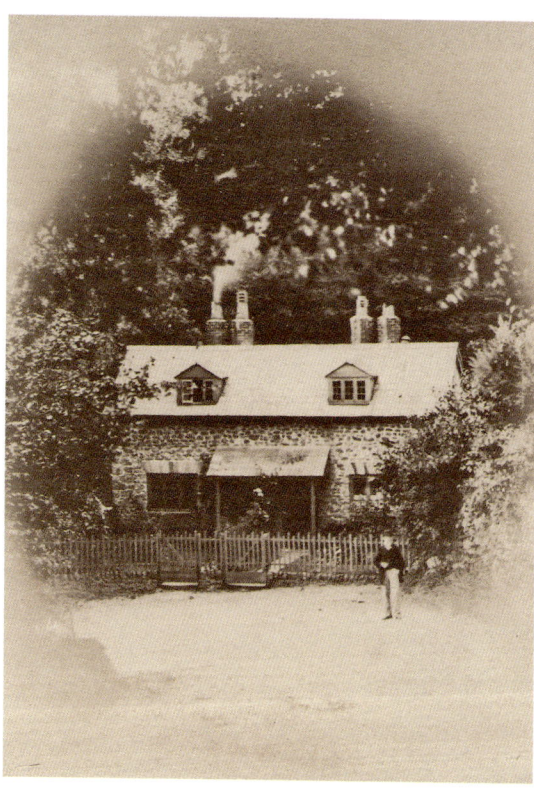

The Gardeners' Cottages

This image from a stereoscopic slide of the 1880s shows the simple but picturesque semi-detached cottages that served as homes for the gardeners of nearby Coombe House. Probably coeval with the early nineteenth-century mansion, they certainly predate the 1840s tithe map of the area. They cling to a bend of the steep and twisting Coombe Lane on the side of the Dingle known locally then as 'Dangerous Hill'. By the turn of the century they had become one of the sights of Coombe Dingle and were both sketched and photographed. In the twentieth century they were enlarged and converted into a single residence called Coombe Cottage. It is now forgotten that the hamlet that grouped loosely around Grove Road on the opposite summit and in the Dingle was called Bowden's Fields rather than Coombe Dingle. The 1959–62 development, Bowden (originally Bowden's) Close, is the only surviving link now with this name.

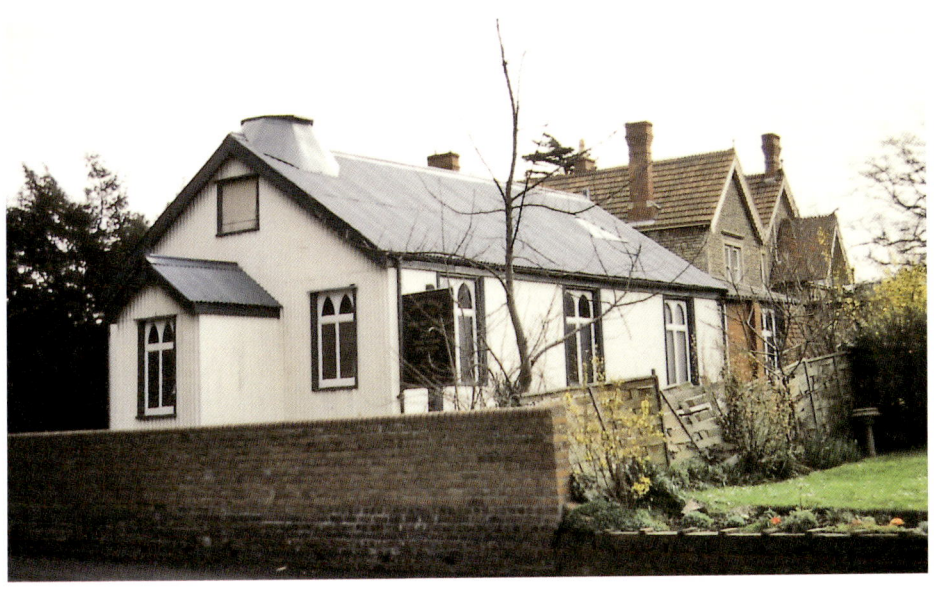

Prefabricated Religion: the 'Pestilence' Reaches Coombe Dingle

The Wesleyan Methodist chapel at 1 Dingle Road, Coombe Dingle, in 1989, before its demolition in 1991 to make way for a house. The rear of William Studley's Coombe Dingle House of 1903/04 in Coombe Lane appears beyond. The chapel's triangular attic roof lights and the circular west window had, by this time, had their stained-glass panels removed. The polygonal base on the roof had originally supported an elaborate wooden flèche when the building opened in 1897, but this had long since disappeared. Originally it had seating for sixty worshippers. There was a great trade in such British prefabricated, corrugated, galvanised iron buildings from the 1840s onward, and they were sent all over the Empire. William Morris deplored them and called their spread 'a pestilence'. Before the construction of the impressive bridge over the Trym, Dingle Road only gave access to the drive of Ebenezer House, a Victorian mansion that has since been replaced by Haytor Park.

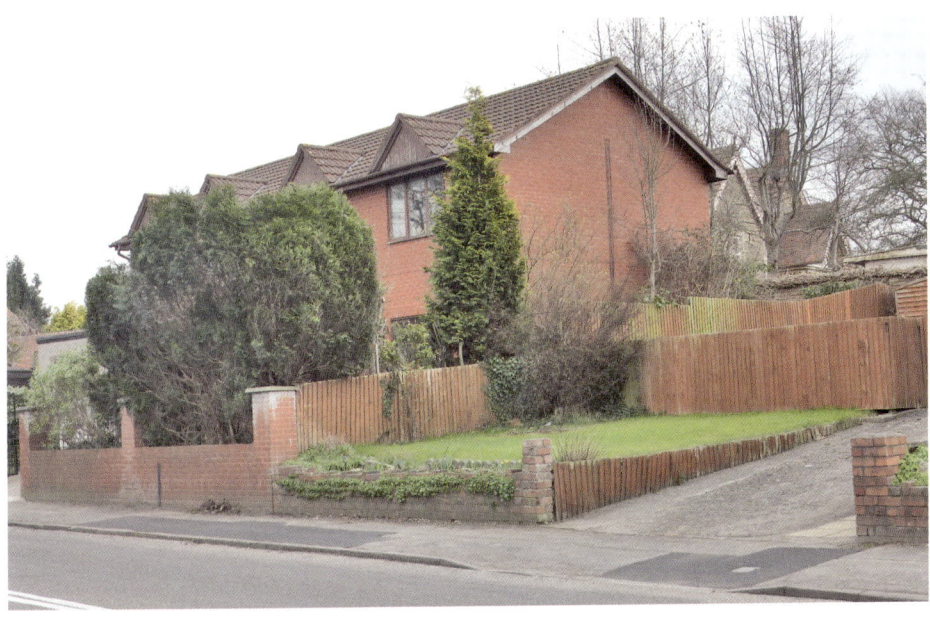

'Nearer the Dingle, Many Palatial Villas Have Been Constructed'

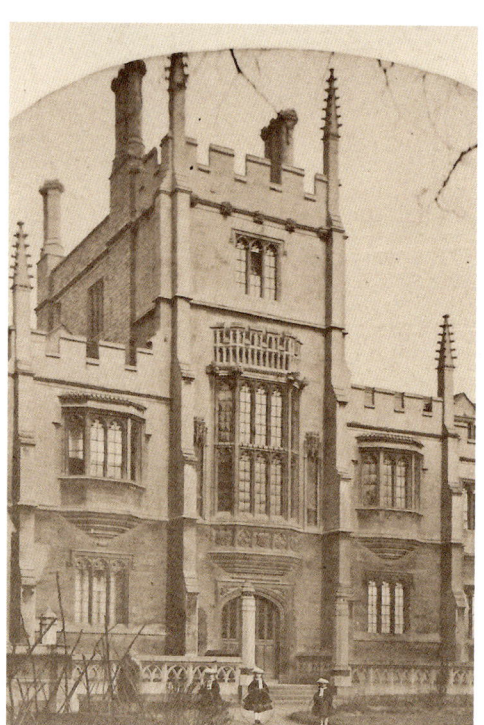

Around 1894, William Edward Studley, a Clifton builder, acquired land west of Coombe Lane, and also some east of Westbury Lane in Bowden's Fields. Over two decades, he transformed Coombe Dingle with his slightly eccentric villas. Studley first built Combe Rocke, his own residence, and dotted the lane with four more houses and several cottages built within their grounds. In February 1897, antiques and modern artworks from Studley's collection were sold in a two-day London sale, possibly to finance these developments. Near the north-west corner of Coombe Lane stands Coombe Dingle House, dating from 1903/04. An exceptionally elaborate Gothic structure, like all of Studley's earlier houses it incorporated salvaged architectural elements of the 1839 Bishop's College (seen here in 1864). Later called 'The Salisbury Club', it was replaced by the City Art Gallery. The stables of Coombe Dingle House would later become 95a Coombe Lane.

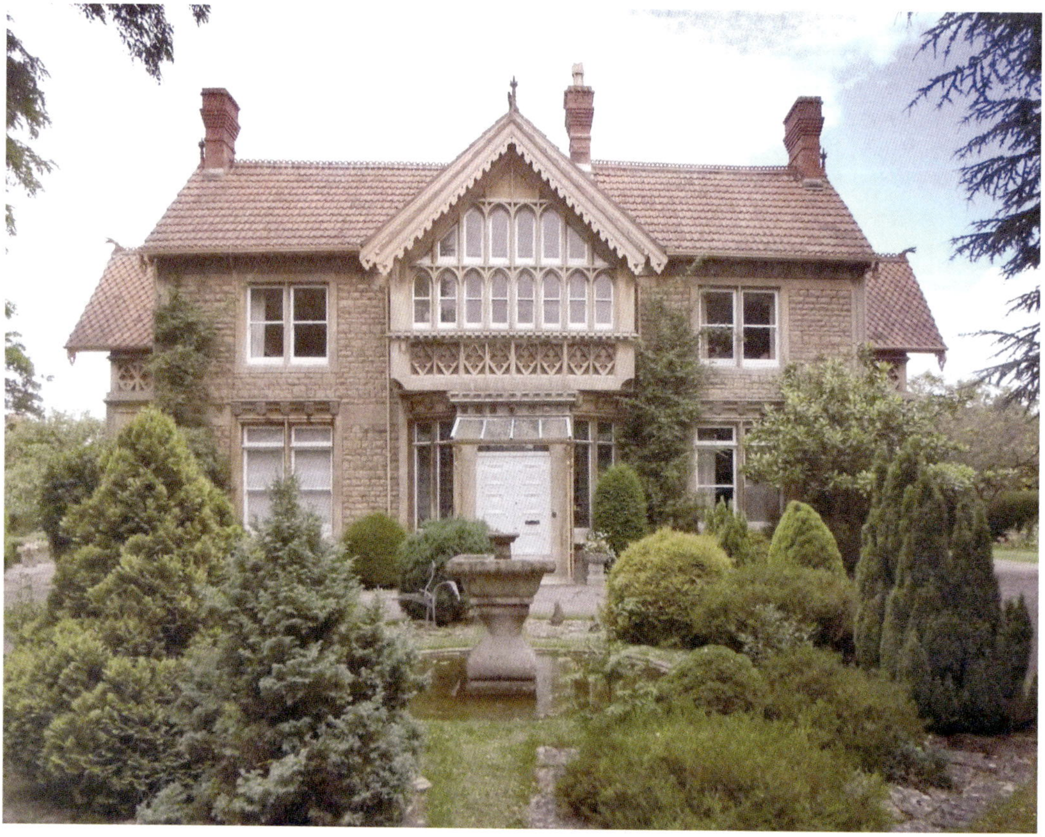

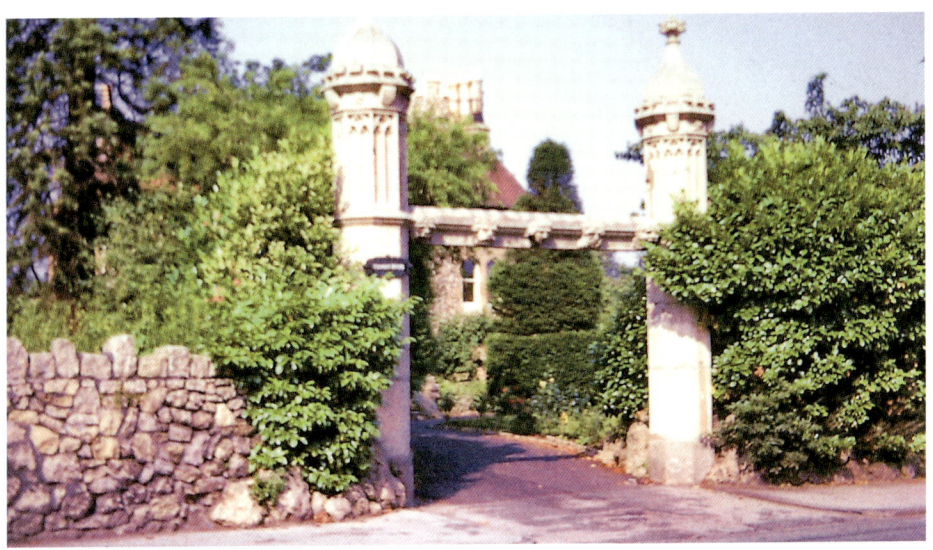

Awaiting Demolition, Combe Rocke, 1895–1966

No clear photographs are known of Studley's residence, but portions visible in views from nearby Ashburnham prove that it differed from his submitted plans. Gothic in inspiration, with pointed windows, a crenellated circular tower rose above the roof at the centre of its north side. The southern entrance façade had two gables and possibly a semicircular porch, but not the proposed corner turrets. The western façade sported a balcony, conservatory, and one of Studley's favourite angled corner window bays. A skylight topped the central staircase. Combe Rocke was finished before he acquired the Salisbury Club's stonework, so its façade was plain compared with his later houses. The magnificent sculptural gateway was adapted from that source, however, and fortunately survives. In 1908 he added a garage, shop and cottage (into which he temporarily moved) in the grounds. Studley moved again in 1910 and finally to Hygrove, his elaborate creation in Grove Road, which overlooks the Dingle.

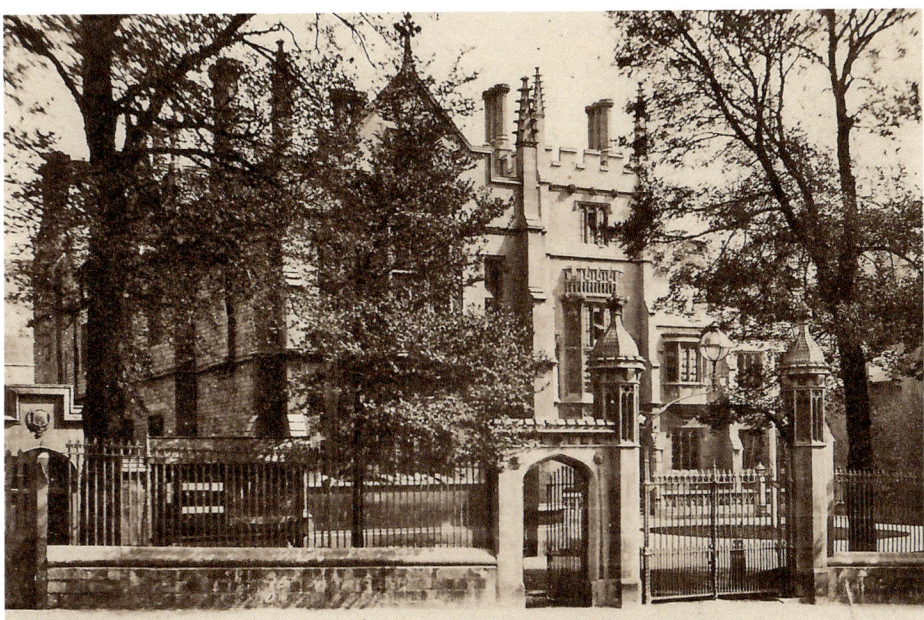

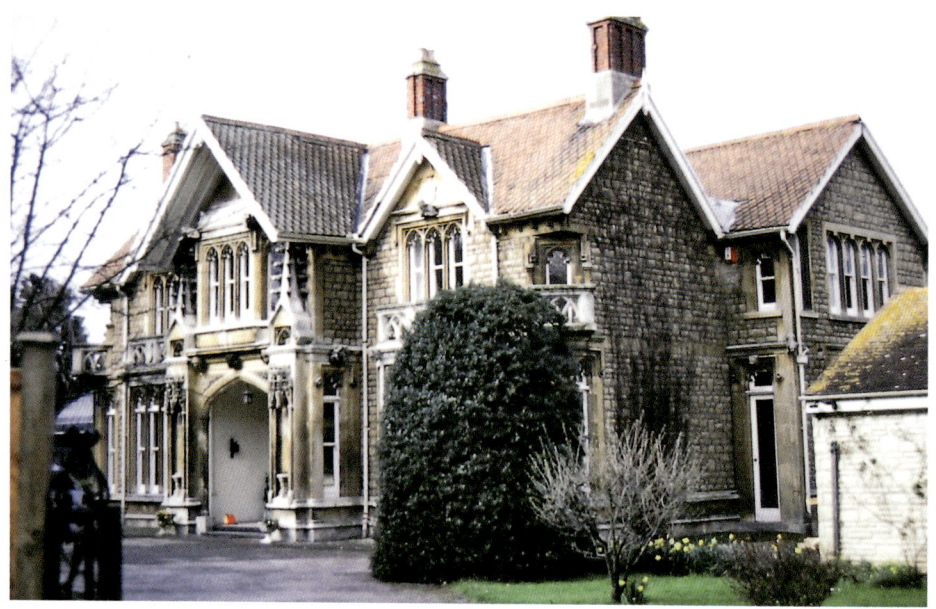

Salisbury House, 1966 and 2013

This was the first house built by Studley after his acquisition of the Salisbury Club's carved stonework and its elaborate façade received the most decorative pieces from its namesake. Larger than Combe Rocke, from 1902 it rose behind the latter, and was approached by a side drive through now lost gate piers that had once formed part of the Gothic balustrade fronting the club. That decorative screen was adapted here for the balconies and in other houses, such as Ashburnham, extended to form the tops of porch screens and windows. A branch of the drive led off northwards to stables and glasshouses behind the house; a conservatory adjoined the western façade. Originally a huge urn stood opposite the entrance porch, as at Coombe Dingle House. Studley built several handsome houses off Stoke Lane (numbers 1–9) in 1906, intending to call the road Studley Avenue. It was renamed Abbey Road in 1909.

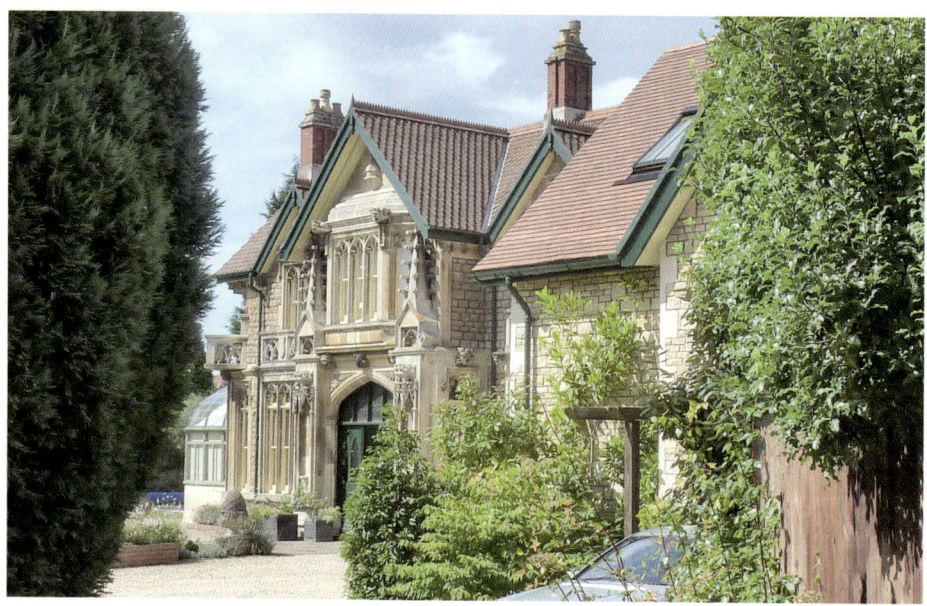

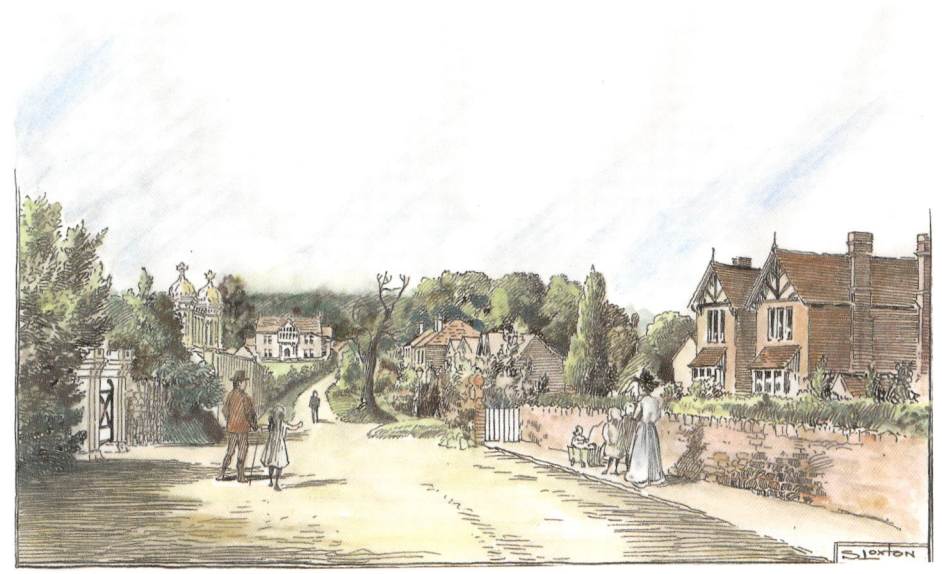

'As far As the Unique Dingle, Beauty Spots That are Unsurpassed'

Coombe Lane (historically 'Combe Dingle Road') was the ancient direct route to the Dingle, continuing Paddy's Well Lane to Bowden's Fields and Lawrence Weston. Although now classed as Stoke Bishop by estate agents and ward boundaries, the area north of the University Athletics Field was historically part of Coombe Dingle. In the 1935 city directory it still appears thus, although the Stoke Bishop telephone exchange embraced the inhabitants. Samuel Loxton's drawing records Coombe Lane looking towards the Dingle from near the corner of Rayleigh Road around 1912. Left are the lost Gothic gate piers of Salisbury House and, beyond, the monumental entrance to Combe Rocke. The attached high wall backed greenhouses, a stable, Combe Rocke Cottage and a shop. In the distance, framed by Brookridge Wood, stands Coombe Dingle House. The small and earliest houses of the lane date from the late 1870s and are in the middle distance.

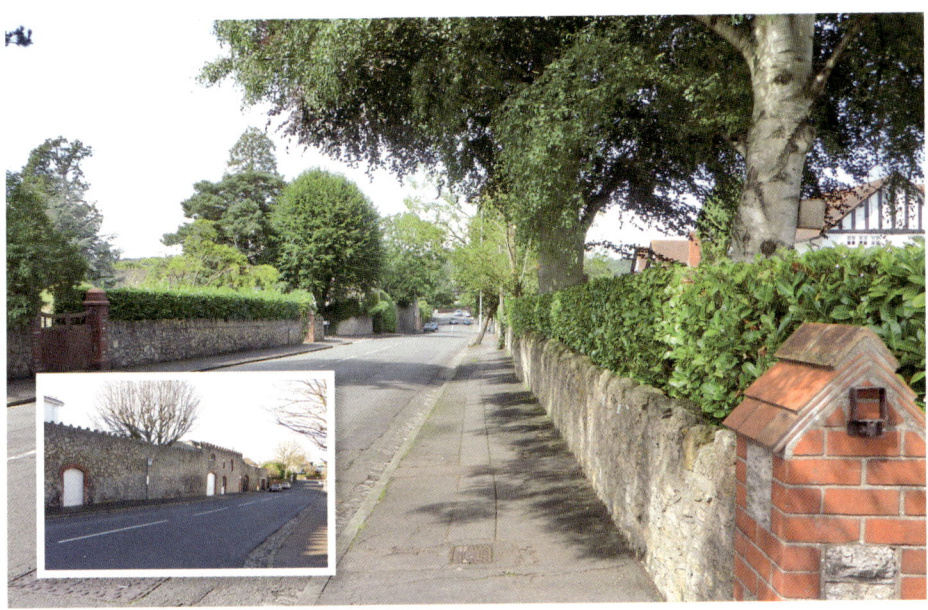

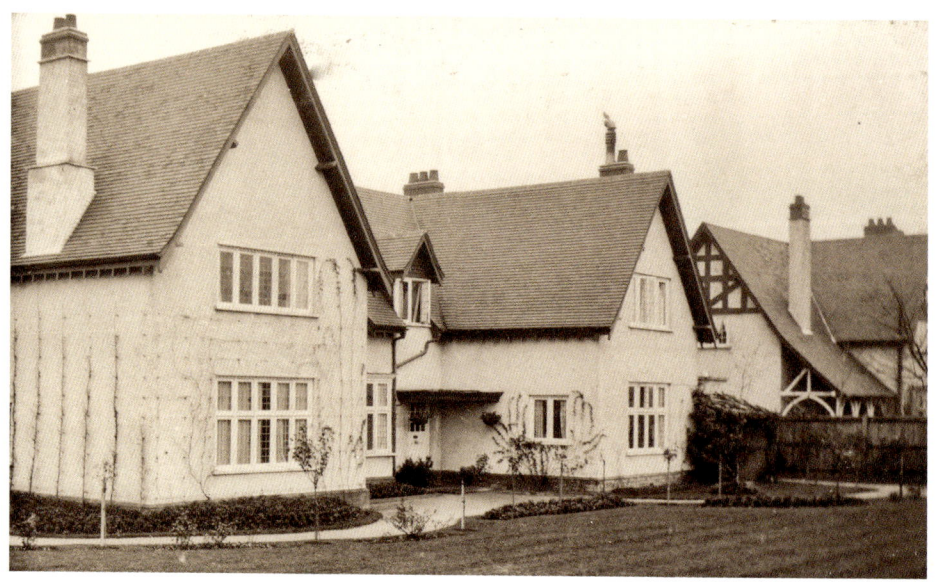

Arts and Crafts in Rayleigh Road

The Gables and its equally splendid neighbour, The White Lodge, as photographed in Coombe Dingle by Edward Sargent on 1 December 1911 while on a house-hunting expedition. The houses had been built around 1905–07 and were the work of the Bristol architects C. & C. Thompson of the Athenaeum Chambers, Nicholas Street. Both houses overlooked the new university athletics field. It is interesting that the Gables (and possibly its neighbour) then had its front door and porch on what is now the rear of the building and away from Rayleigh Road – from whence the modern photograph is taken. The Gables was then owned by Douglas Smith, and the White Lodge by Cuthbert Hicks. The semi-detached and smaller houses of Rayleigh Road and Coombe Lane were the earliest of the new developments for those seeking rural solace in Coombe Dingle. They were joined by the detached mansions after 1900.

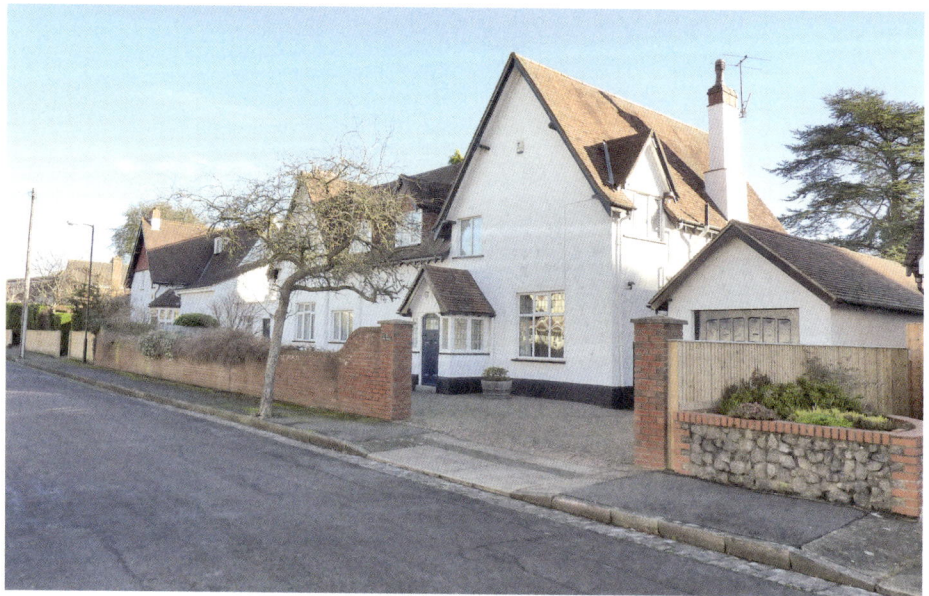

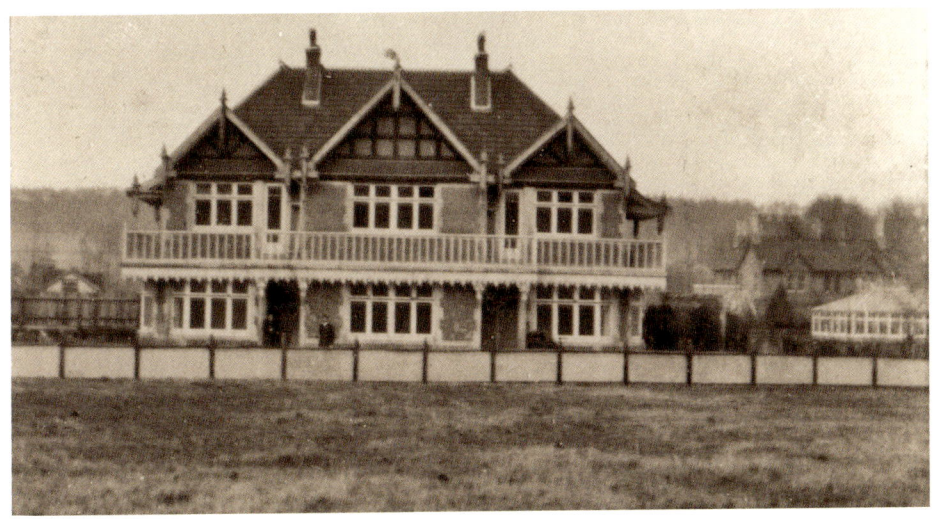

'Ashburnham, A Possible Future Home'

In 1911, Edward Sargent, a highly respected ex-banker, philanthropist and leading member of the Baptist church in Bristol, along with his equally philanthropic wife, Emily (herself religious and concerned with female refuge), decided to sell St Austell, 94 Pembroke Road, Clifton, and to retire to the country. On 4 January 1912 they viewed Studley's recently completed Ashburnham and were photographed from its hayfield. They purchased it. Studley built neighbouring Glenrose (now South Lodge) in late 1909, seen in the Storey family's picnic photograph of 31 March 1913. Its twin, Ashburnham, was originally to be placed beside it on what would later become its croquet lawn. The Sargents effected alterations, removing the pagoda roofs above the side balconies and repainting Studley's buff-coloured timberwork (as still employed at Coombe Dingle House) with darker hues. Both photographs afford rare, if distant, glimpses of Combe Rocke beyond Glenrose's lost palm house. The Sargents resided at Ashburnham until 1931.

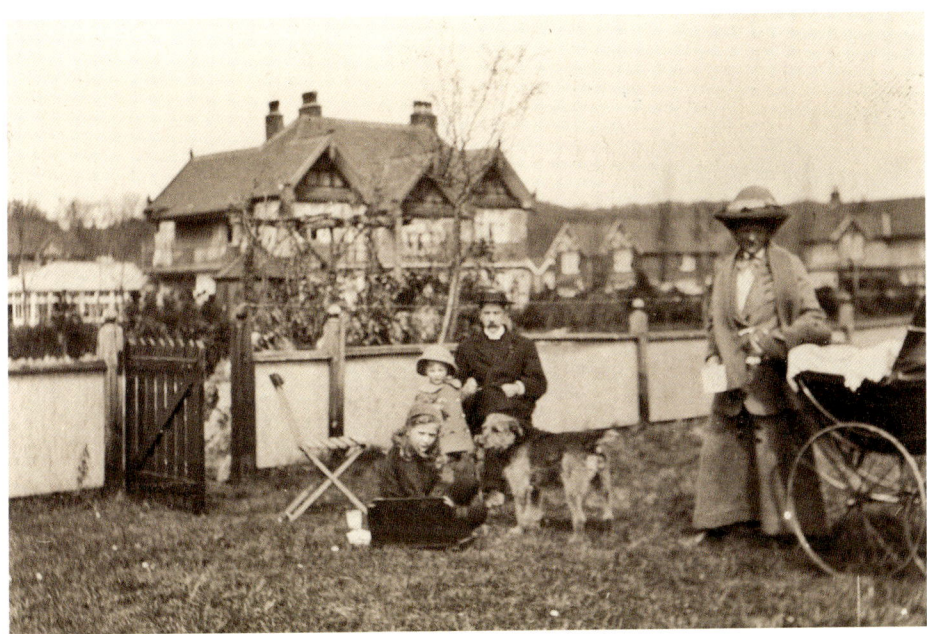

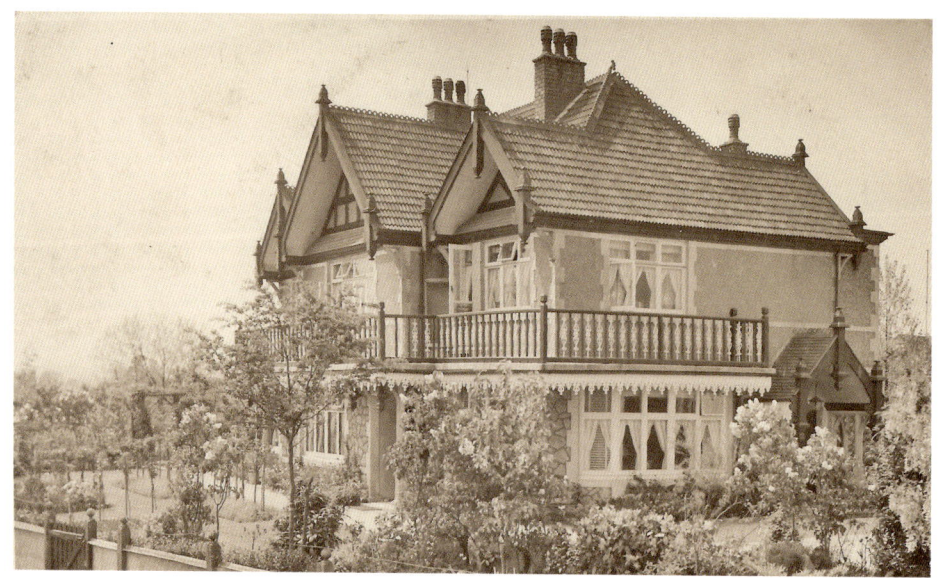

Coombe Dingle Lace Work

Ashburnham, looking its prettiest amid its gardens in 1913. The house incorporated many of the features found on Studley's other villas in Coombe Dingle. It still retains original decorative details, although the fretted gingerbread and original woodwork of the balcony has rotted away, as have the bracketed heavy pendants adorning bargeboards on the gables and porch. Less monumental stone versions of these still survive elsewhere at Harford Lodge, Westbury Lane, and especially at Studley's final residence, Hygrove in Grove Road, pictured below. There, bracketed stone and wooden pendants survive, although in part renewed, on both house gables and the original gate porch. The Gothic screens of Ashburnham's garden façade and porch incorporated stonework from the Salisbury Club's balustrade. By 1911 Studley, aged sixty-six, was living in Westbury Lane with his long-time housekeeper, forty-nine-year-old Mary Griffin. They married in 1912.

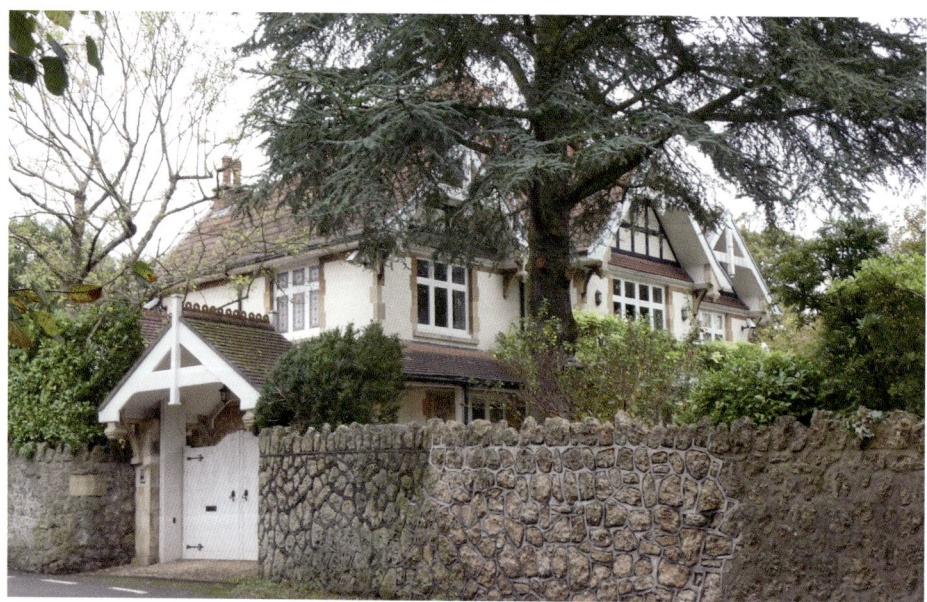

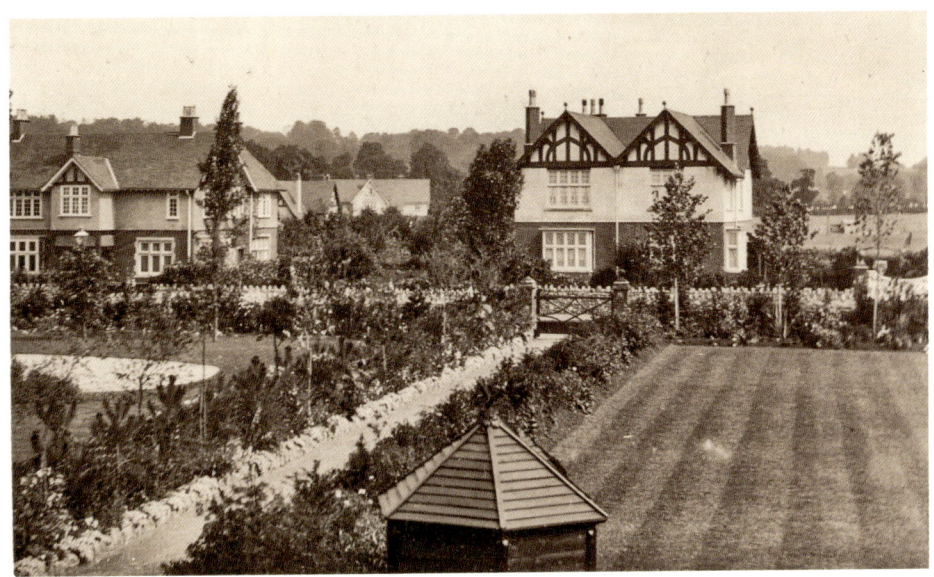

The View Towards Westbury, 28 August 1912

Within eight months of acquiring Ashburnham, the energetic Edward Sargent had created splendid gardens. As was usual with most of Studley's houses of this era, the principal façade of the house turned from the road and faced south-east. Here, the view from the side veranda looks along the carriage drive with its newly planted Austrian pines and over the summer house and croquet lawn. Two of the great Edwardian houses in Coombe Lane that fortunately still survive appear beyond. Sitting Stones on the right enshrines the name of the field it occupied. Behind are the roofs and chimneys of The White Lodge and Wheatleys, the great Arts and Crafts style house, then owned by James King. It sat at the top of Rayleigh Road and was demolished for the Greenacres flats in the 1960s. To the right may be seen part of the university athletics field with the new Canford Cemetery beyond.

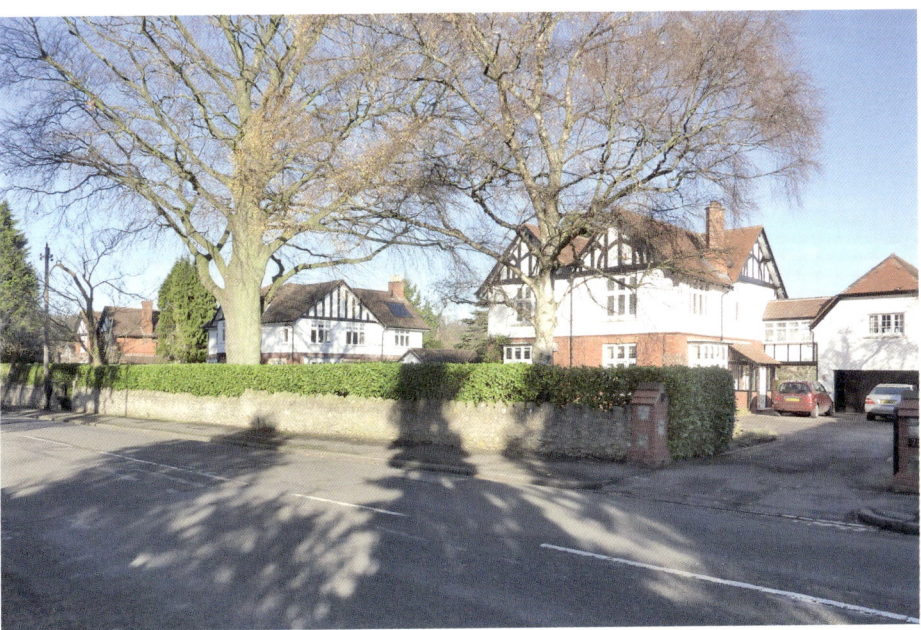

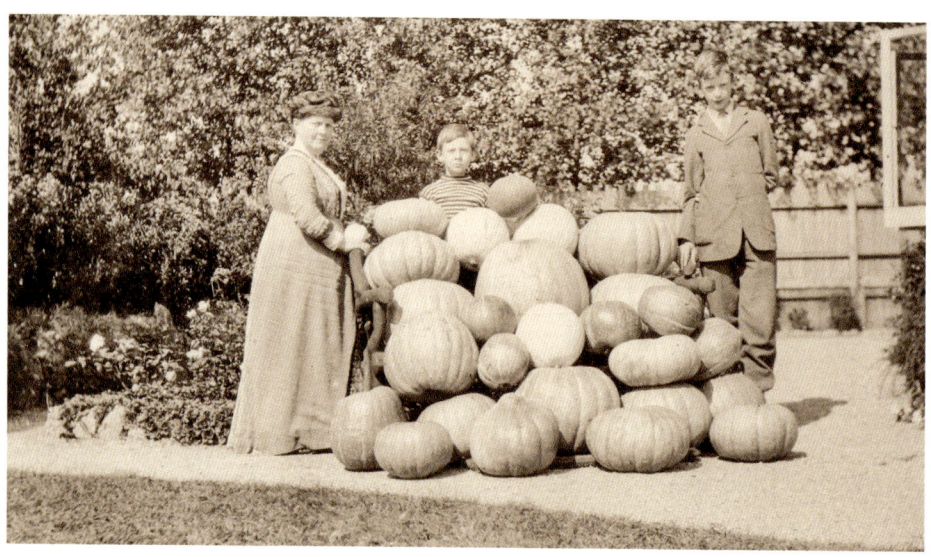

All are Safely Gathered In

The rich soil of the valley of the Trym between the Durdham and King's Weston Downs once supported a series of nurseries, allotments and successful dairy, sheep and arable farms. Medieval Westbury could even boast of vineyards on its slopes. Not only commercial ventures prospered from the fertility of the region, but domestic kitchen gardens also benefited. Here, Emily Sargent and two grandsons proudly pose by Ashburnham's pumpkin harvest of August 1914, and in June 1913 Kingsley Storey and Eric Sargent pick strawberries in the kitchen garden backed by the façade of Salisbury House, its garage, and the minor buildings of Combe Rocke. East of Coombe Lane, the area around Hutton Close was then occupied by Coombe Nursery's long glasshouses. In the distance, open fields, as yet untouched by the building of the houses of Coombe Dingle and Sea Mills, slope up to the woods of King's Weston Down.

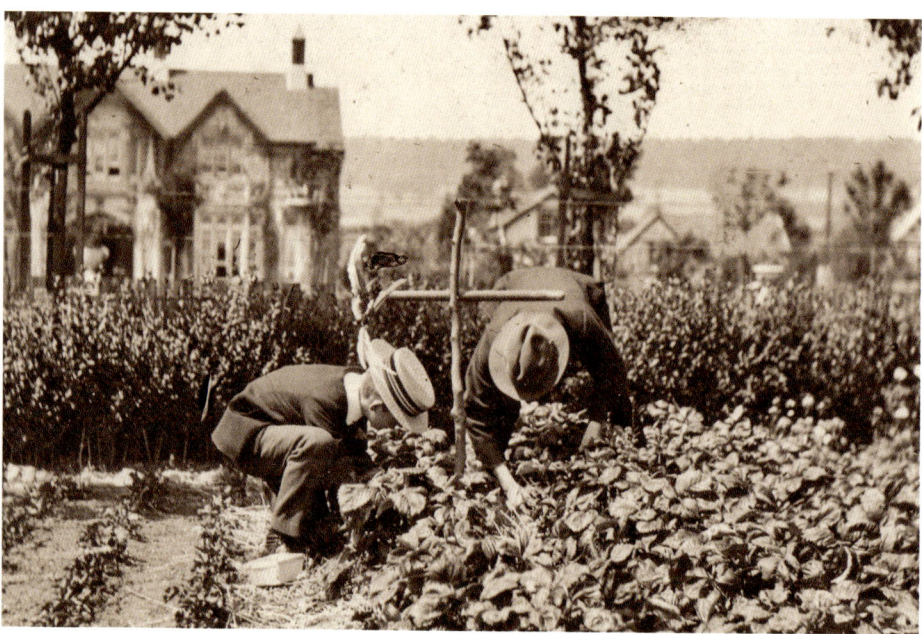

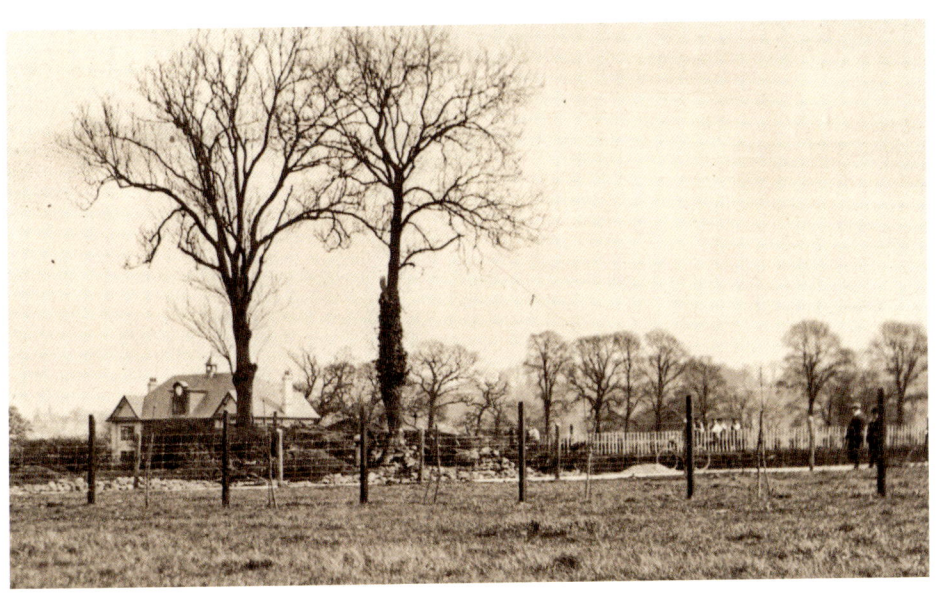

'And Then There Was One', the Varsity Ground Before 'The Outrage'

Seen from Asburnham's Field, on 31 March 1913, onlookers watch the removal of one of a pair of ash trees in the hedgerow in Coombe Lane bordering the recently opened Coombe Dingle University Athletics Field. The acquisition of the 12-acre ground from Coombe Lane's Red House Farm was made possible by the gift of £4,000 from George A. Wills in 1911. John Spry, head groundsman at the County Ground, gave advice as to its arrangement and £1,000 was spent on landscaping. Three football pitches and a hockey ground catered for winter sports, while tennis courts and a bowling green were included. The rarely photographed but elegant Pavilion cost £1,000 and achieved notoriety when, on 23 October 1913, it was destroyed in a Suffragette arson 'outrage'. In retaliation, the Suffragette offices in Queen's Road were burned by undergraduates. The rebuilt Pavilion, seen here in 2013, imitated the original design.

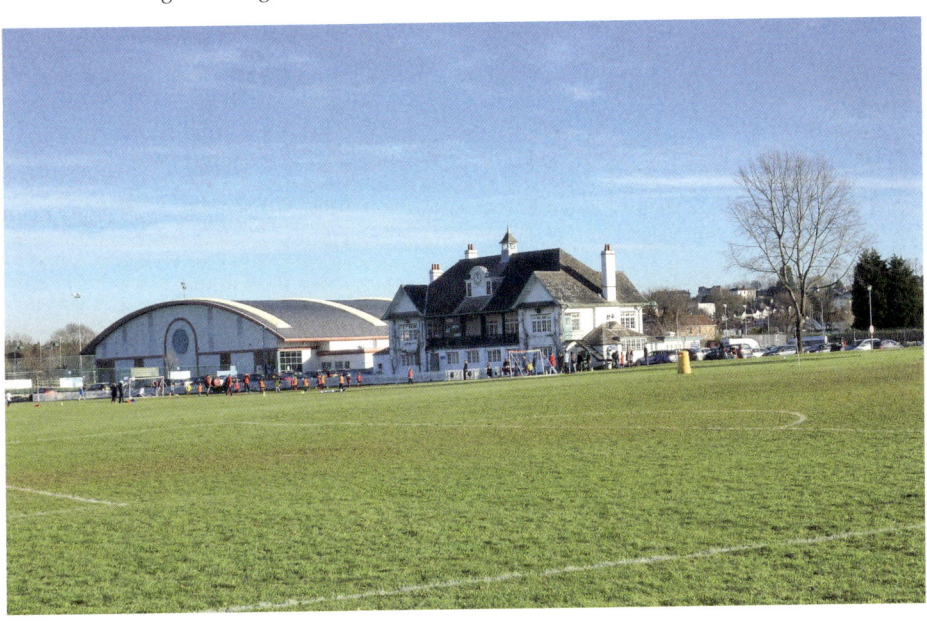

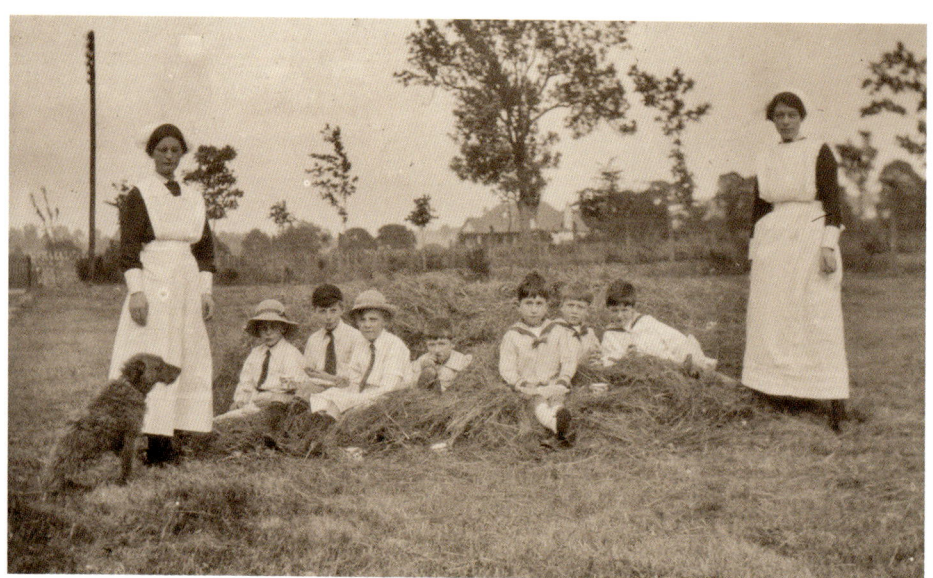

Making Hay While the Sun Shines

Many substantial country homes in the first decades of the last century had a hayfield either to feed their livestock or to sell the hay on. Haymaking could be turned into an annual party. The Sargents of Ashburnham seem to have turned it into an event for the family's children and their friends, presumably after the gardeners Pyke and Ambrose had done the real work of mowing. Here, Caesar the dog and loyal maidservants Scuse and Chapman round up the boys for a photograph in the summer of 1918. The rebuilt university sports pavilion may be seen in the distance beyond the hedges of Coombe Lane. The other photograph shows Gladstone Sargent taking precautions to keep a recipient of the hay away from young chestnut trees in April 1913. The view looks towards Stoke Lane. Since 1931 the Sargents' hayfield has been beneath the houses and gardens of Woodland Grove.

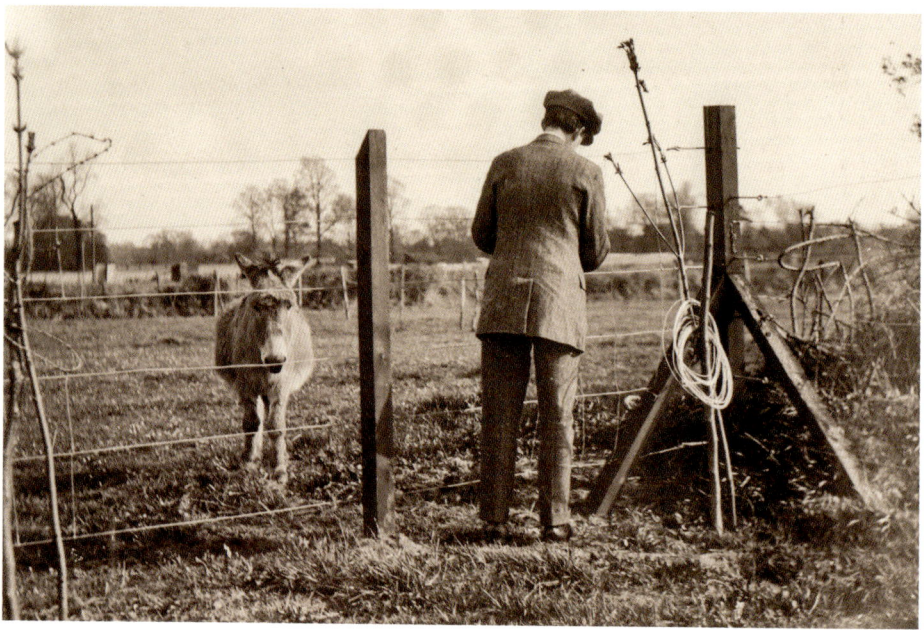

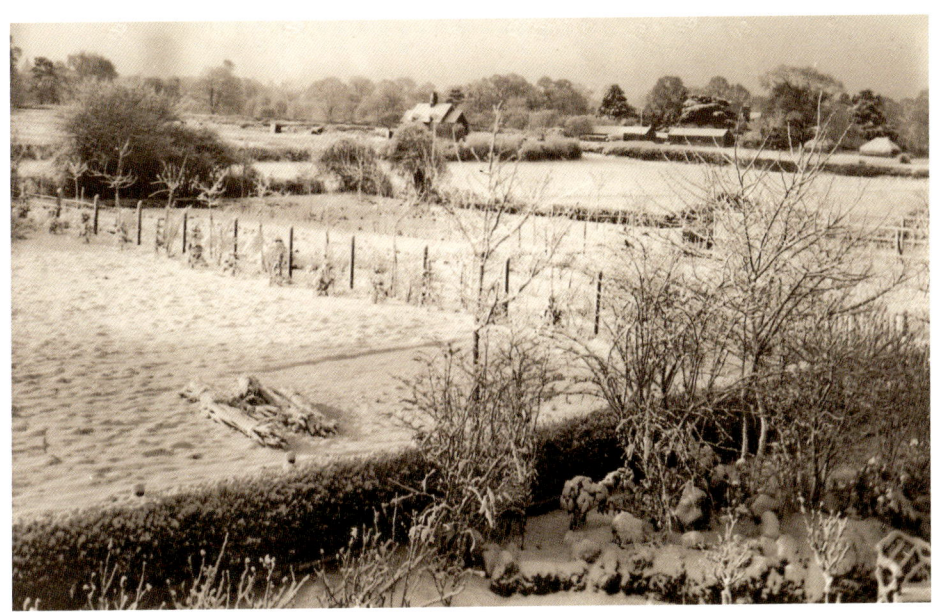

The View Towards Stoke Bishop, 22 March 1917

This winter view from Ashburnham's balcony towards Druid Stoke shows nothing in the way of houses beyond the entrance lodge and outbuildings of Stoke Lodge that nestle beyond them behind the great cedar tree. Two haystacks sit on the far right. The fields fronting and to the left of the lodge belonged to Cross Elms, and were described as 'allotment gardens', all of which are now covered by gardens and houses. At the far left, trees mask the site of The Grove and the new mansions of Druid Stoke. Sargent divided up his land, planting fences and trees, many of which survive in modern boundaries and, together with houses, now block this view. His poultry enclosure appears on the far right. In 1931 Woodland Grove was laid out across the scene. The modern photograph reverses the view, looking towards the lodge and Blaise woods beyond.

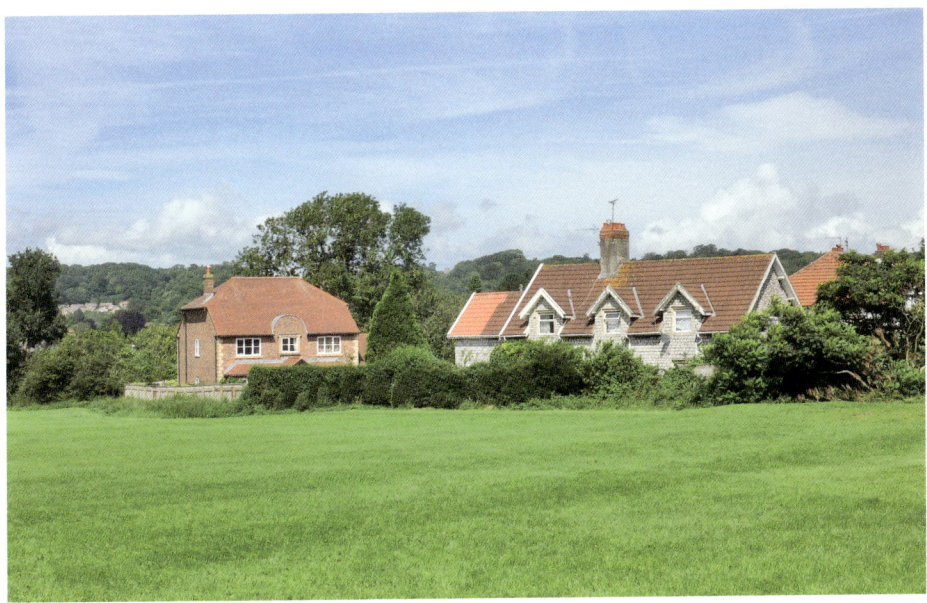

Walk 3

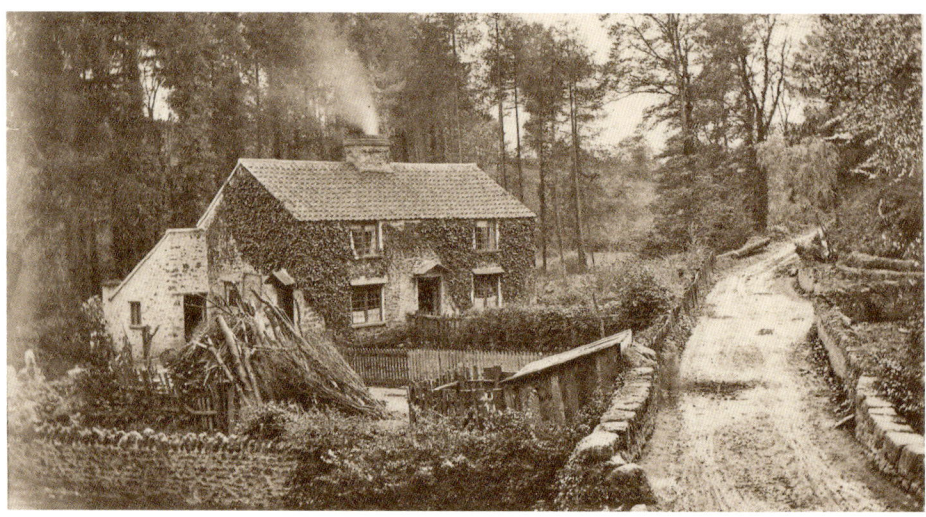

White-Washed and Ivy-Clad, the Cottage by the Bridge

The Dingle's Ivy Cottage was much featured on postcards. This, however, is the earliest image known of it and is one of five previously unpublished photographs of the area in the 1860s by William Barton. The Westbury to Shirehampton road crossed the bridge over the Trym in the right foreground. The river skirted the garden walls to the left and looped behind the house, backing the line of tall trees. Brookridge Wood sparsely covered the slopes beyond that Dingle Road would later crown, and provided a striking contrast with today's tangle. Out of frame to the left of the viewer was the hamlet's pump and the only source of drinking water. Residents used yokes and buckets, as seen in the delightful 1910 photograph, while the local tea gardens obtained their supplies from it in churns by pony cart. Always prone to flooding, the cottage was demolished by the council in 1942.

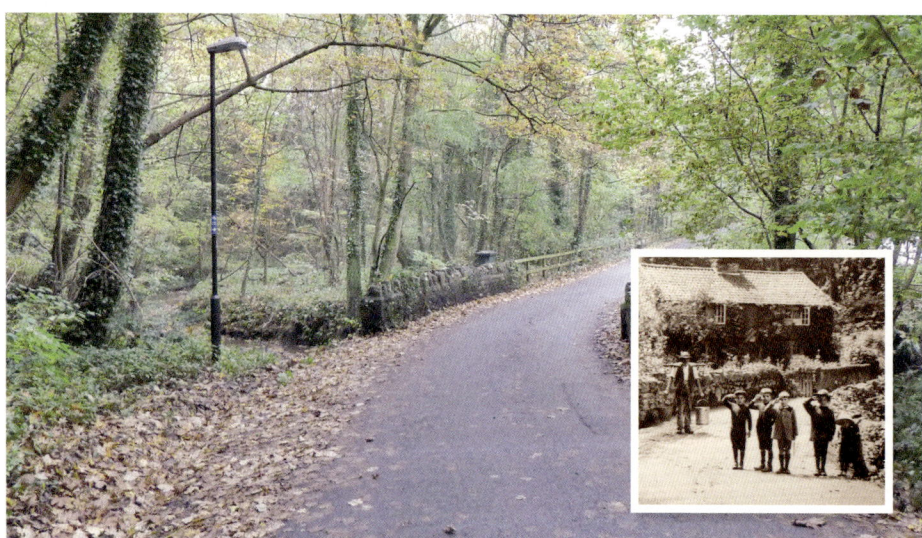

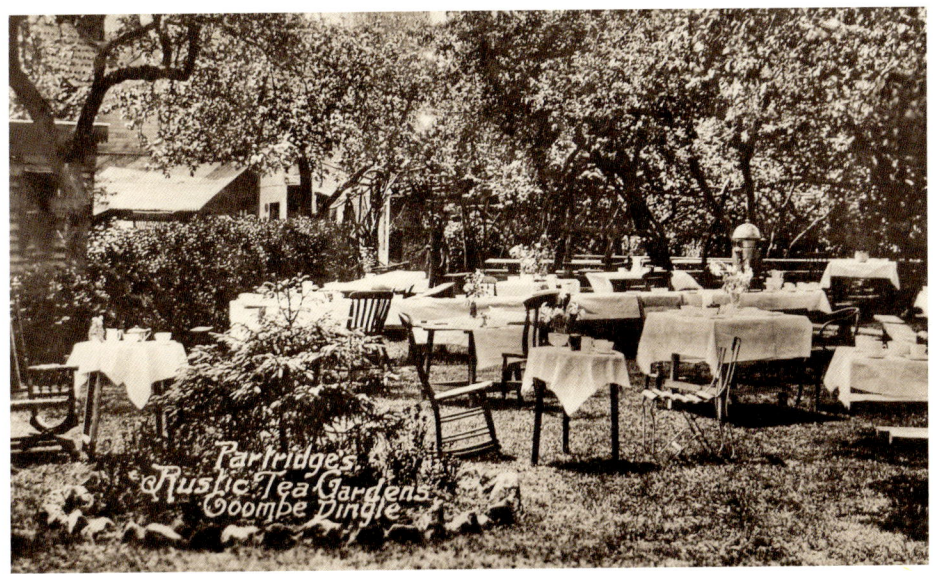

A Rustic Industry

Coombe Dingle's visitors supported a thriving local 'hospitality industry' in the form of tea gardens. Bowden's Fields boasted substantial ones by 1912, issuing their own postcards, but enterprising farmers and cottagers might also find at least one spare table in the garden for rambling guests. John Clark's Rose Cottage, in Grove Road, could serve up to 350 customers in an afternoon in its trellised booths. Appletree Tea Gardens lay opposite it and large groups would be split between them when necessary. Adjacent to Rose Cottage, at Grove Lodge, were Mrs Jane Lee's Refreshment Rooms, previously the Grove Side Tea Gardens. Partridge's Rustic Tea Gardens, with its booths for inclement weather, lay nearby. Directories list other gardens, such as Charles Gould's at Treborough, and E. J. Robertson's exotic Coombe Dingle French Garden. The gardens encouraged the local economy in their needs for external staffing, cake and bread-making, dairy produce, and laundering.

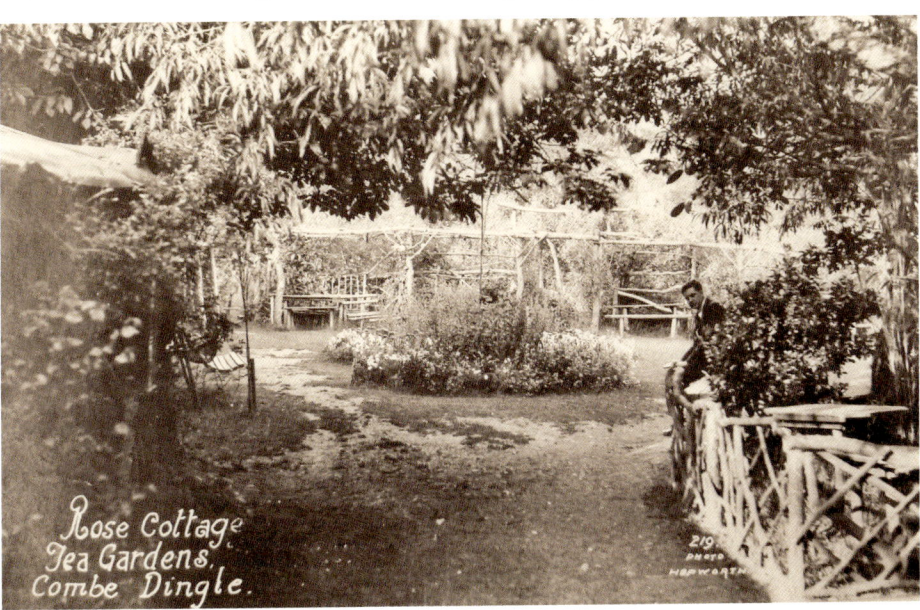

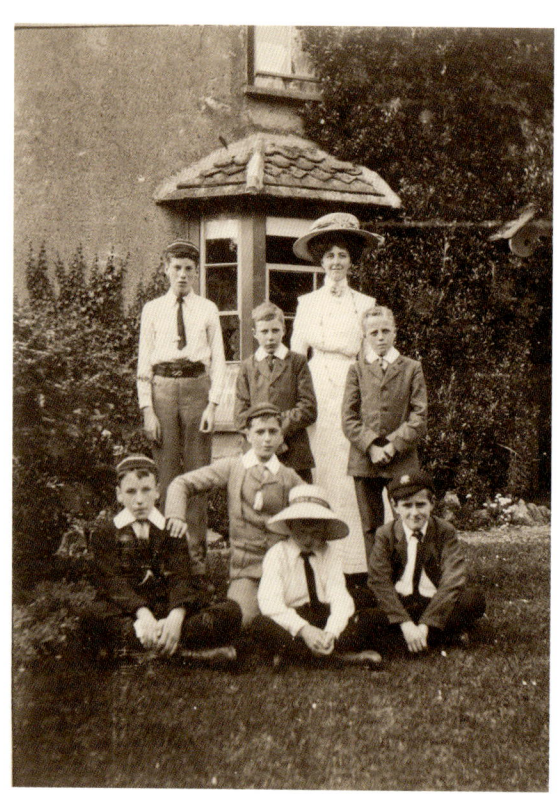

'Ruby at Appletree Farm, Coombe Dingle, 1909'

Ruby Sargent and some rather glum boys from her Sunday school class stand, hoping for refreshment, before the façade of Appletree Tea Gardens in The Dingle (then Westbury Lane). Newspaper reports state that thousands of Bristolians explored the near countryside on public holidays. At other times the Coombe Dingle tea gardens catered for visiting church and men's groups, athletic and other club outings. Appletree utilised its large orchard and provided benches and tables throughout and swings for amusement. Chocolates, cigarettes and other necessities were sold from small shops at the gardens. Speculative infilling in the last fifty years has unfortunately seen at least five houses built on Appletree's grounds.

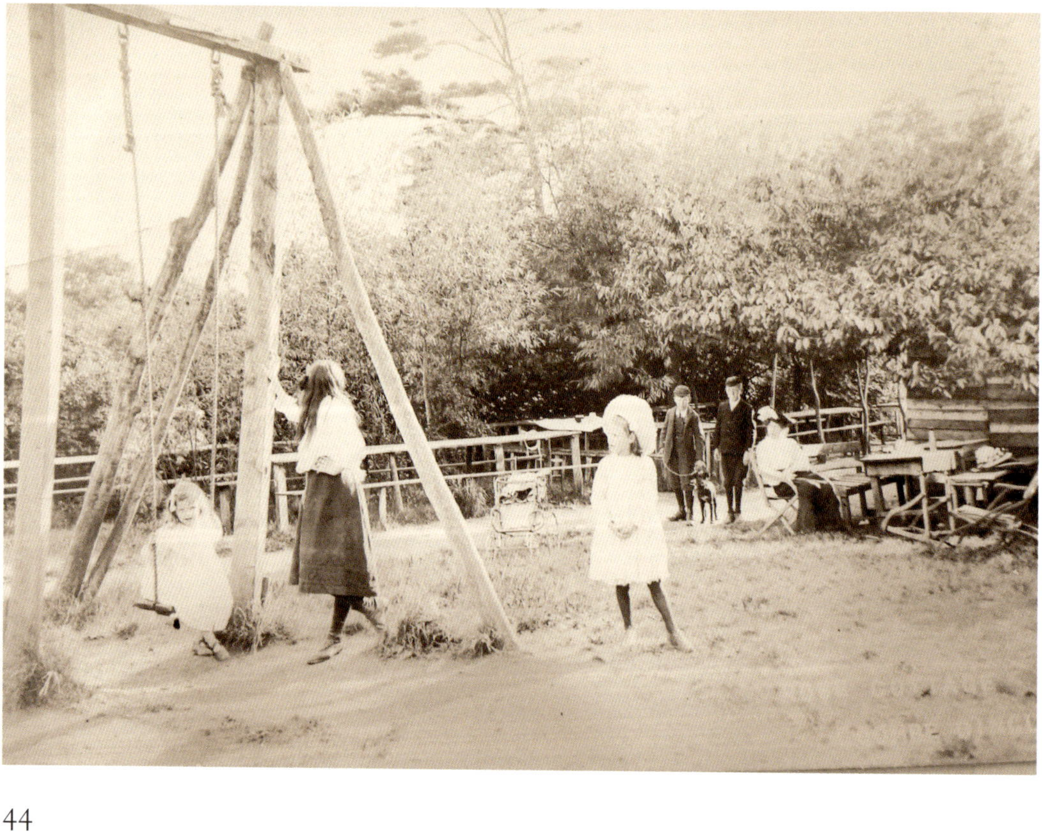

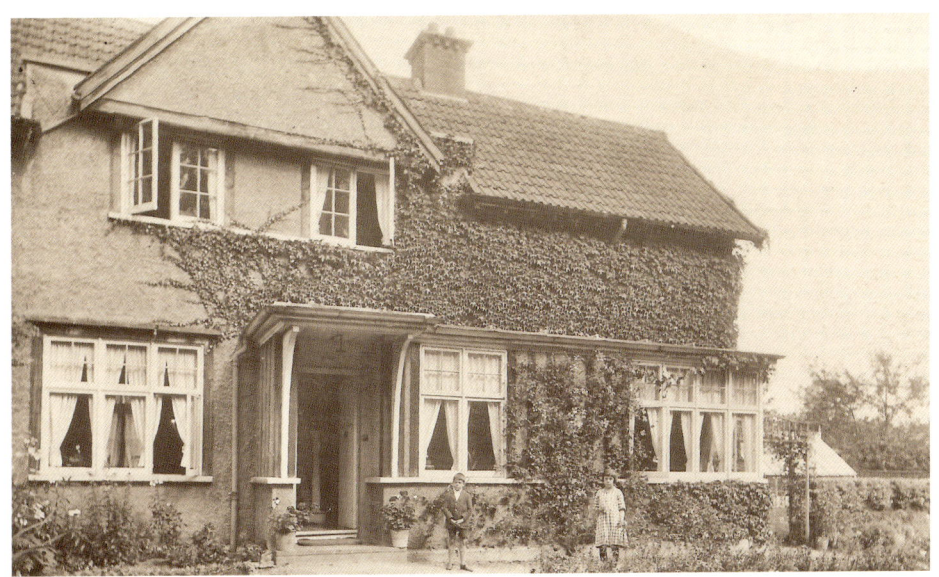

Young Harts at The Birches, 1925

The Birches (now 2 The Dingle) is one of a series of semi-detached and detached residences built in Westbury Lane in the teens of the last century. In Westbury Lane and that section now renamed The Dingle, houses such as Nutgrove (now Byways), Harford Lodge and numbers 16–22 all display William Studley features, such as angled corner windows on the ground floor and pendant gables. The Birches and the neighbouring properties up to Grove Avenue may also be his work, but from a slightly later era. Unlike its attached neighbour Staddle Stones, The Birches seemingly never possessed a balustrade above its projecting lower windows. From around 1915 until at least the late 1930s, The Birches was the residence of Frank and Dorothy Hart, whose children feature in the photograph. Before the construction of the bridge over the Trym, the Shirehampton to Westbury road ran past The Birches.

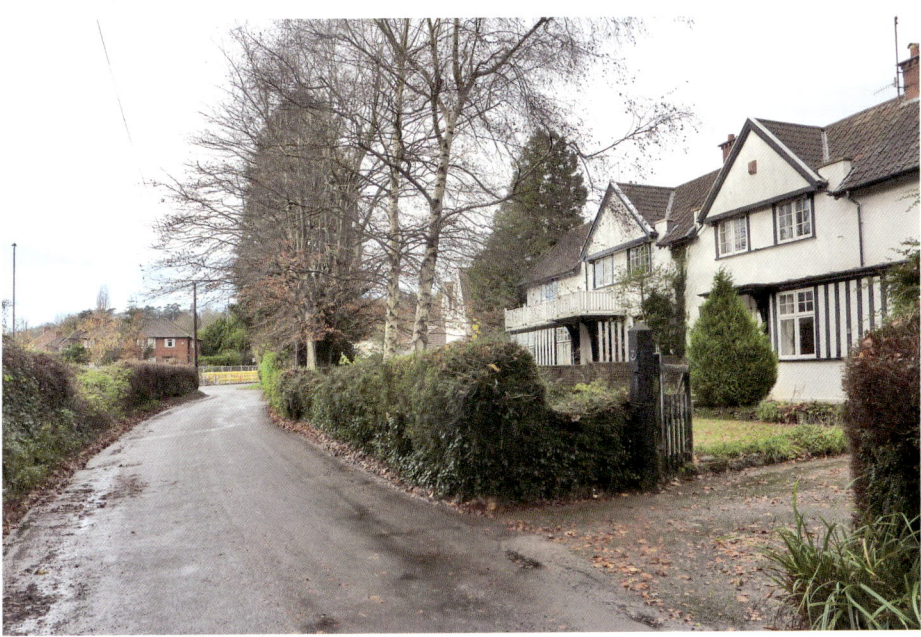

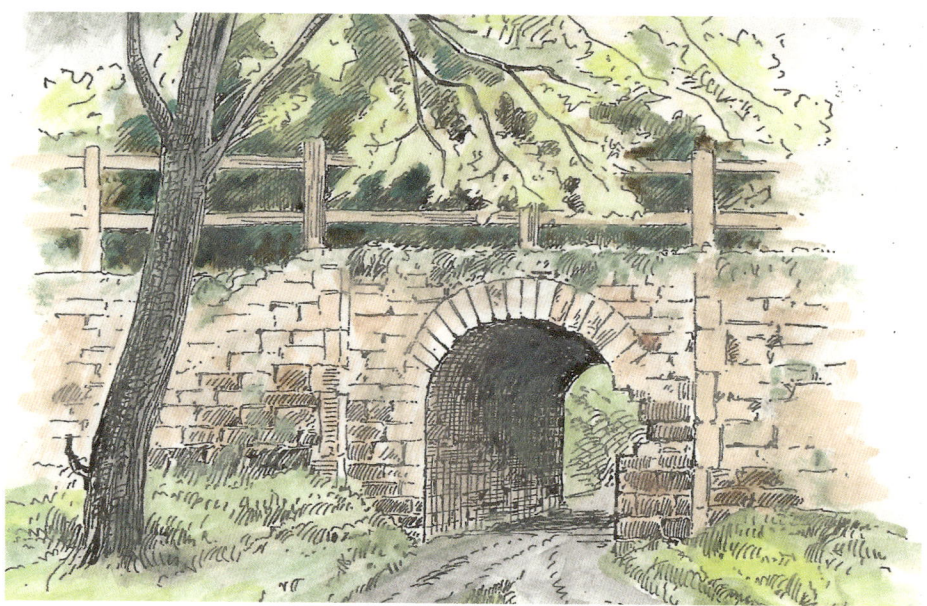

The Mysterious Archway

The lane from Grove Road towards Penny Well ends before a substantial archway. Descending as a footpath, it emerges beyond into Blaise estate, where it divides. One branch ascends towards Arbutus Walk while the other descends to the historic, but now elusive, Penny Well. The *raison d'être* and history of the archway are generally unknown, but rather than an entranceway, the structure was actually a bridge that once supported a carriage drive over the footpath. The drive ascended from the bridge near the pond below, and ran along the hillside before curving back to be carried spectacularly over the archway, finally joining the lane. It may date from Farr's day, as do other Blaise bridges, or from the 1812 drive improvements. That no trace remains of the drive's exit on the 1883 Ordnance Survey map suggests it was long disused. Loxton's drawing from around 1915 shows a handrail but the structure appears semi-ruinous.

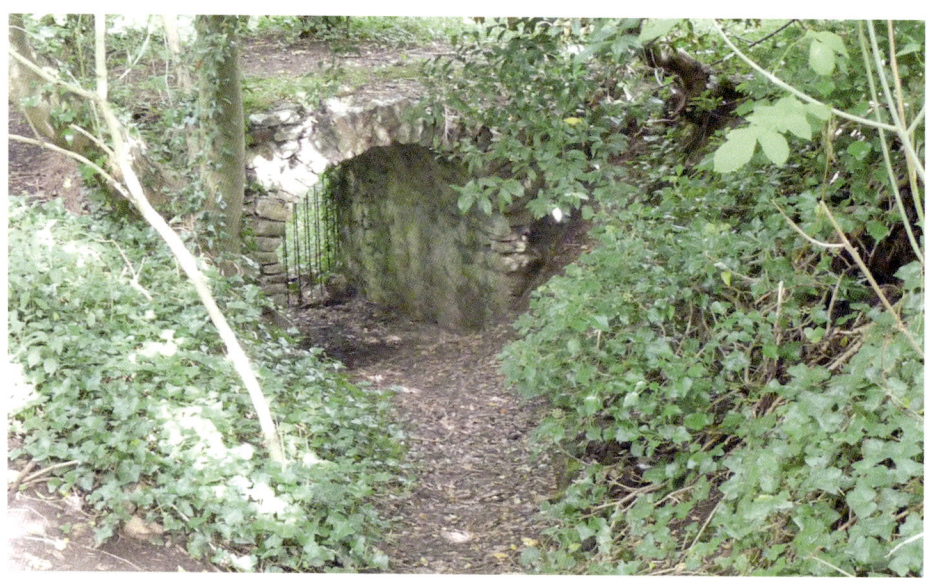

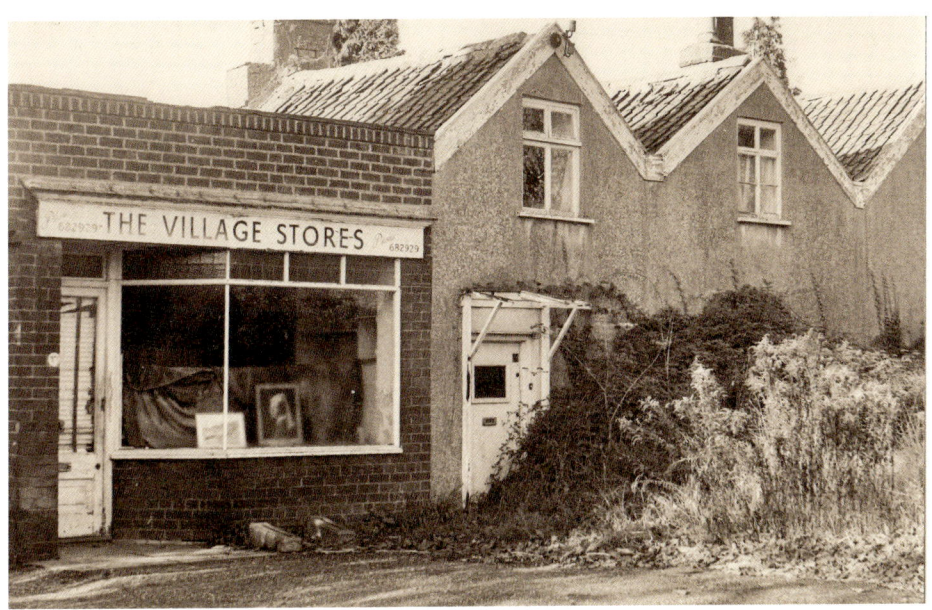

'Closed': the Village Shop and a Lost Sarcophagus

Wren's and three of the Bowden's Fields early cottages await demolition in 1978 to make way for new houses. Bert Wren built the shop in Grove Road in 1936, which traded until the mid-1970s when it finally closed. It survived for a while as a distribution centre for Mrs Beatrice Pearce's newspaper-delivery service. Vermeer's *Girl with a Pearl Earring* long ornamented the empty shop's window. Somewhere nearby, a beerhouse had catered for the villagers' needs in the nineteenth century. Local tradition grants Grove Road a Roman origin as the route from Abonae (Sea Mills) over the Down to the settlements in the Lawrence Weston area. A stone sarcophagus, found in 1972 during the building of Cedar Court, Pitchcombe Gardens, suggests the presence of a nearby Roman villa supporting the tradition. Although the sarcophagus was saved for the City Museum, now it (and even its photograph) is reported as 'lost'.

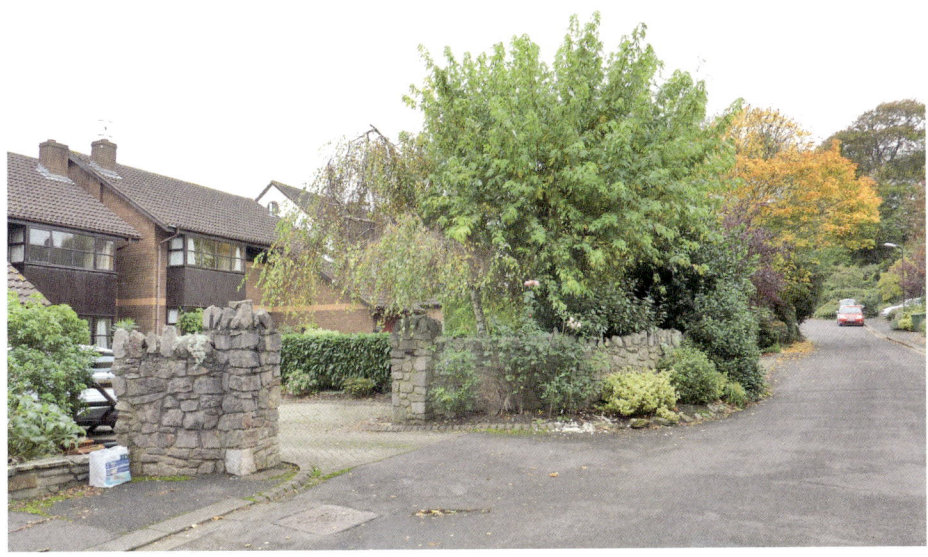

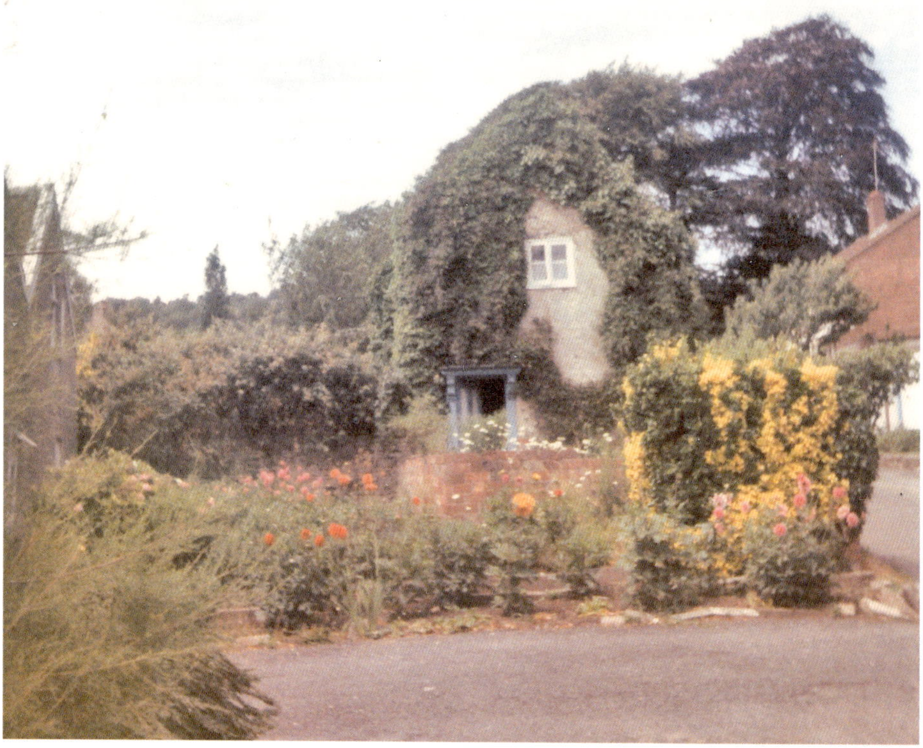

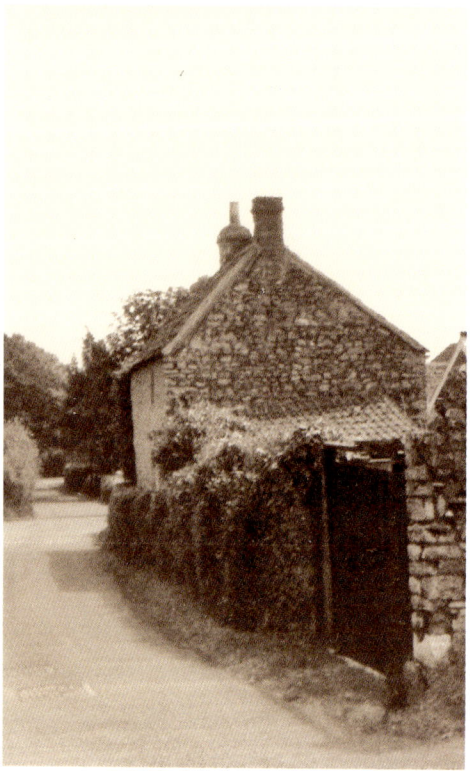

Just Like a Helen Allingham Painting

One of the oldest cottages of Bowden's Fields, 37 Grove Road, ivy-mantled and with its burgeoning cottage garden, is seen in the mid-1970s prior to its unexpected demolition in 1979. The cottages attached to the village shop appear to the left. To the dismay of local residents, number 37 was demolished to make way for two houses built in its garden and to 'improve road safety' by straightening the road. Demolition showed the roof beams to consist of unworked timbers. Disquiet at the urbanisation of Coombe Dingle and infilling around Grove Road led to its inclusion in a conservation area. This notwithstanding, infilling has continued since. Concerns were raised as early as 1926 concerning the damage to the local environment by commercial enterprise and protests arose again in April 1960 after the zoning of Coombe Dingle by the Corporation for housing. Much damage has been done since and it continues to be threatened.

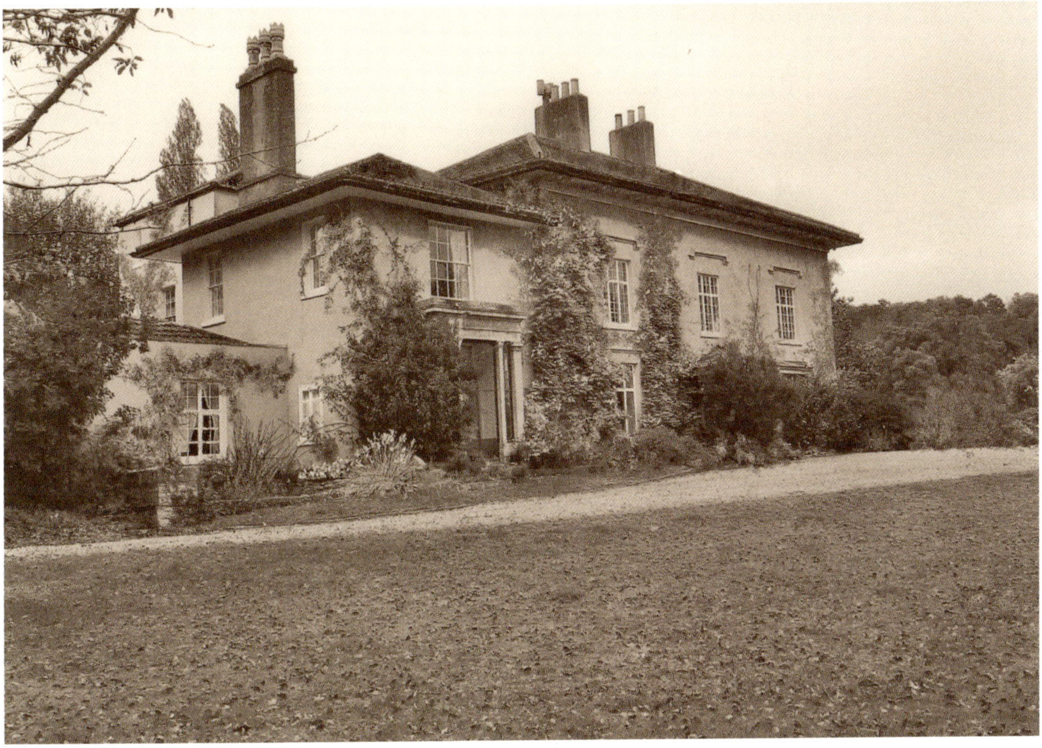

An Artist's House in the 1930s

Hillside in Grove Road was for many years the only gentleman's house in Bowden's Fields. It is believed to date from 1805, although it may have enlarged and aggrandised an earlier structure. It was extended and remodelled in the 1830s. Tudor-style stone windows still light the upper floor of the rear block, and hood-mouldings remaining over the windows of the main façade hint at earlier fenestration there as well. A conservatory once fronted the low extension on the left. From the 1900s until his death it was the home of widely exhibited artist and banker Edward Hamilton Chetwode Chetwood-Aiken, PS (1867–1935), whose family also owned the Glen, Stoke Bishop. He painted landscapes and flowers and was a passionate gardener and designer of rockeries. In 1911, four servants and a governess attended on three Chetwood-Aikens. During the Blitz, Hillside was hit by a stray incendiary bomb but sustained minimal damage.

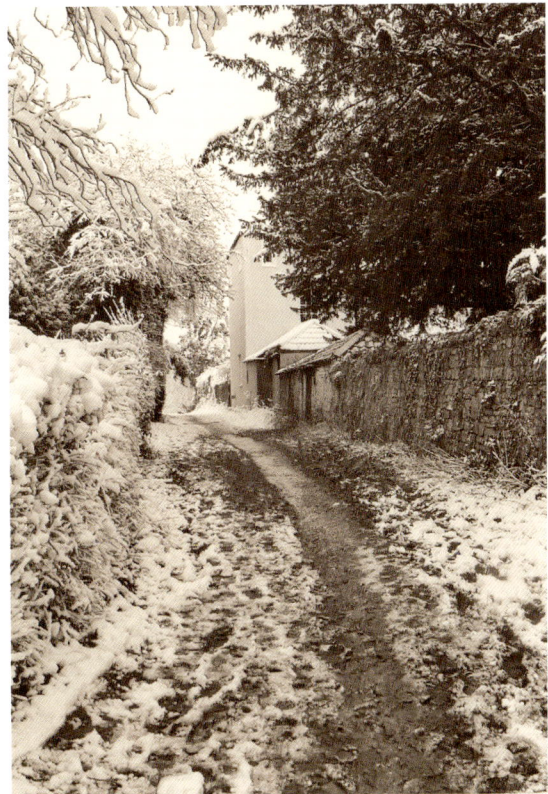

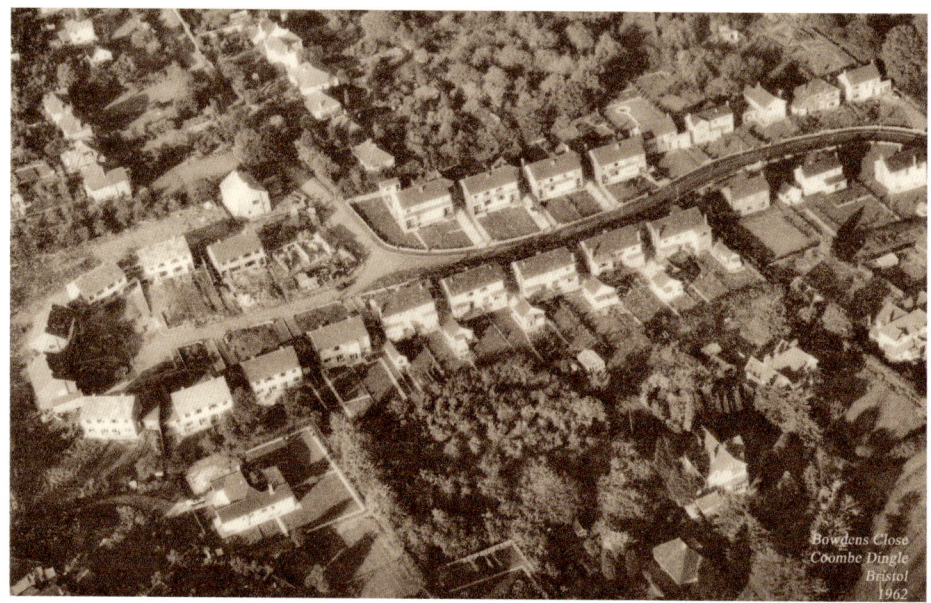

Bowdens Close
Coombe Dingle
Bristol
1962

A Hamlet's Namesake Rises, 1962

The 1950s saw the permitted expansion of housing in Coombe Dingle with the extension of the 1930s Grove Avenue to Westbury Lane over former pasture and nursery land, as seen to the middle and right of the photograph. There are local stories of bankruptcies and suicides among small builders who overreached themselves in the enterprise. Bowden Close at the left, and also in the modern photograph, arose between 1959 and 1962 on the site of historic Bowden's Field Farm. It preserves the name of Bowden's Fields (sometimes Boulton's Fields), the hamlet that straggled around Grove Road. The complications of tithings set it within Lawrence Weston, although isolated plots belonged to Westbury. Tennis courts once occupied the land where the house in the left foreground above stands, and Harford Close would soon sweep away the orchard to its right. Long Acres Close and The Grange have since infilled half of the bosky rectangle behind Grove Avenue.

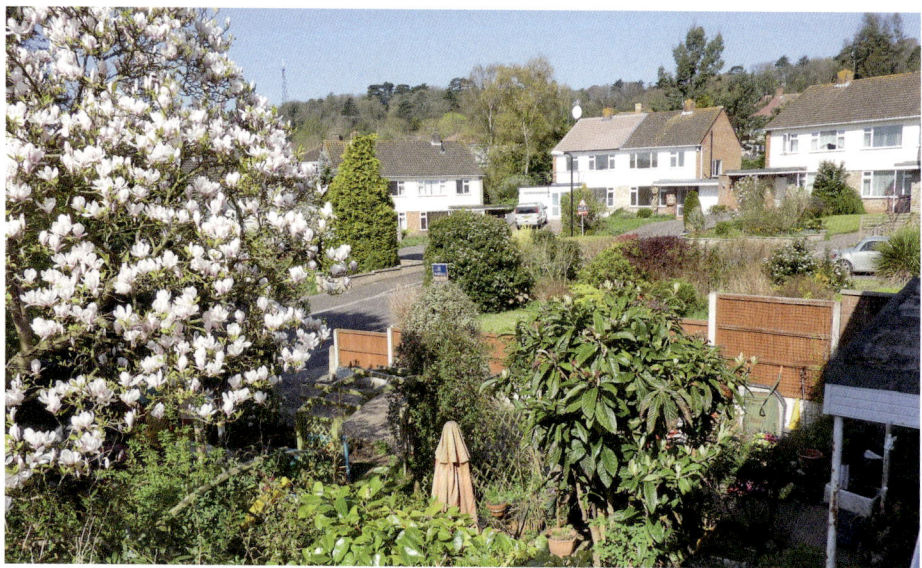

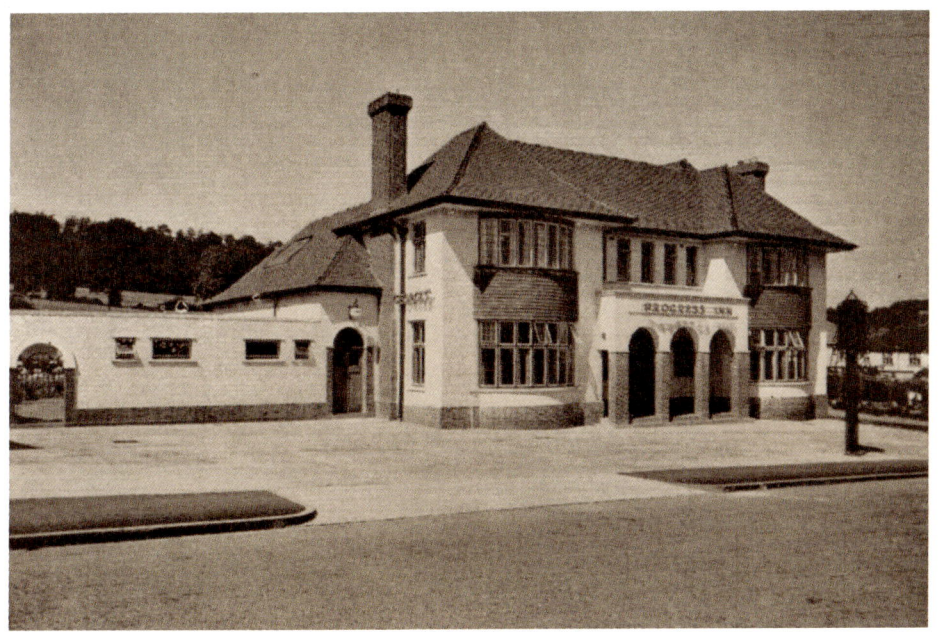

'This Place of Cheer … 'Mid Storms Unkind'

Sea Mills estate, on the western side of Westbury Lane, was without a public house, and it was not until the sale of King's Weston land that Georges Brewery saw an opportunity to build the Progress Inn next to the new rank of shops. They submitted plans in August 1936. Aldercombe Road and the Southwood estate had not then been developed and the building was backed by fields and woods. Georges, mindful of hikers and visitors from the city, lauded its 'country setting within easy reach of Bristol'. A handsome building, designed to cater for families, its delights included a walled garden, skittle alley and a smoking room. Opened in 1938, it inspired the Revd A. C. Stratton to compose a rondeau in its honour in his *Songs from the Ship and Castle*. Renamed The Iron Bridge, it eventually closed in 2011. Now beautifully restored, it houses the Red Bus Nursery.

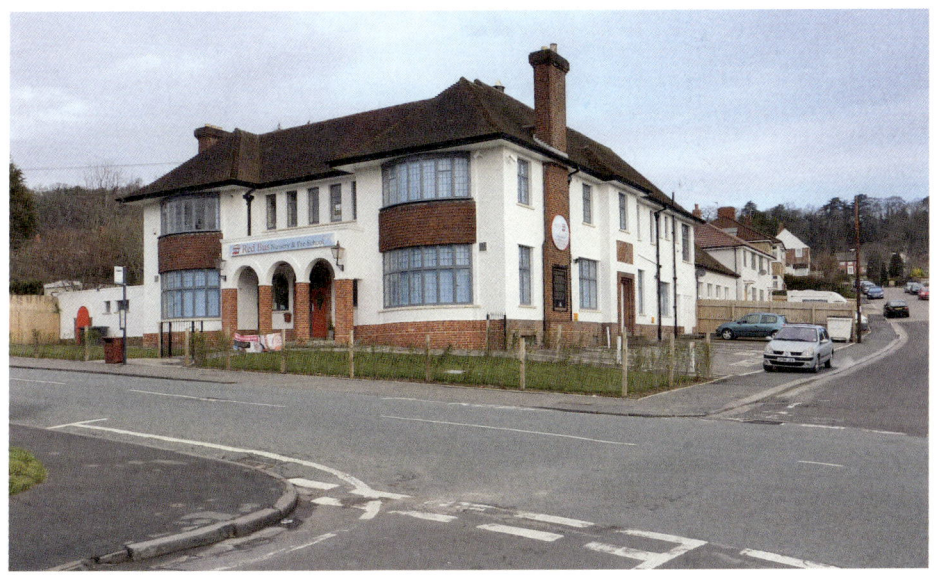

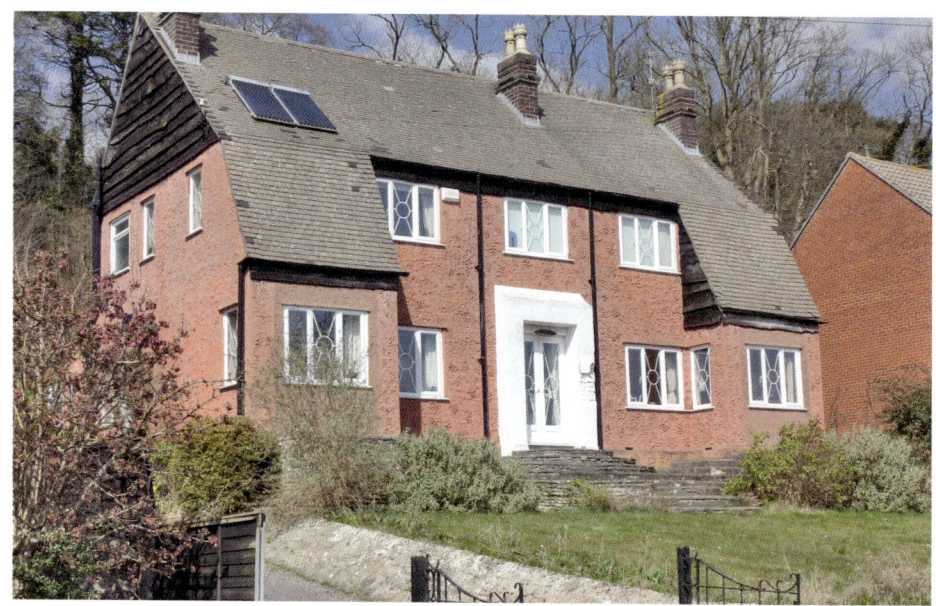

Beyond Westbury Lane, 1933

In 1938, the builder William Henry Martin, who owned the meadows behind Westbury Lane (seen here above Sea Mills estate in 1933), submitted plans for forty-eight houses called the Southwood estate. By July 1939, he had submitted applications for a further ninety-nine houses and two bungalows in Southwood Drive, Southwood Avenue, Aldercombe and Overcombe Roads. He built the Red Barn at the top of Aldercombe Road for his sailor son, Bill, humorously giving it 'porthole' glazing bars. Two oaks from its pony field still exist nearby. Another son, John Delair Martin, constructed the roads. This proved difficult because intractable bedrock broke drill bits and the steepness of the hillside made traction difficult for horses and vehicles. The war ruined the Martins' business and destroyed their homes in Henleaze. The council then bankrupted them by compulsorily purchasing their Coombe Dingle land for social housing before many of their houses could be built.

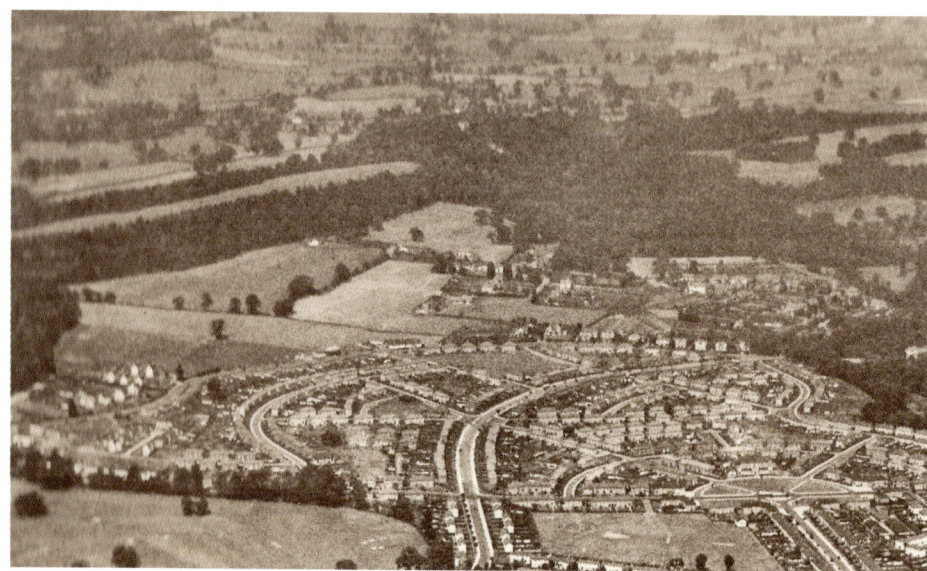

Homes for Heroes, 1929

In 1929, the recently established Charitable Trust, the Douglas Haig Memorial Homes, laid out a small estate of twenty-four houses near the top of Westbury Lane, on land donated by Philip Napier Miles. From around 1925, properties had started to colonise this virginal territory to take advantage of the views to the south. Field Marshall Haig (whose bas-relief image overlooks the estate's central garden) had been concerned over the plight of ex-servicemen and their families in 'Civvy Street', especially those disabled by conflict. The Trust aimed to provide homes at affordable rents to these; it now has over 1,300 properties in Britain. Wyvern Villas, the Haig flats in Falcondale Road, Westbury, occupy a building acquired from the Ministry of Defence in 1993 and refurbished in 2007/08. In 1955, two brick dormer bungalows were added at either side of the entrance to Haig Close. The top photograph dates from 1968.

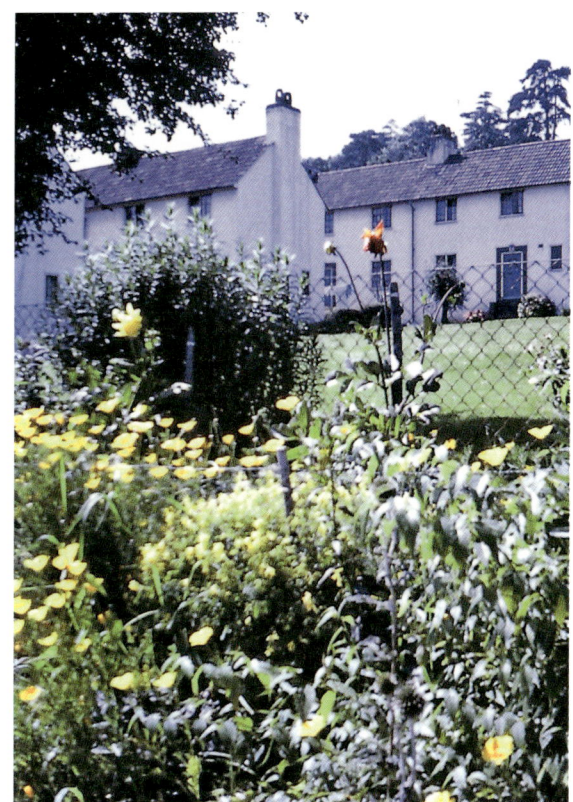

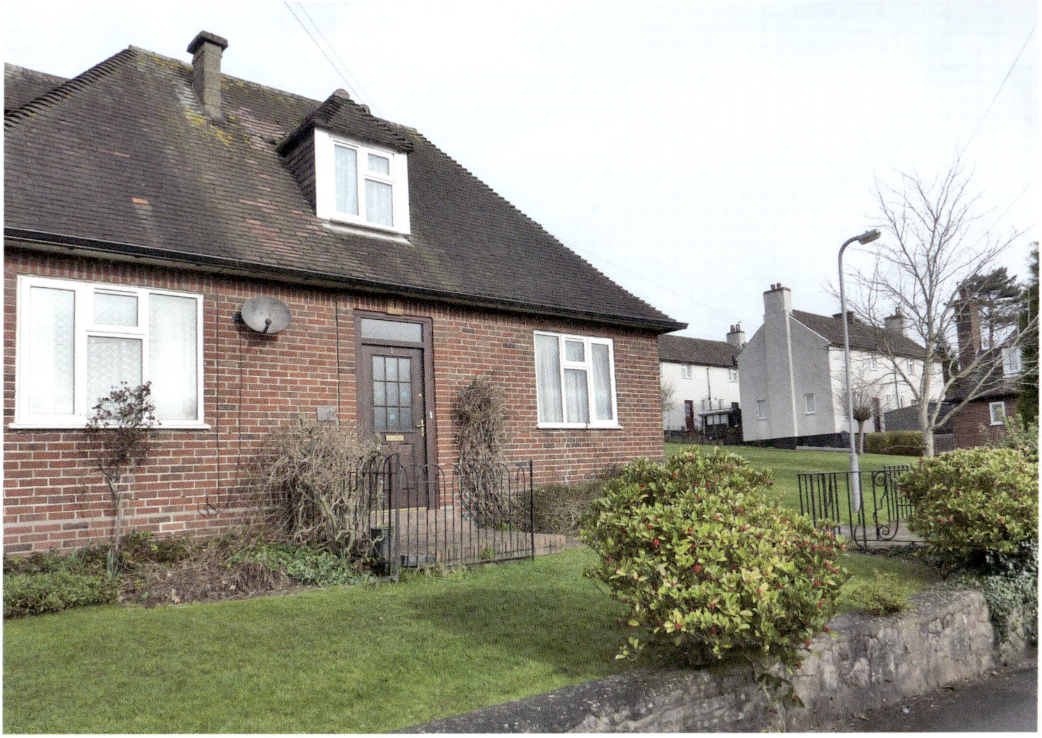

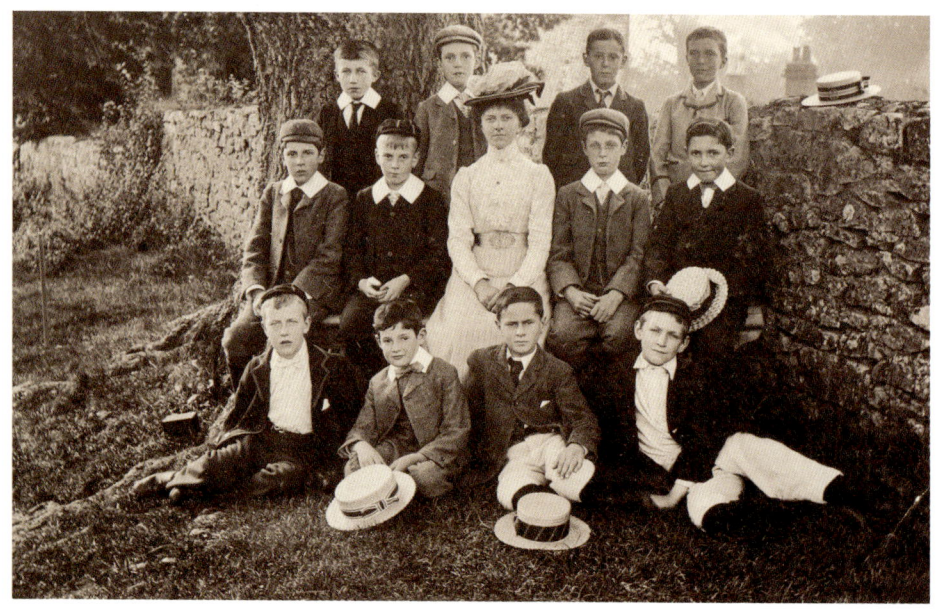

'A Convenient Place to Leave Carriages and Servants'

Norma Walters and her Sunday school class in 1904 pose seriously in the tea garden behind Vanburgh's remodelled King's Weston Inn. Pocket handkerchiefs, watch chains and bow ties adorn her charges. The northern corner of the inn, and cottage chimneys, appear behind the wall. The hill behind the inn had always been lauded as affording some of Britain's most stunning panoramic views. Alas, the cessation of grazing, and uncontrolled tree growth have robbed the modern visitor of this delight. The inn was an important venue for visitors to House and Down, and Georgian Bristolians took a dish of tea there on Sunday evenings. It is now cottages, and the main façade appears below. The cutting and footbridge date from 1819 to 1822 when John Loudon McAlpine upgraded the road to Henbury into a turnpike. Further improvements followed the death of the Miles's coachman near this corner in 1854.

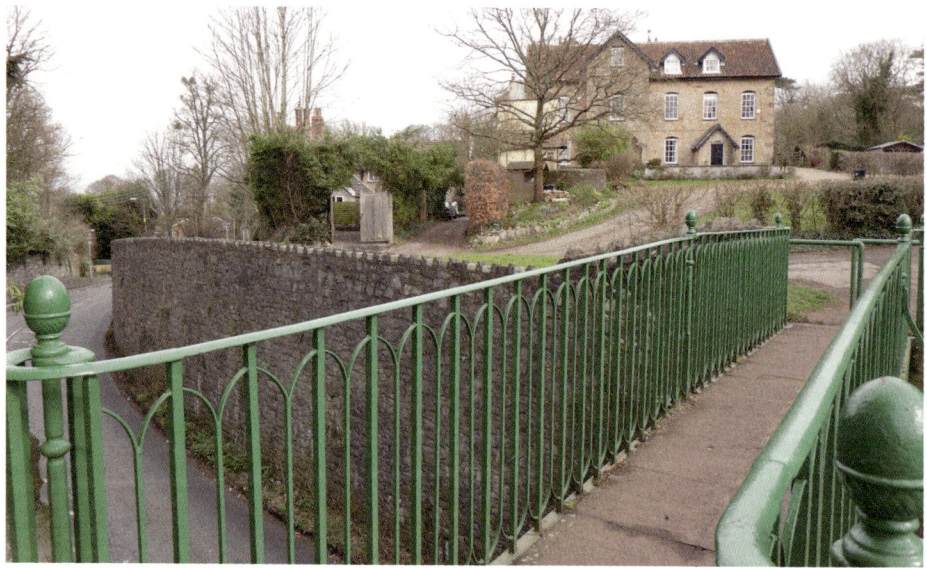

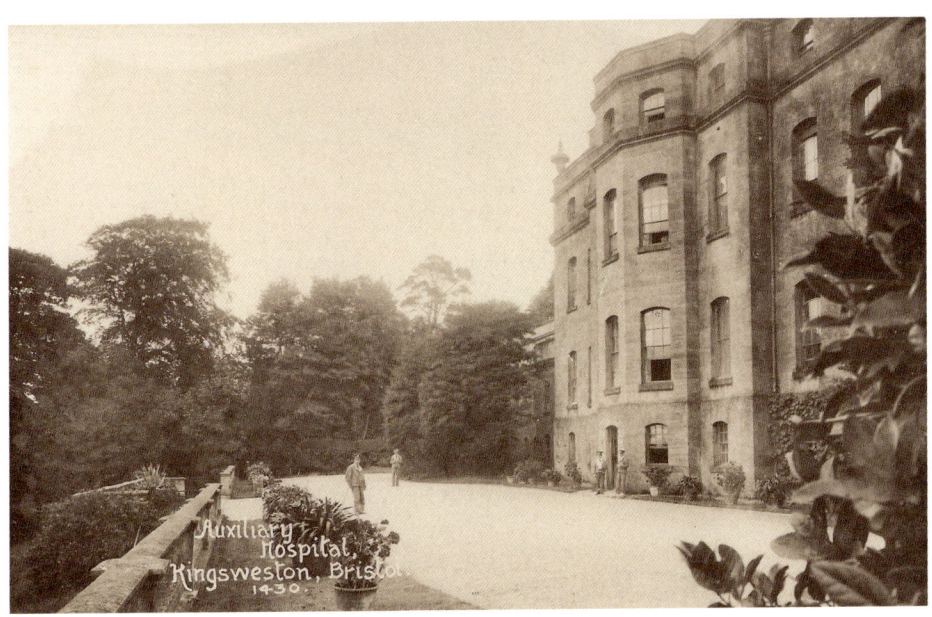

King's Weston House at War

Philip Napier Miles (1865–1935), the last squire of King's Weston, might well be described in the words of *1066 And All That* as 'a good thing': cultured, kind, forward-thinking and protective of his tenants and estate. In many ways, his tenure was a golden age for north-west Bristol. He was generous with gifts of land both to protect its beauty and to foster development. During the First World War, the house became an auxiliary hospital with Mrs Miles as matron. Following Philip's death, the estate was sold to pay Death Duties. Bristol Municipal Charities acquired Vanburgh's house with the intention of moving Queen Elizabeth's Hospital School there, and partial demolition was followed by the first stages of work on Maurice Webb's new school, seen on the right of the lower photograph. Wartime requisition halted construction and, after various post-war uses, in 2013 it was acquired by Norman Routledge, who has laudable plans for the building.

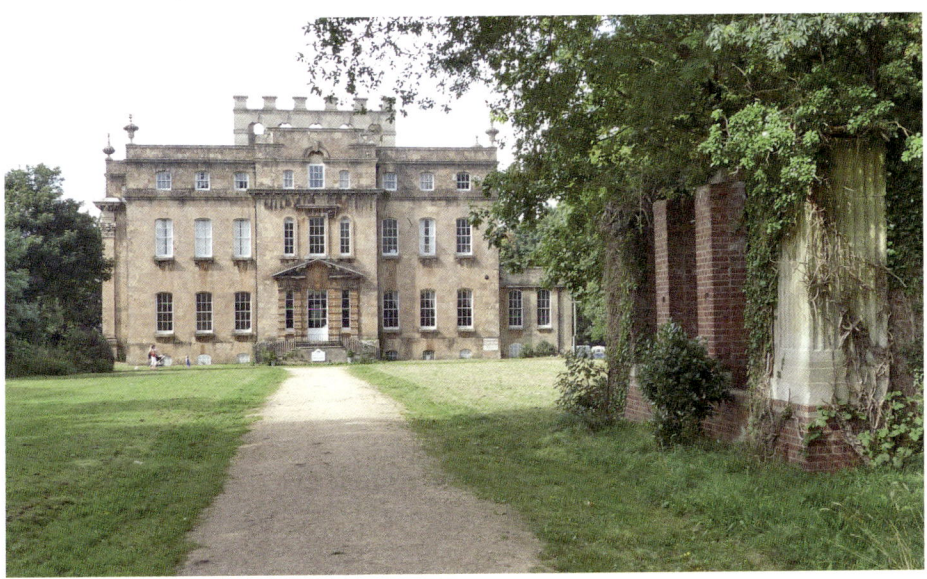

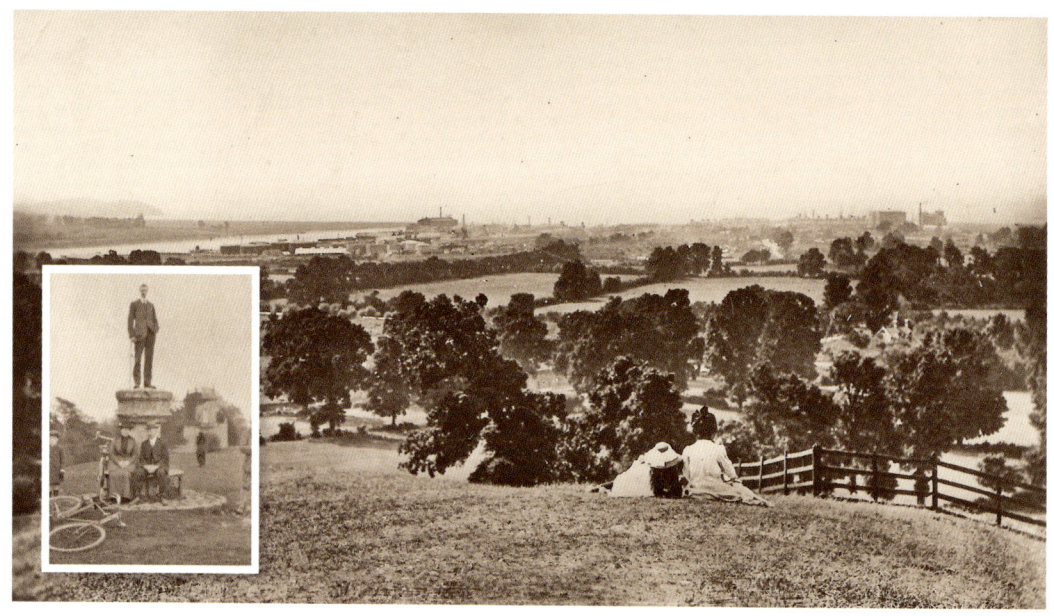

'The Finest View in Europe'

Visitors who flocked to King's Weston came not only to view the house and its superb gardens, but also to experience the wonderful panoramas, sunsets and pure air both from the ruined windmill then on King's Weston Hill (above the present Ardern Close), and from Penpole Point. There, the seventeenth-century dial, and Vanburgh's noble Penpole Lodge (demolished by the Council in 1952) marked the traditional viewing places. The magnificent views are still there, albeit less romantic, but are now obscured by a wall of self-seeded woodland, the result of Council neglect since the 1950s. The admirable and energetic Kings Weston Action Group has done much good work recently on the estate, including the clearing of undergrowth from the Penpole Lodge ruins, but a greater commitment is needed from the Council. The photographs from 1907 and 1957 illustrate the great expansion of Shirehampton and Avonmouth in fifty years.

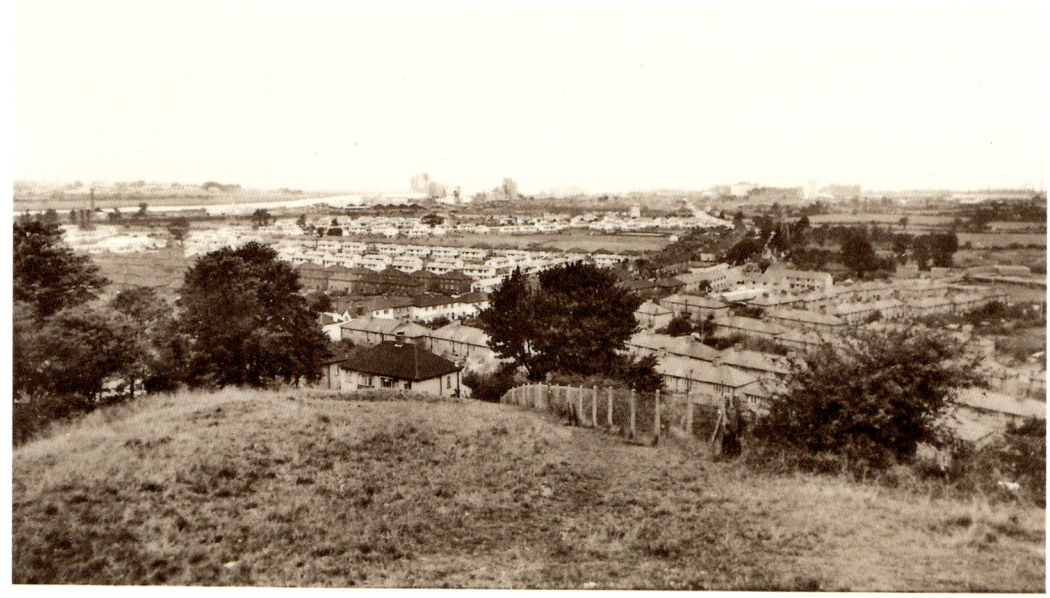

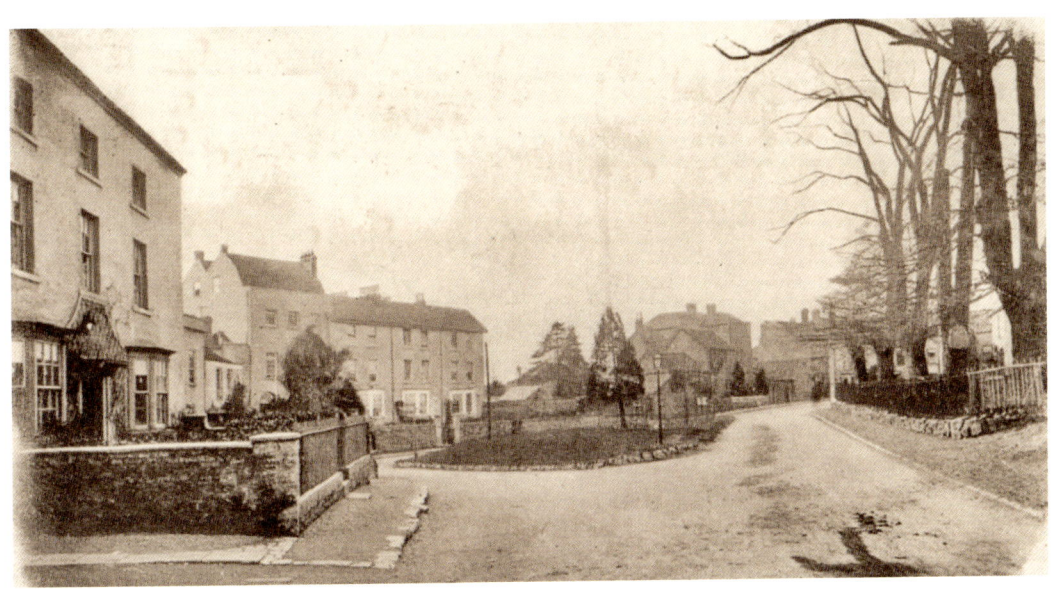

'The Elegant Village of Shirehampton'

Keswick House, The Terrace and The Green around 1905. Once referred to as 'the prettiest village in Britain', Shirehampton provided sheltered winter accommodation and was much frequented during the summer by genteel visitors. Like Westbury it attracted Bristol's wealthy merchant class in search of convenient country dwellings. The development of Avonmouth and the influx of an industrial class began an unstoppable change in the social fabric of the village. The twentieth century dealt unkindly with Shirehampton, with the loss of its squire and its assimilation into Bristol destroying much of its beauty and, as with Henbury, swamping the original inhabitants with new housing estates. Still affectionately called 'The Village' by locals, it retains a strong, bustling, and healthy identity. An unusual local peculiarity, perhaps resulting from the influx of Bristolians, is to abbreviate some words and sentences. Thus a request to a bus driver for a ticket to Shirehampton becomes 'Shire, Drive'.

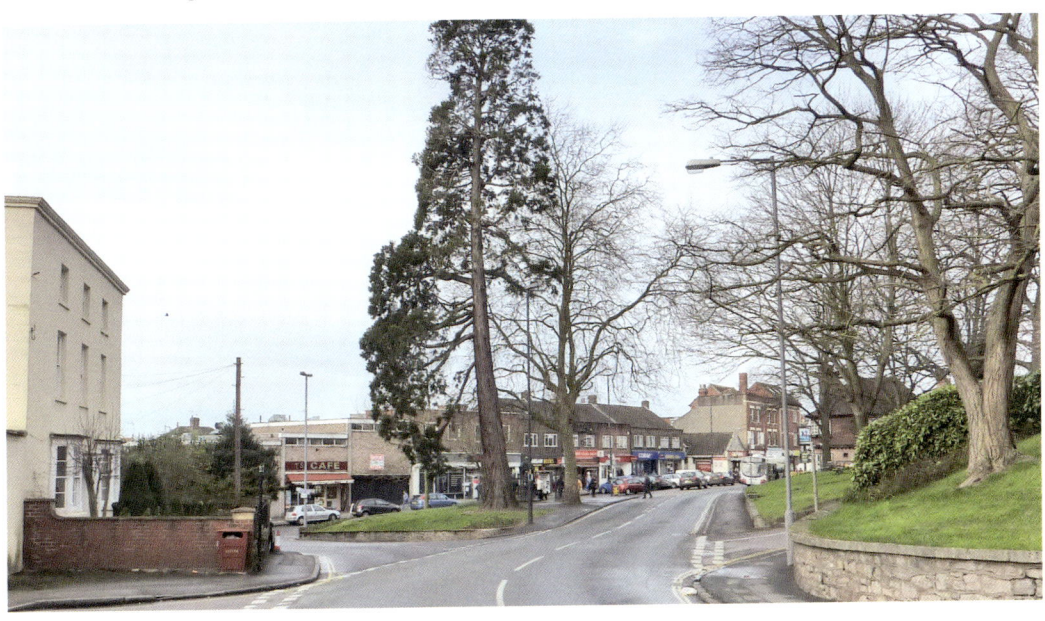

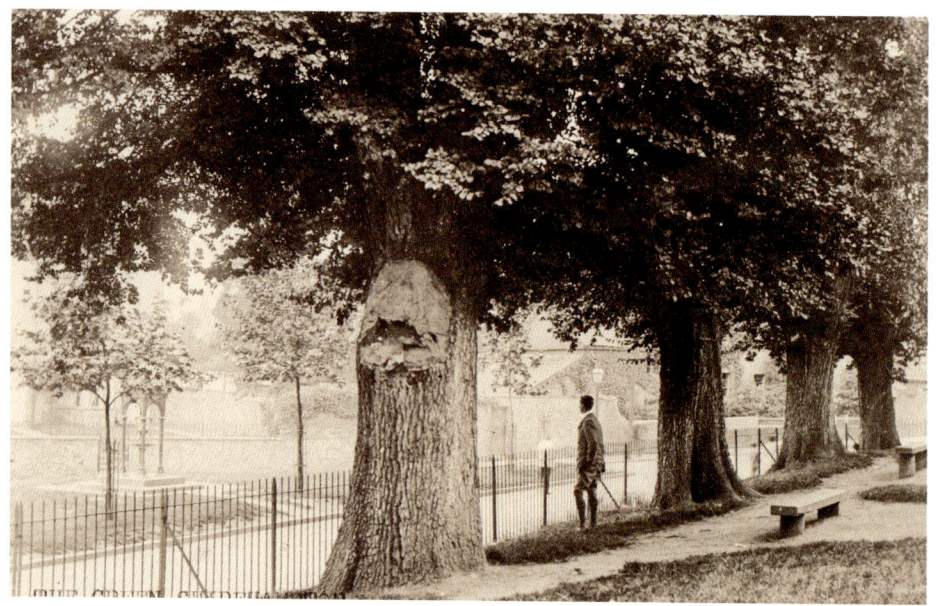

'Plenty of Nice Young Men Here': Shirehampton, 1904

Whoever 'A. L. M.' was, or whatever their sex, the weekend spent in the fleshpots of Shirehampton in November 1904 was sufficiently stimulating to be described as 'a bit of alright' on their postcard shown here. A young man gazes from the natural colonnade of ancient elms at the Jubilee drinking fountain on the island of the Lower Green beyond. The wall of The Terrace closes the scene and gardens and creepers complete the idyll. All is peaceful, genteel, orderly and lost forever. The later replacement of the houses of The Terrace and neighbouring Walton House with wretchedly inferior commercial buildings completely ruined the enclosed domestic ambiance of The Green. The Lower Green's Wellingtonia replaced the famous Stocks Tree. This was an elm shadowing the village stocks that, even in 1793, was remarked upon for its great height and for the amazingly picturesque way in which the roots had penetrated the protruding bedrock.

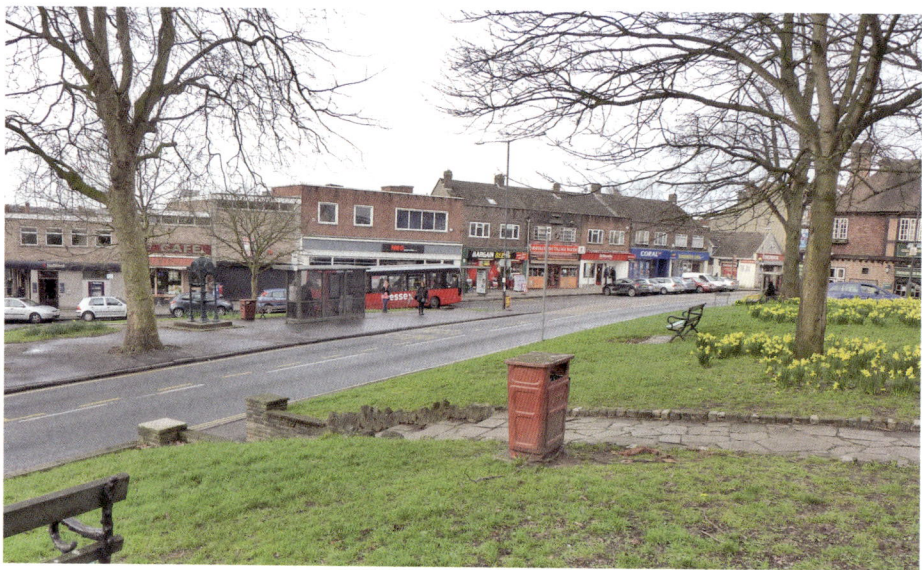

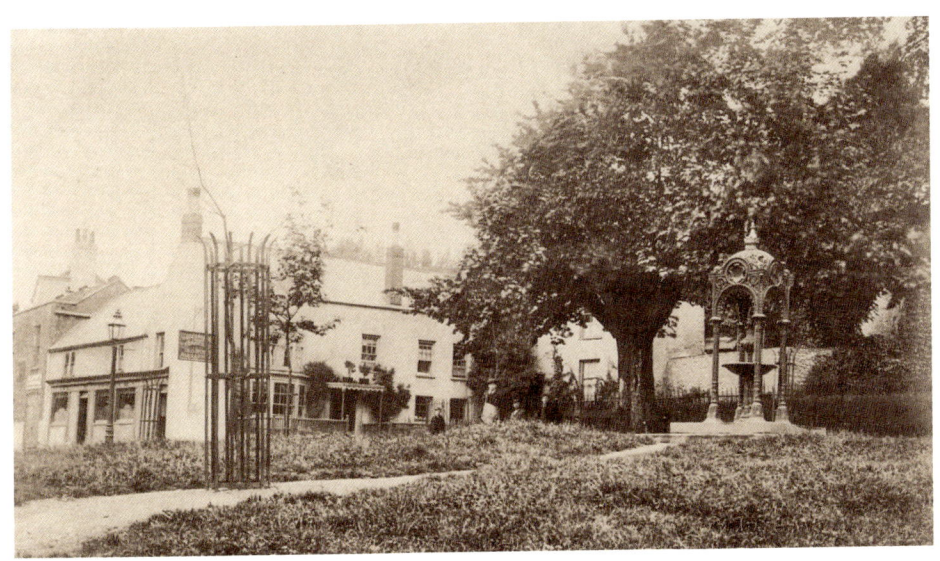

Of Inns and Incendiary Letters

The George, Shirehampton Green, is one historic inn that remains from the village's past, although it was rebuilt in the 1930s. In 1835 a residence beside The Green, then occupied as a beerhouse and called 'The Travellers' Rest', was advertised. The sale included recently built cottages at outlying Shirehampton Marsh, near the river mouth. In January 1761 a spate of so-called incendiary letters alarmed Shirehampton. These were a common form of blackmail, whereby anonymous threats to set fire to property enforced payments or demands from the terrified recipients. The landlady of The Ship, on the riverbank at Hung Road, was threatened with fire if she did not pass on the letter to a Mrs Jackson demanding the dismissal of her coachman or to face the flames. That evening, an arsonist set fire to a woodpile adjoining the property. A Mrs Waterman was also threatened with a demand for staff dismissal and payment of five guineas.

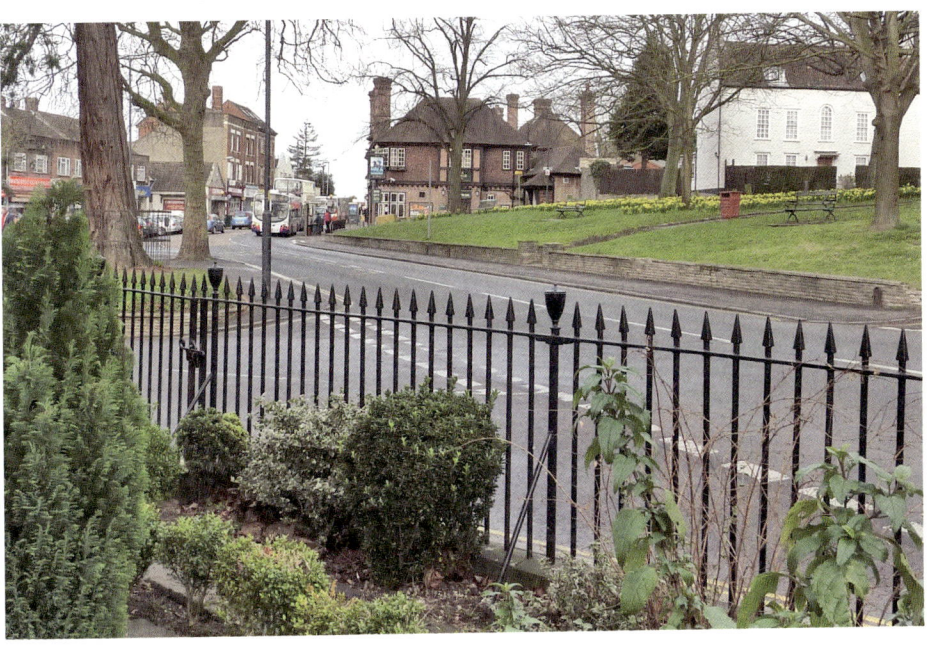

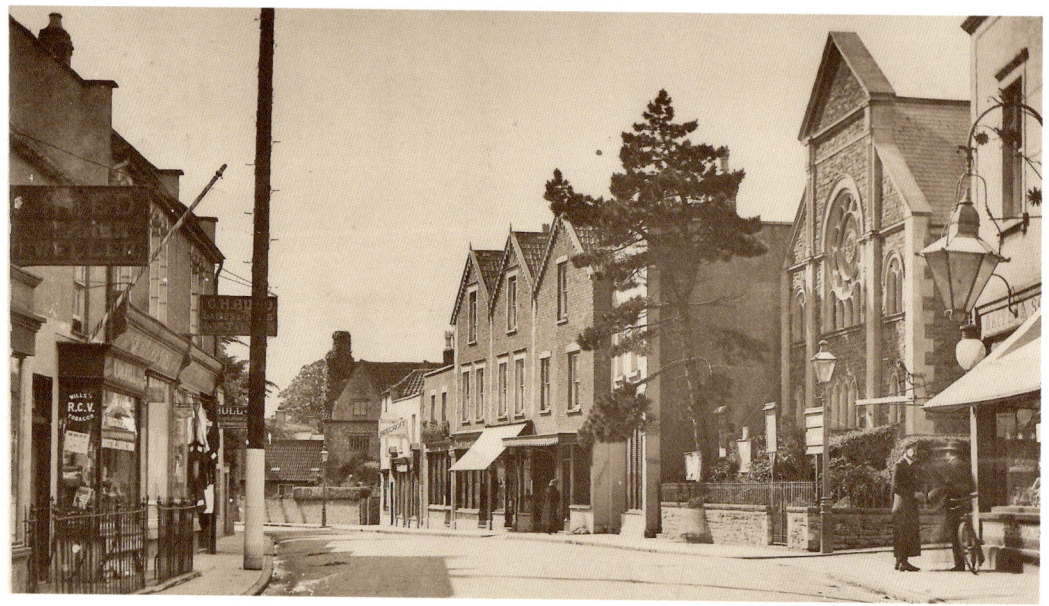

'There are a 1,000 Soldiers Billeted Near the House'

Shirehampton High Street on a postcard sent by a nurse in 1918 working at King's Weston House, which was then a military hospital. A dog snoozes on the pavement outside Codrington's the butcher while, distantly, one of the four gables of the Manor House appears. Sometimes called 'The Elizabethan House', it was tragically lost to road widening in 1936; a symbol of the despoliation of the village that was to come. An established shrubbery fronts R. Cosslett Jnr's 1886 Methodist church at the corner of Penpole Avenue. The church singularly has cinema seating installed in the 1930s. The tall, gabled shops have now been rendered and lost their pretty bargeboards. A large and picturesque lantern hangs outside of Mrs Hack's grocery shop. Among the selection of businesses in this section of the High Street were three banks. All of the buildings on the left have now been replaced.

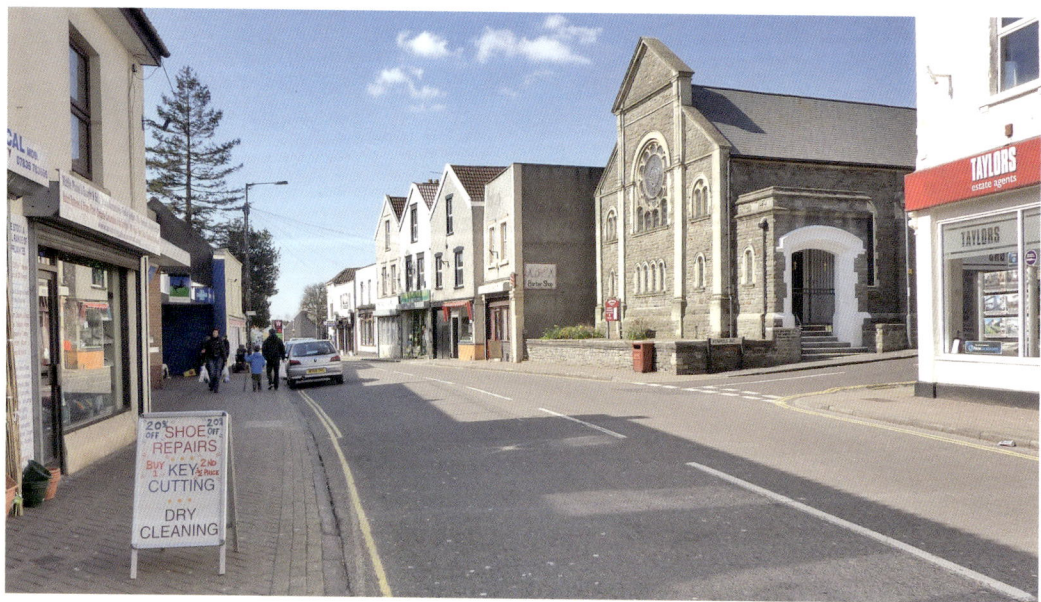

Window Shopping in the High Street

An elderly couple consider the delights offered by the window display in Bert Britton's sports shop at 22 High Street, Shirehampton, in this 1973 photograph by Jim Hale. Chico's Barber Shop now occupies the premises. The unusual wooden canopy, more reminiscent of a railway station than a shopfront, still protected pedestrians from the rain and produce from the sun over William Clarke & Sons at number 24. A bright fabric canopy has succeeded it. Their butcher's shop carried on the tradition of their predecessor, Codrington, at the same address, as does now the firm of W. B. Butchers. The garden wall of the Methodist church appears beyond and Penpole Avenue with The Paint Shop (now an estate agent's) that replaced the earlier ironmongery. The loss of the trees from the church garden is regrettable. In the distance in both photographs, buses take on passengers below the towering 1887 Wellingtonia.

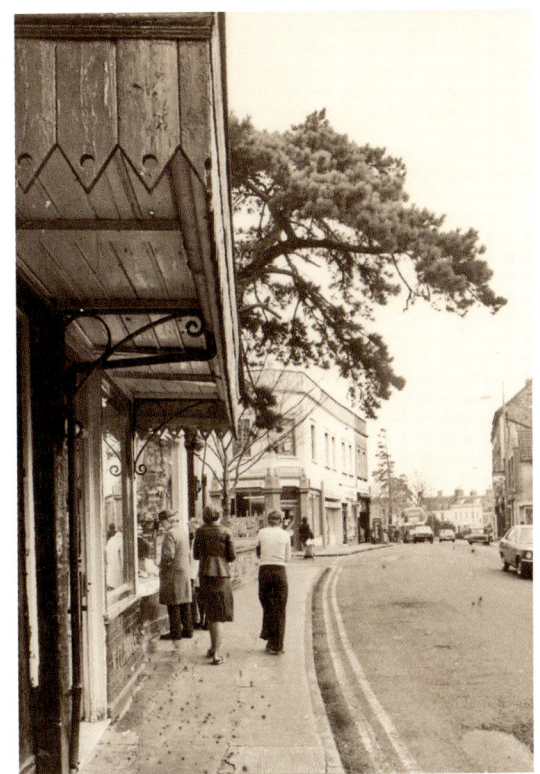

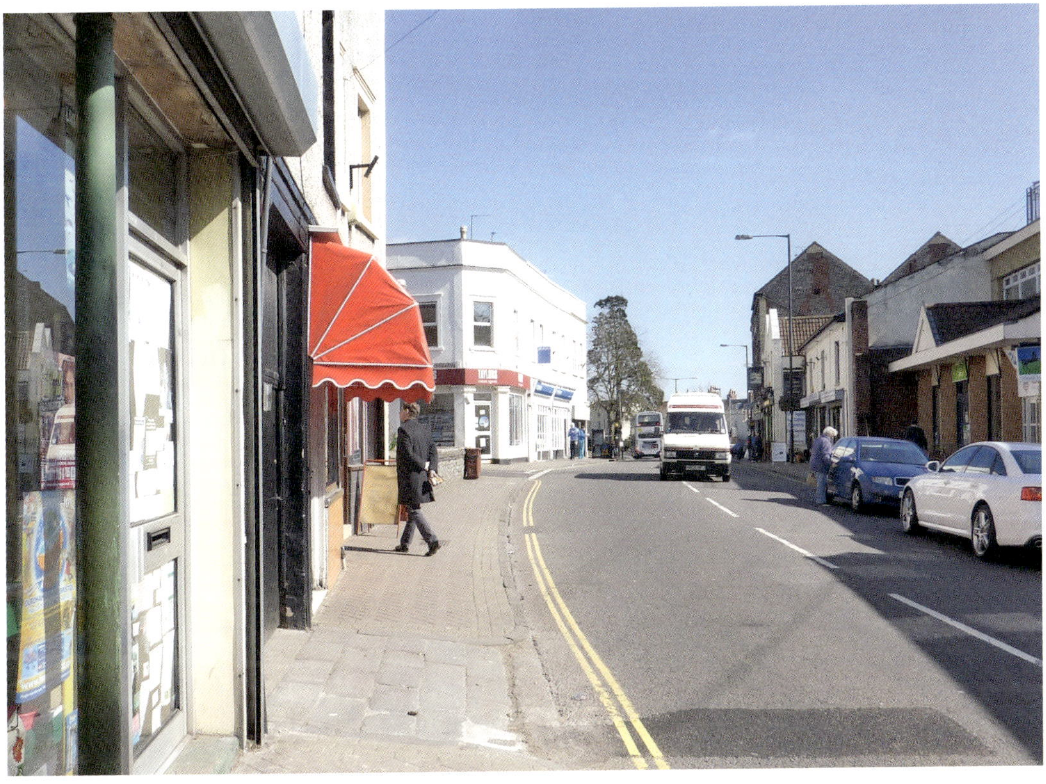

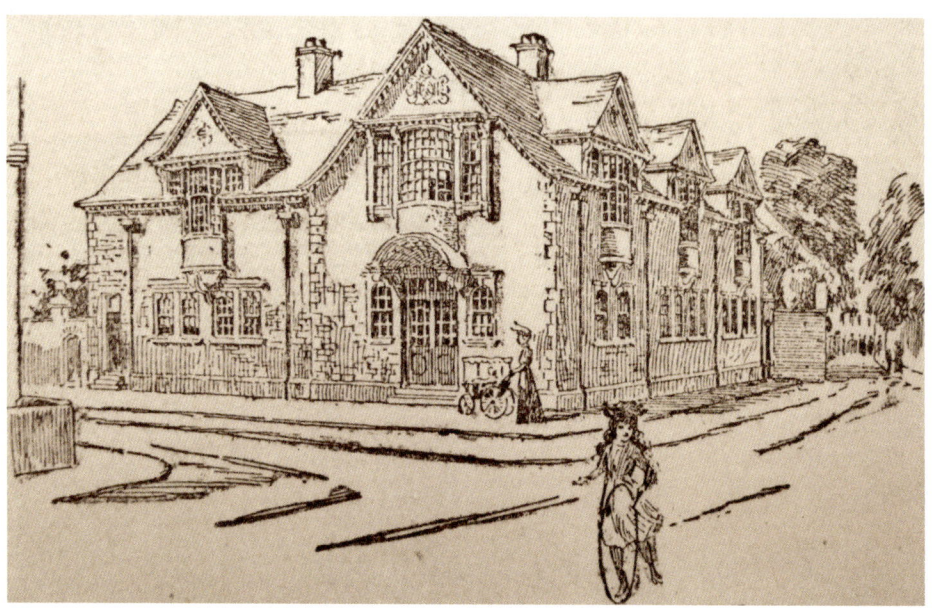

'A Handsome Estate Office for Mr Napier Miles Commands Attention'

Frederick Bligh Bond designed the King's Weston Estate Office for the corner of High Street and Waverley Road in 1902. The superb new building housed the vastly increased estate staff occasioned by the developments at Shirehampton and Avonmouth. Its rusticated masonry was of 'a pretty stone' from the Penpole Hill quarry, with dressings of pennant. Rough green Precelly slate 'of striking appearance' clad the roof. The gables and bases of the oriels were covered with buff roughcast stucco and all the paintwork was white. The stuccoed gable, high above the great shell-hooded entrance, bore the Napier Miles arms. The attached land agent's house was by 1919 called Westward Ho! (an allusion to Philip Napier Miles' 1909 opera of the same name). The Estate Office later became the Shirehampton Men's Social Club, but was demolished in the 1950s to make way for a garage; a poor exchange at any rate.

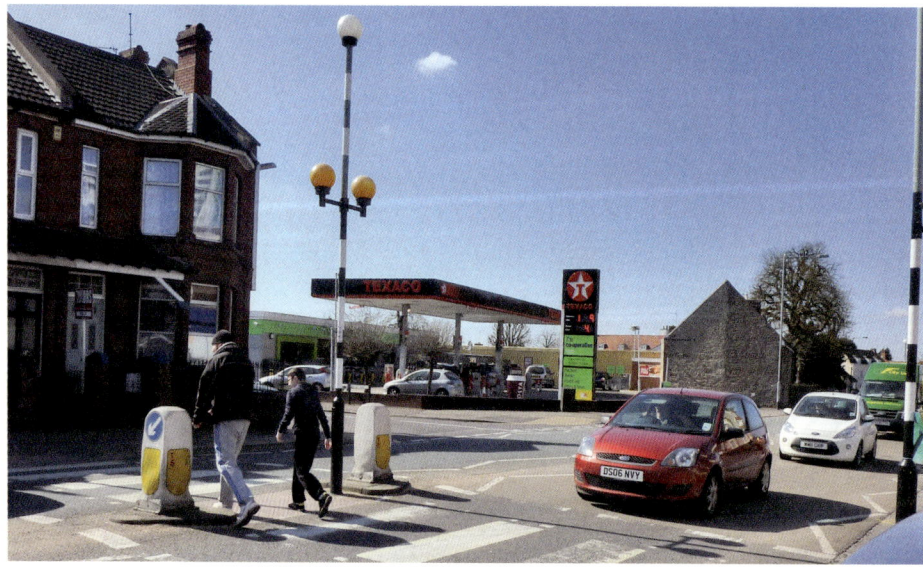

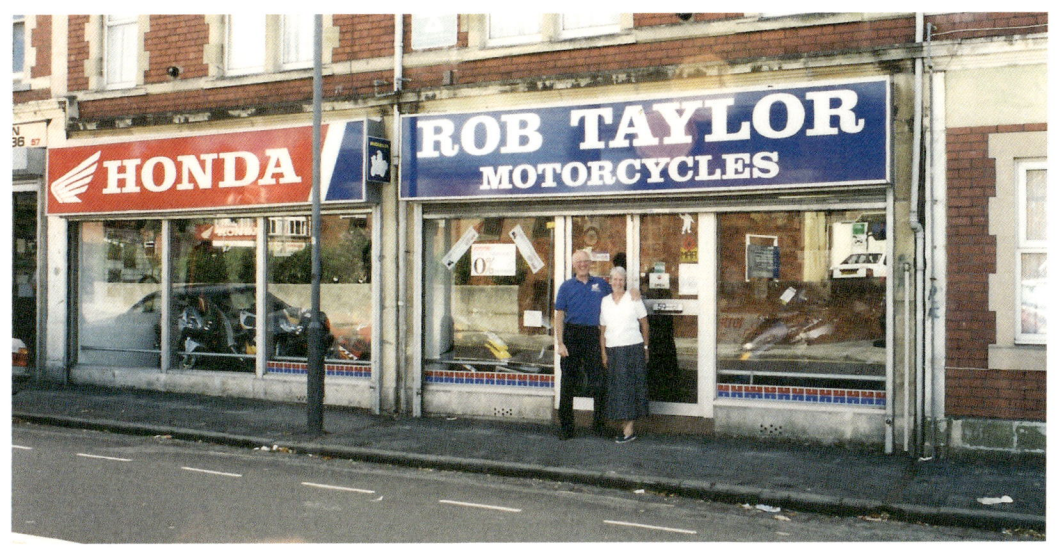

Bikers' Bazaar

In any community, commercial businesses wax and wane; one popular, if specialist, Shirehampton example was Rob Taylor Motorcycles. Founded in 1966 at 10 The Parade under the name of Shirehampton Scooters, by 1967 it had become Shirehampton Motorcycles. Business boomed, and in 1975 it moved to 59–61 Pembroke Road, into premises previously occupied by Chilcott's Hardware. In 1978 the business expanded into number 63. Mike Drayton had come to work in the shop from Dorset in 1967. In 1994 he and his wife June (seen together in the photograph) bought the business and ran it from numbers 59 and 61. Rob Taylor then converted number 63 into a house. In 2001 the Draytons retired and the business became George White Motorcycles, which unfortunately failed in 2008. This shopping terrace with its Flemish gables was designed by Heard's building firm between 1906 and 1909, and bears plaques to C. and A. C. Heard.

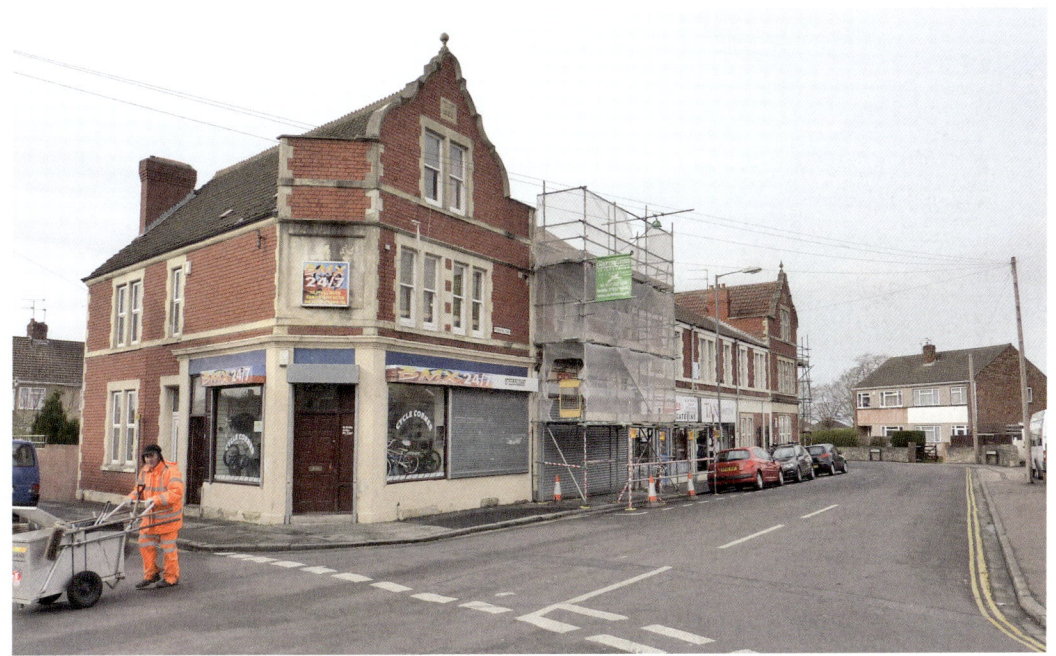

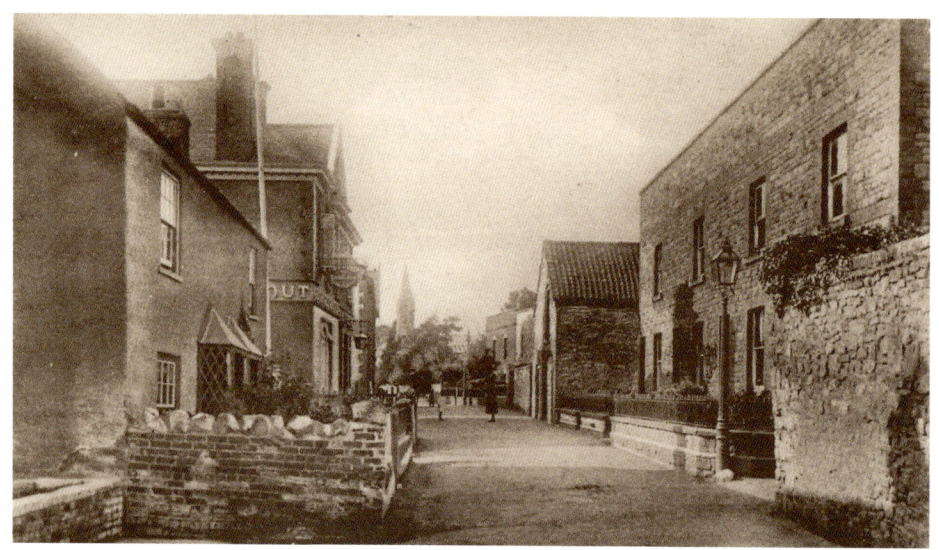

The House of the Rising Sun

Pembroke Road around 1912, looking north. On the right, only the two cottages in the distance remain virtually unchanged. Ellenborough Place, the slightly bleak terrace of houses in the foreground, and the adjoining stable, survive only as a palimpsest on the old wall bordering a car park. Its 1965 replacement is aesthetically uninspiring and this stretch of Pembroke Road badly needs softening with trees and shrubs. On the left much remains as it was although now refaced. The once attractive cottages in the foreground with their front gardens have lost their trellised porches and been modernised into sterility. The Rising Sun's Edwardian façade adjoins and remains intact although, since 2008, no longer fronting a hostelry. The establishment was in existence by 1871. Plans from 1889 for enlarging number 2, the road's smithy (now an undertaker's), show its yard's arch was originally whimsically designed aping a horseshoe. Structural practicalities resulted in a more prosaic entrance.

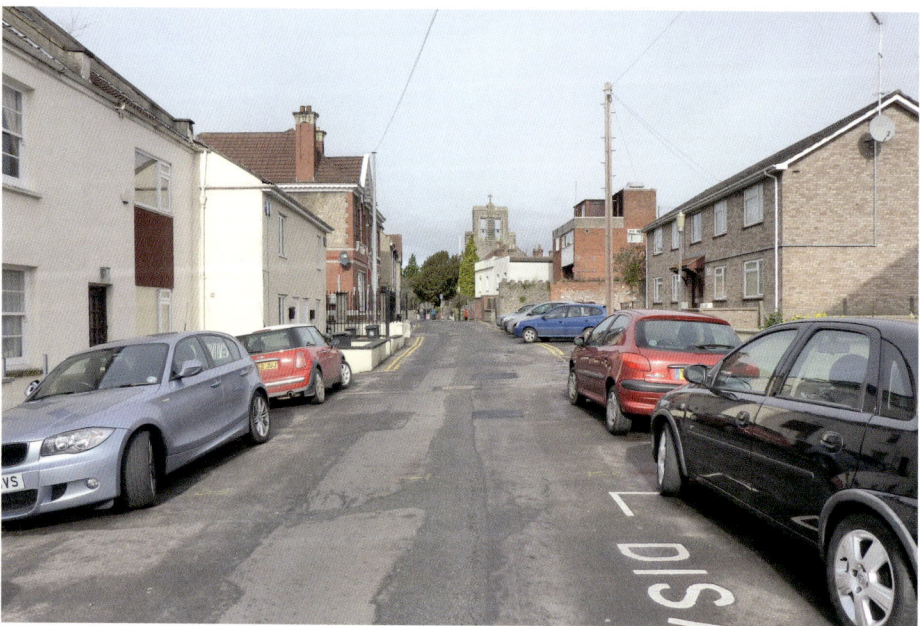

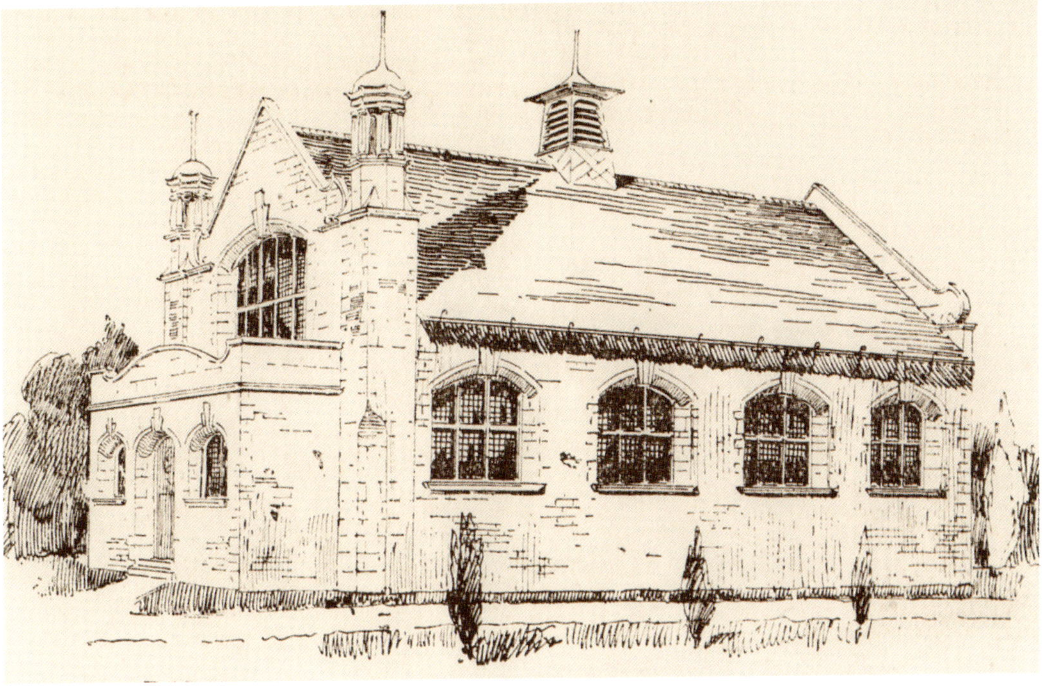

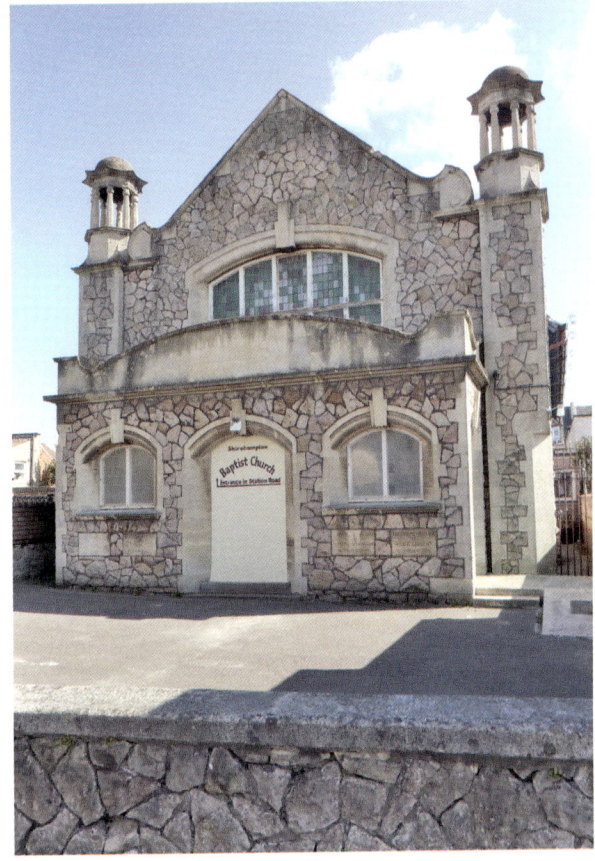

The Floating Domes of Pembroke Avenue

In December 1904, Emily Sargent was one of the four local ladies who laid ceremonial foundation stones for a new Baptist school chapel in Pembroke Avenue. Designed in a restrained Arts and Crafts style by Benjamin Wakefield, it was erected in 1904/05 at a cost of £2,044 and using King's Weston stone. The entrance was through a narthex with a curved pediment set before the main west façade. This bears centrally a variant of a thermal window, the style used throughout the building. The gable is turned into a pediment with half-leaves acting as acroteria. Beyond these are delightful domed tholoi with polygonal columns, but now missing their finials. Originally a louvre or bell-cot sat midway along the roof-ridge. Inside, the walls had fold-out panels that could form classrooms. In 1962 a new Sunday school building and Youth Hall was added to the east side.

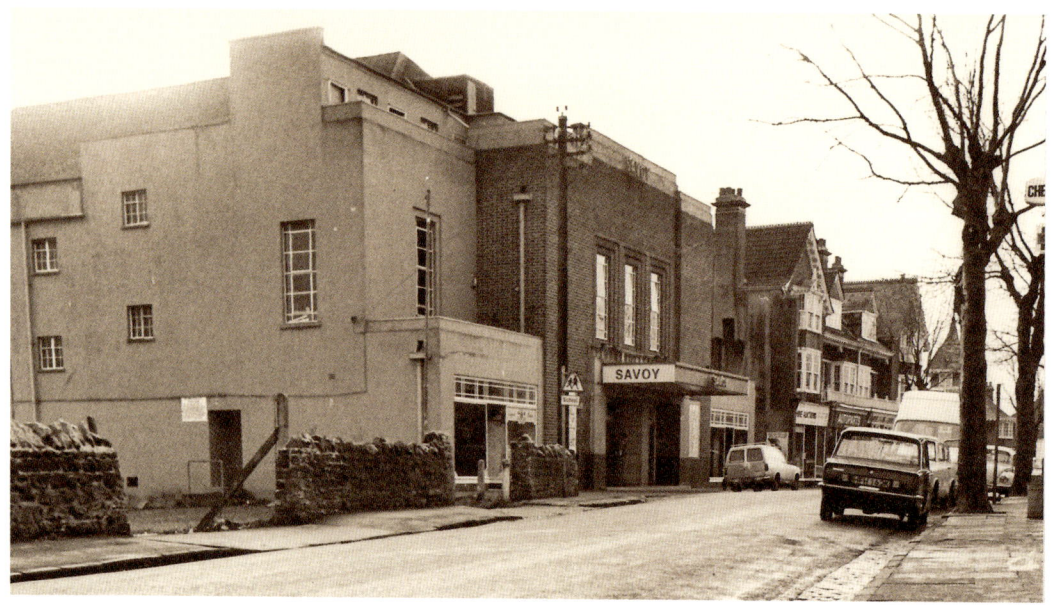

Bingo at 'the Cabbage'

The Savoy Cinema, affectionately known locally as 'the cabbage' after the Savoy cabbage, was opened in Station Road in 1933. Its architect was W. H. Watkins, who also designed Westbury's Carlton. Owned by Emanuel Harris, it had seating for 700 in the stalls and 200 in the circle. Each screen curtain was emblazoned with an elaborate 'S'. With the decline of cinema, it closed in 1962 but had a new lease of life as a bingo hall, finally closing in June 2000. Plans to convert the building to a supermarket were opposed and it was acquired by a property company and finally demolished in 2003, notwithstanding its rating as a Grade II listed building. The block of flats subsequently erected on the site and on the adjoining playground of the 1892 Shirehampton National School bears its name. Jim Hale's photograph shows the Savoy around 1978.

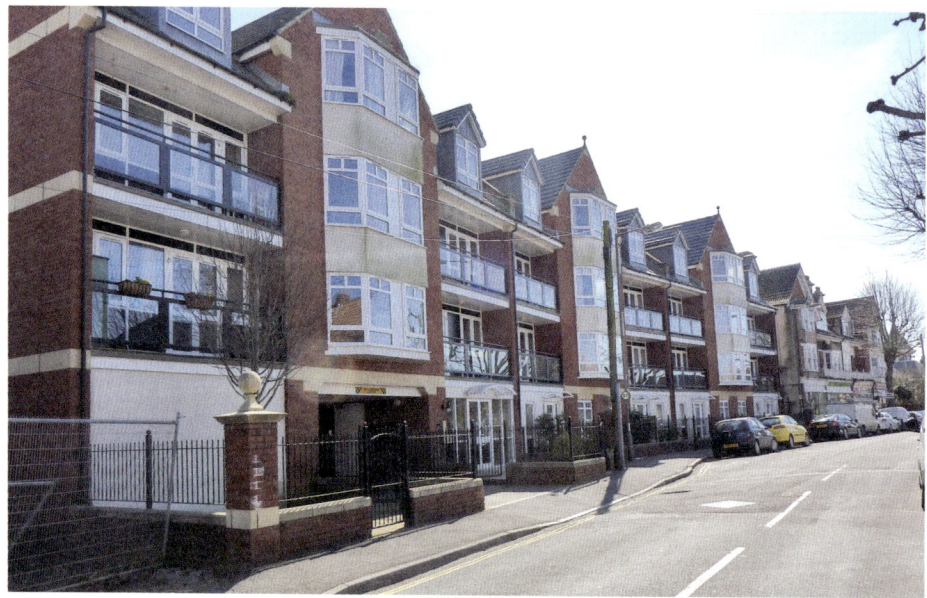

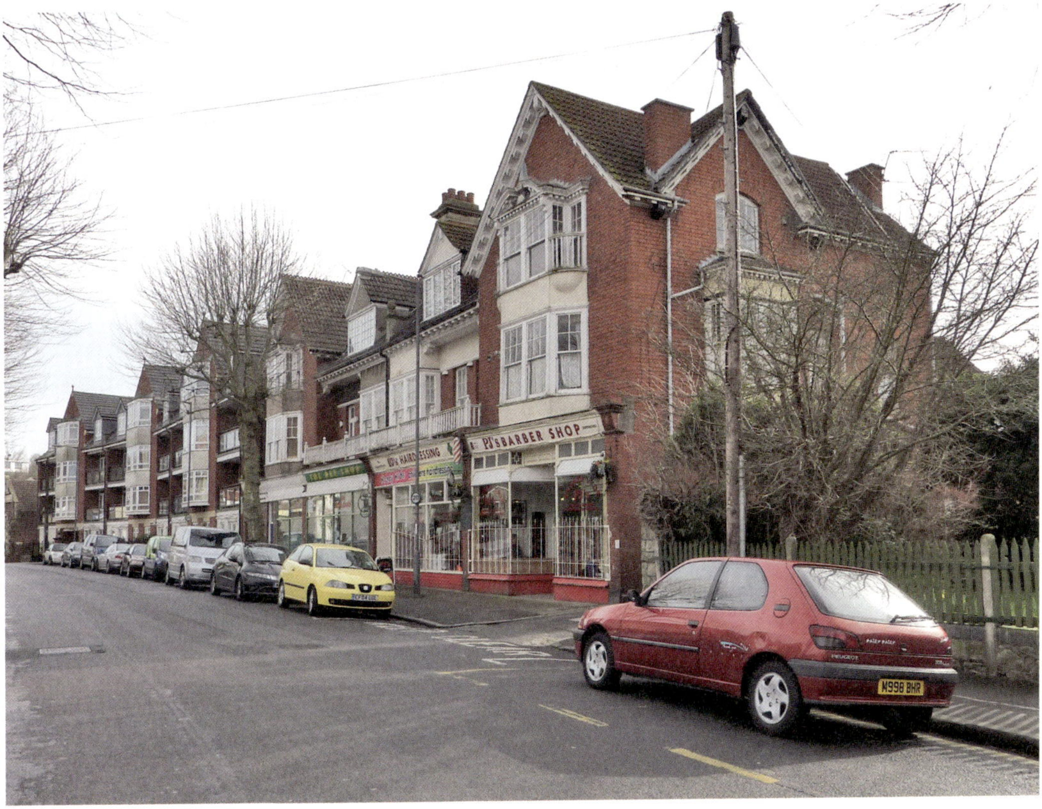

'The Way to the Railway Station has Been Much Widened'

The building programme, started in Shirehampton by Squire Philip Napier Miles and later endorsed by the Corporation, when the village became part of Bristol, shows to good effect in Station Road. From 1905, Miles's estate architect, Frederick Bligh Bond, submitted plans for twenty-three houses alone in this road that were built by such builders as J. Stride, C. Carter and Couzens & Co. His delightful Parish Hall of 1903/04 vies with his house The Wylands in the High Street as being the finest building remaining in Shirehampton. Often overlooked is Winchester Buildings, Bligh Bond's highly interesting parade of four shops, here illustrated by Samuel Loxton, which bears comparison with his two shopping parades in Avonmouth Road. Wooden curved and broken pediments, obelisks and balconettes adorn it and mostly survive; red brick contrasts with white paintwork. Only the P. J. Barber Shop now retains its original Edwardian shop window.

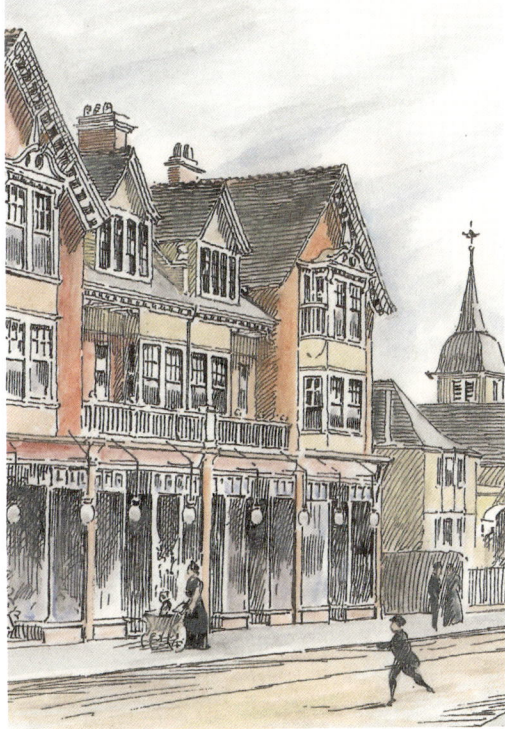

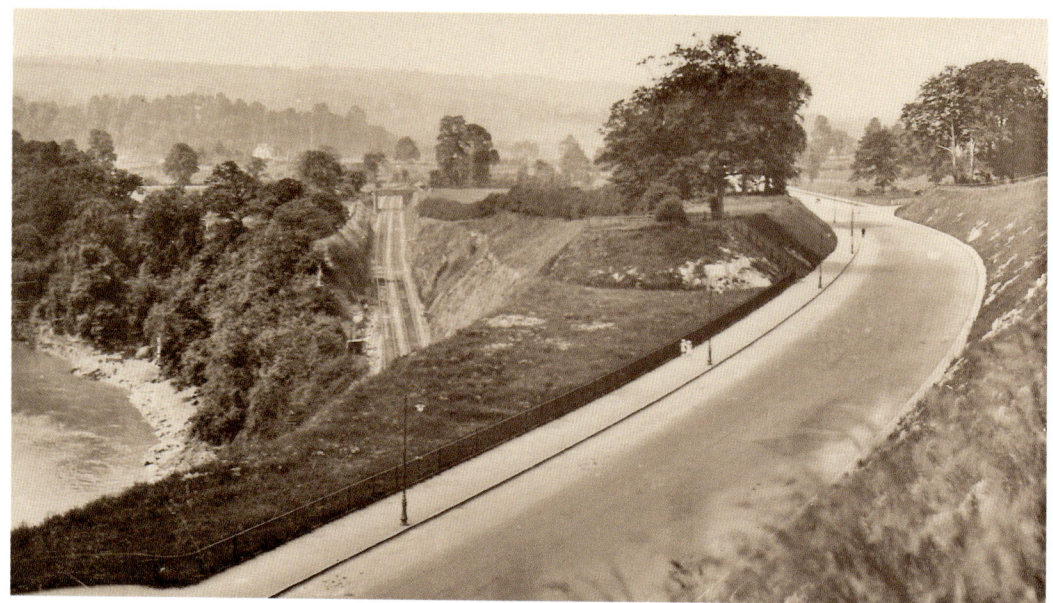

River, Rail and Road: Three ways to Avonmouth

Over 6 miles in length, and varying in width from 65 to 100 feet, the new Portway, between Hotwells and Avonmouth, cost £800,000 and was, when built between 1919 and 1926, the most expensive road to have been constructed in Britain. The need for a modern access road between Avonmouth docks and the city had become obvious during the First World War when the narrow lanes of Shirehampton had been unable to cope with the traffic. This resulted in the widening of the High Street and the demolition of a number of historic properties. The 1926 view is taken above Horseshoe Bend in sight of the corner of Park Road. Houses would soon rise along its length between there and Avonmouth. Between 2011 and 2013, a new mixed housing development (seen on the left of the 2013 photograph), designed to merge successfully with the 1930s houses, replaced 'prefabs' at Valerian Close.

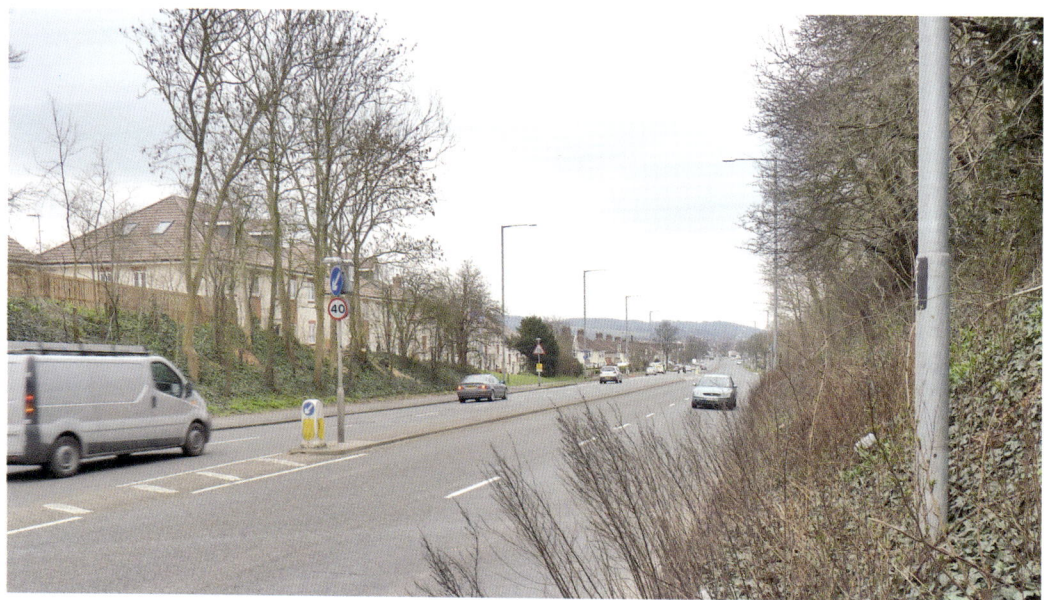

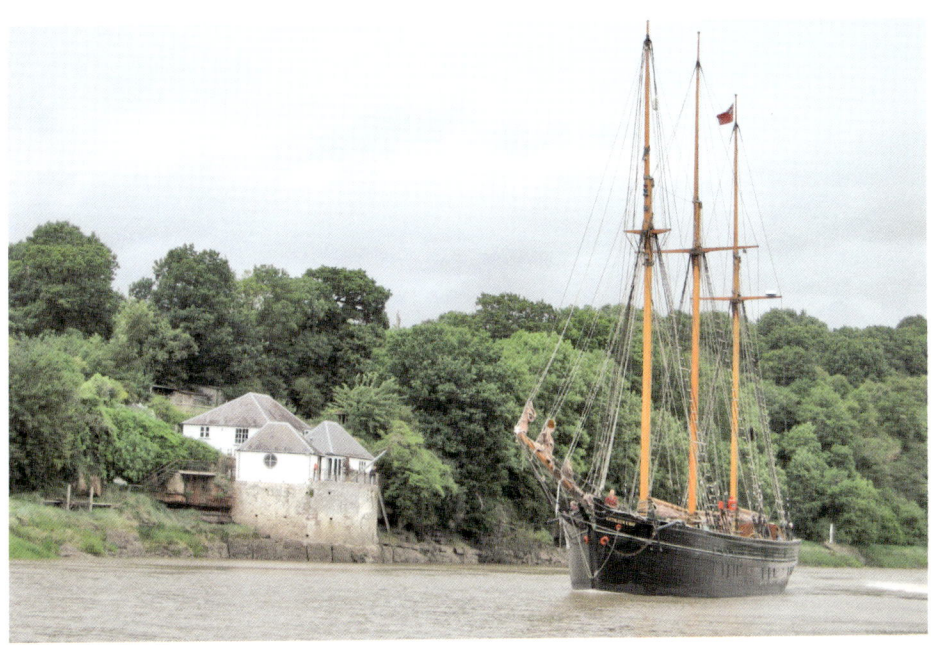

'The Grand Magazine of Powder'

On the Shirehampton side of Horseshoe Bend stands the Powder House, where vessels deposited their gunpowder to alleviate the risk of explosions in the city. It has been here since at least 1775, but the author has discovered the earliest account of its existence and one, either suggesting the timidity of the local inhabitants, or that it may once have stood closer to the village. The *Bristol Chronicle* of 14 June 1760 reports that around 11 a.m. on Wednesday 11 June, a thatched cottage near the Powder House at Hung Road caught fire. Within five minutes the roof collapsed, terrifying the people of Shirehampton, who feared that the Powder House, then containing over 150 tons of gunpowder, would also catch fire. Everyone abandoned their houses and fled to Penpole Hill until the danger had passed. Stuart Cory's photograph shows the *Kathleen and May* passing the house.

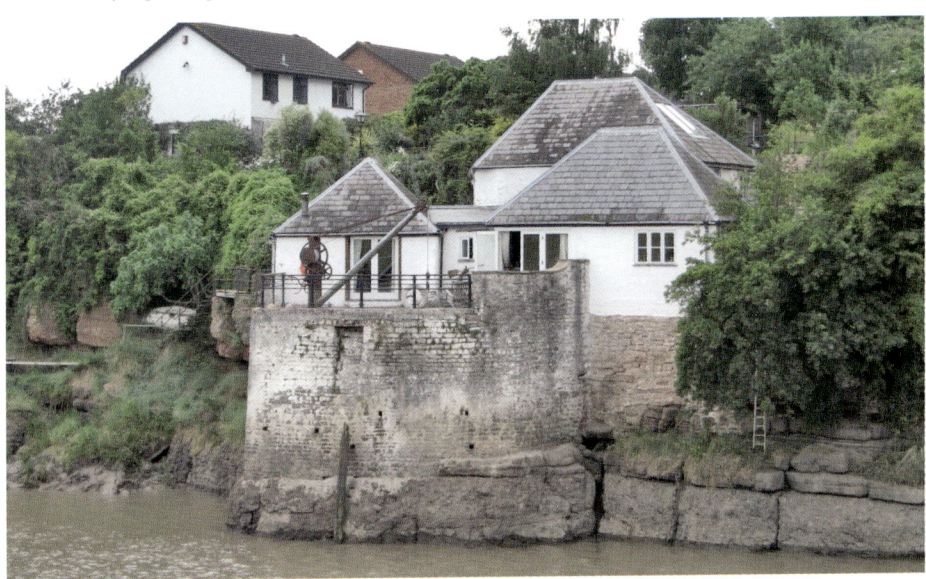

Walk 4

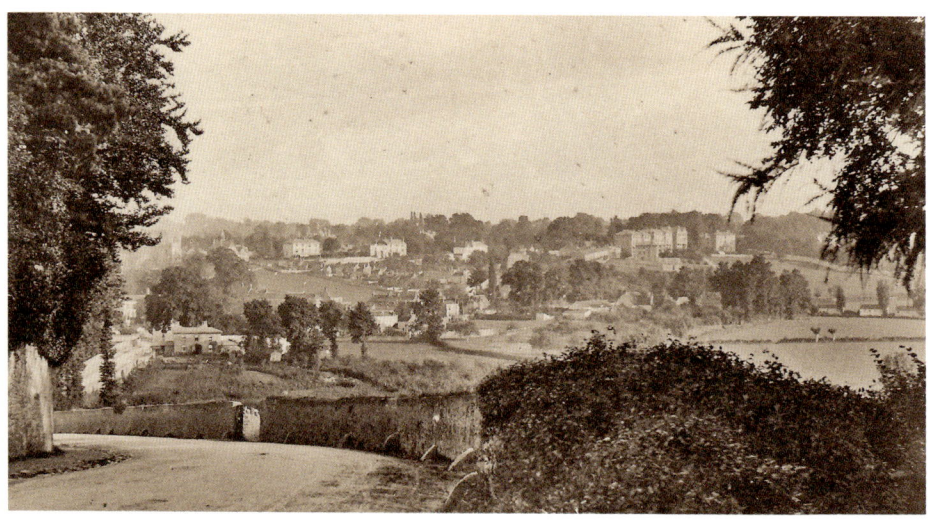

'Extremely Pleasantly Situated': Westbury from Henbury Hill, 1879

This view of Westbury, which confronted travellers from the Severn Passages on descending Henbury Hill, is now blocked by later houses and trees. A nursery is in the foreground and Henburyhill's boundary wall appears on the left. The tower of Westbury church appears to the right of this in the distance, enveloped in smoke from the Chalk Lane limekilns. Next to this are the gables of the Parish Rooms and the white block of the ex-workhouse. Houses in the Butts (Eastfield Road) frame the chimneys of The Priory. The line of houses in East Hill and Betty Waters Lane lead down to the High Street. Westbury Court Farm's buildings appear mid-centre and the spaced cottages in Canford Lane are to their right. Westbury Hill and its houses appear at the top far right, ending with Southey House and Cotebank. The modern photograph is taken from the grounds of Henburyhill.

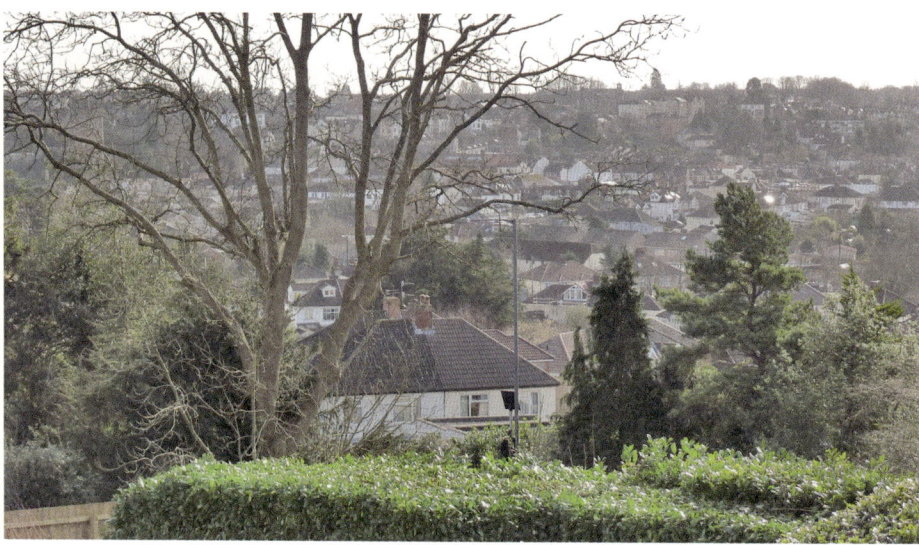

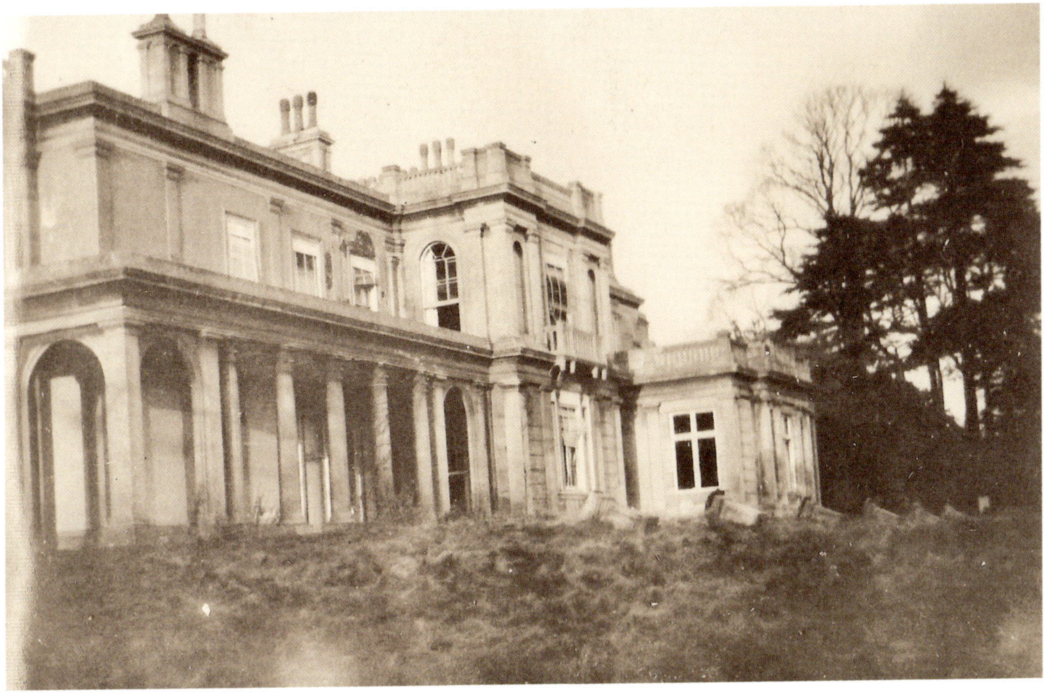

The Last Days of Henburyhill

Westbury's Henburyhill gazes forlornly over its fallen garden urns and awaits demolition in 1938. This once spectacular early nineteenth-century house was possibly also the work of the Reptons, designers of Brentry House (1802), with which it shared several features. It boasted a Corinthian portico topped by a viewing terrace with seating there formed from the colonnade's architrave, enabling those viewing the beautiful views towards Westbury to do so at their ease. Further terraces were placed on the eastern wing. In 1841, Mr Franklyn of Henburyhill commissioned Charles Abraham to sculpt a 14-foot statue of Wellington for the lawn in front of the house. It became one of the sights for travellers en route to the Passages. Henburyhill was replaced long after demolition by the houses and flats of Westover Gardens. The house's fine panelled lodge gate survives at the bottom of Henbury Hill as a rarely preserved curiosity.

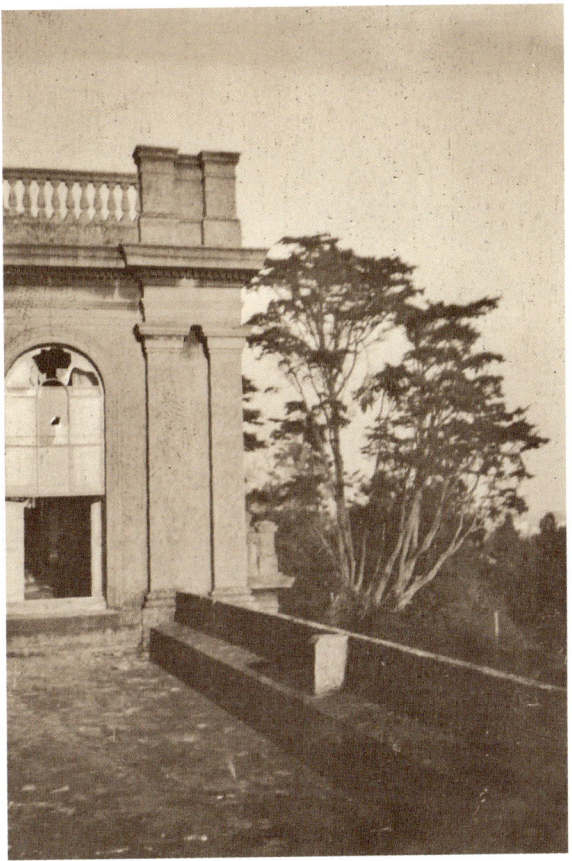

71

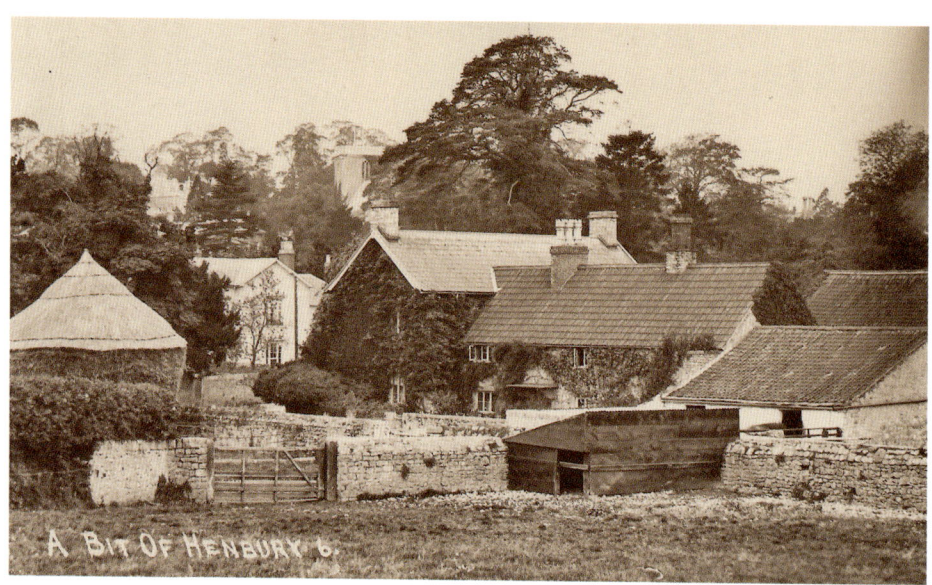

'Dastardly Treatment ... Had the Germans Done This We Should Not Have Felt Surprise'

Once referred to as 'an opulent village', Henbury was absorbed into Bristol by 1935. This was ultimately disastrous for the inhabitants. In May 1947, newspapers estimated that 1,500 property owners in the Henbury, Brentry and Westbury areas had received notices by registered post informing them that their land and houses were to be compulsorily purchased in order to build an estate of 2,000 houses on 442 acres of land. For example, Raymond McEwan Smith's Westmoreland Farm, on Crow Lane (seen here around 1910) had 117 of its 146 acres taken. Until that time it had produced 36,500 gallons of milk a year for the city. Protest meetings were held and objections submitted. Even the BAC objected to the proximity of the estate to their new Brabazon runway that had itself obliterated the village of Charlton. In December 1947 the Ministry of Health granted permission for the Corporation to proceed and modern Henbury was born.

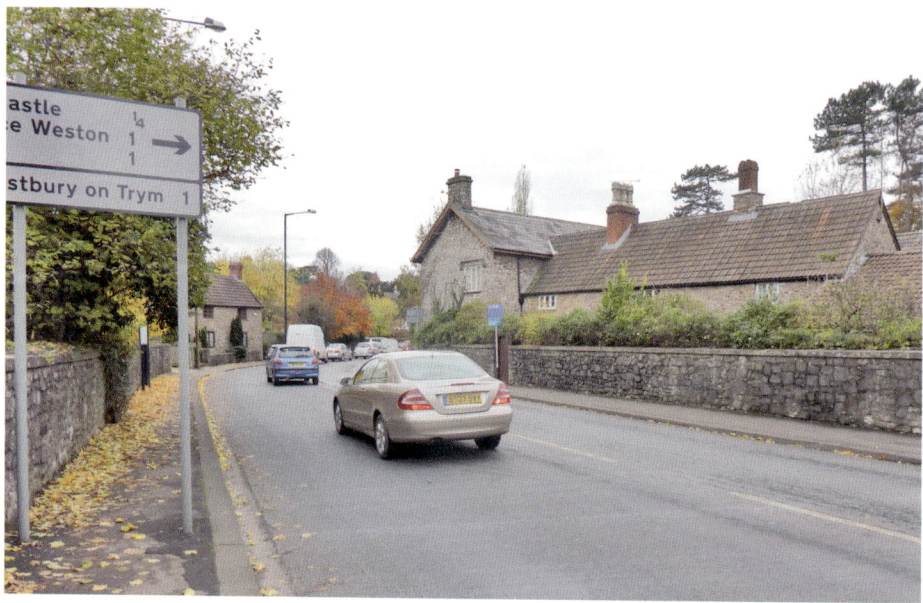

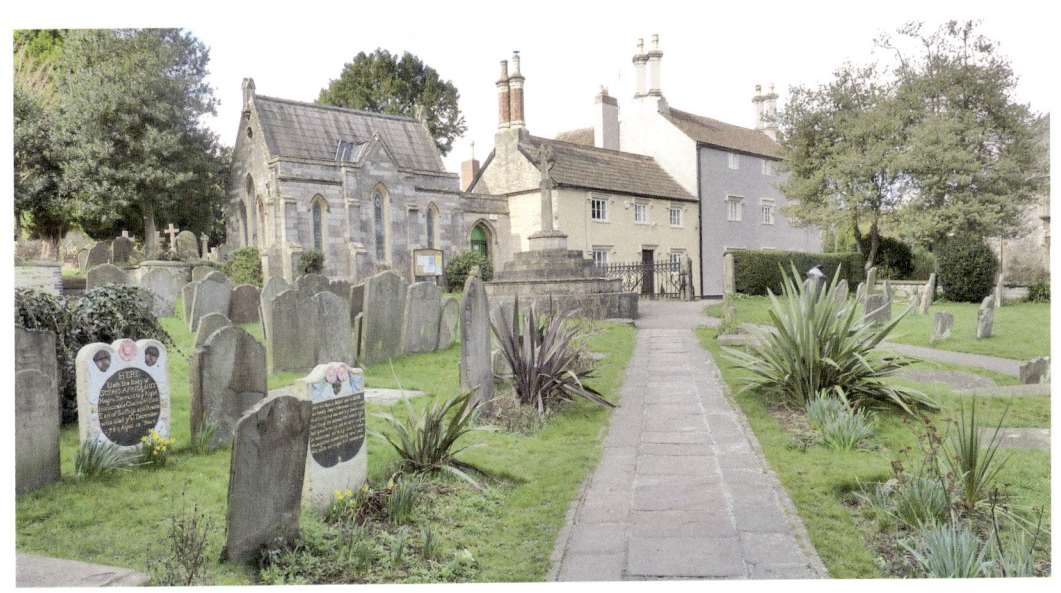

Under English Skies ... A Problematic Grave

Near the door of St Mary's church, Henbury, is the grave (much visited by modern politicians) of the servant Scipio Africanus, recently the subject of an historical evaluation commissioned from Colin Godman, MA. This found the 1721 burial unrecorded and the gravestones unlisted in Ralph Bigland's careful recording of churchyard inscriptions made later that century. An 1830s engraving of the churchyard omits them, and they were probably placed as a tourist curiosity about 1887. Godman wonders if Scipio (as a family favourite) may have been buried in Henbury's Great House's gardens where the stones were possibly discovered. They were first textually mentioned in 1910, but even Arthur Mee, that great collector of local curiosities, ignored them. The footstone is actually a reused headstone and its inscription, the only record of Scipio's slavery, a nineteenth-century pastiche lacking long 'S's. The stones were first painted around 1930, with the cherubs blacked up by 1951.

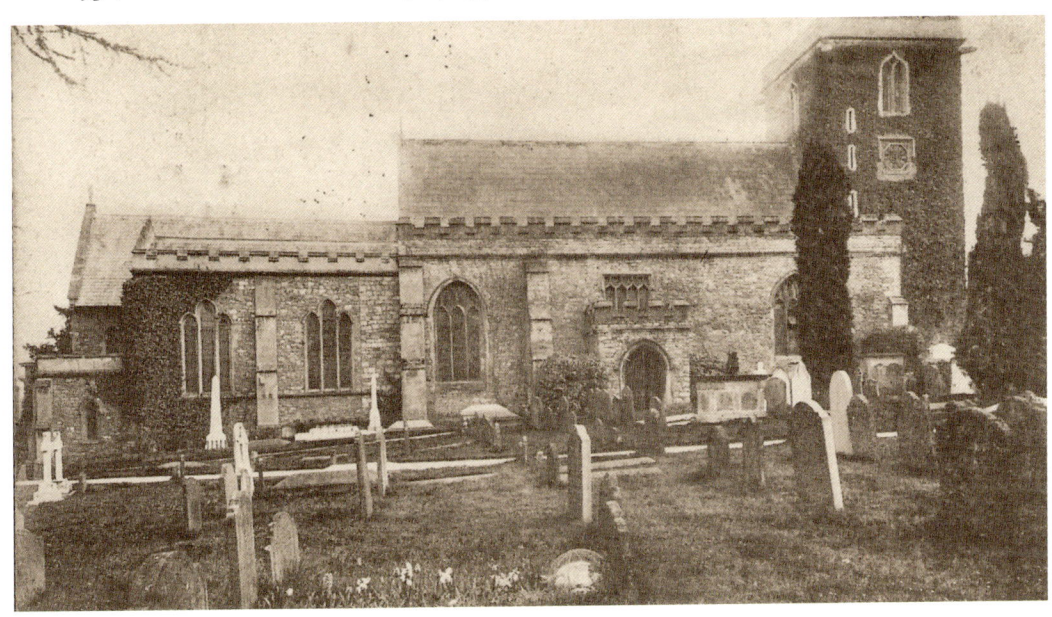

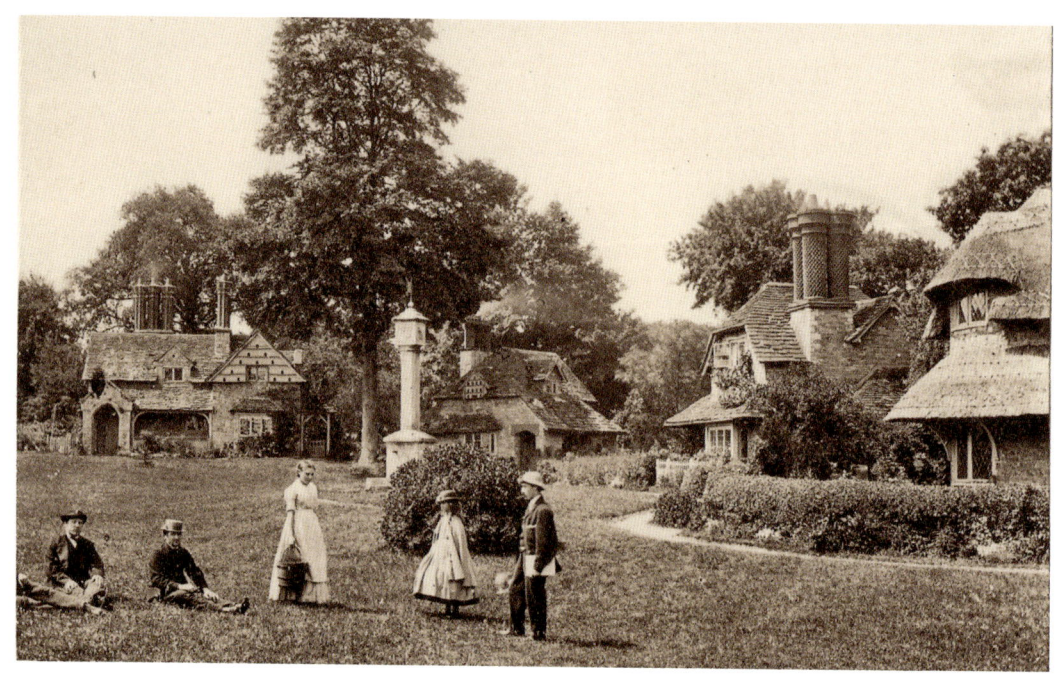

'These Cottages Cannot Fail to Gratify the Visitant', Blaise Hamlet, 1866

Carefully posing for W. H. Barton, genteel visitors and a villager gather on the green at Blaise, in what may be the earliest surviving photograph of the hamlet. The architectural ensemble was commissioned by Blaise Castle's owner, John Scandrett Harford, from the architect John Nash, and built from 1809 to accommodate ten households of 'decayed retainers' from his estate in its nine *cottages ornée*. Nash was assisted by George Repton during his absences. Each cottage is unique in this very early example of an English planned community and all vie for picturesqueness below their great Jacobethan chimneys. The lower photograph, taken from Vine Cottage, shows more of the hamlet around 1880. Featured from the left are Diamond, Double and Rose cottages. To the right of the sundial are Dial, Circular and Sweetbriar cottages. Blaise Castle was bought by the Corporation in 1926; the hamlet became a National Trust property in 1943.

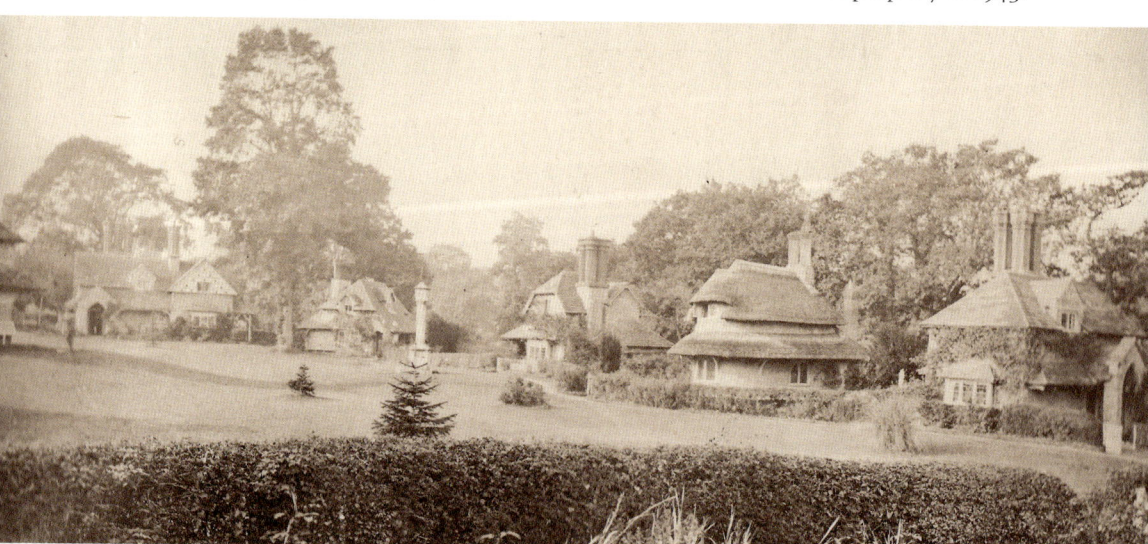

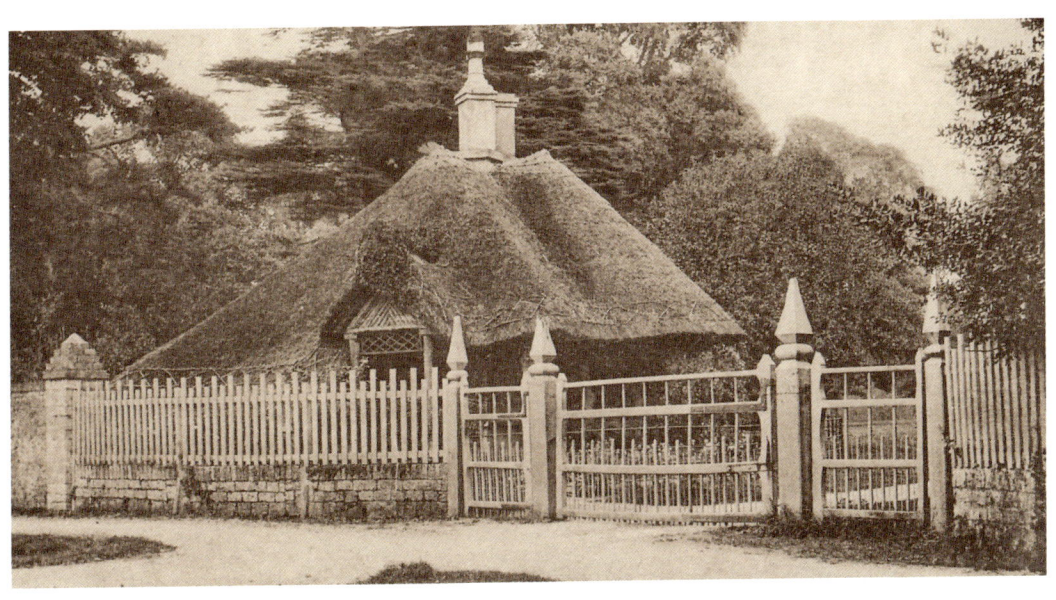

At the North Gate, on King's Weston Road

Blaise Castle's delightful, but lost, North Lodge was presumably made of brick, but coated with a rustic, patterned covering of trunks, branches and roots; very like the Inner Lodge on the Westbury side of the estate. There was much of the *cottage ornée* about it, with its large central chimney, sweeping thatch and rustication. Its date is uncertain, but it appears to have been the lodge that so entranced a visitor in Thomas Farr's day that he left a poem inside praising it. Certainly the lost Root Arbour, sketched by Samuel Hieronymus Grimm on a visit in 1788, is of this era. Considering its situation on the estate, the North Lodge was, perhaps, the inspiration for the Romantic style of the later adjacent Blaise Castle Hamlet. It survived up until the 1940s but succumbed either to a stray bomb or, in another more likely version, to the billeted troops.

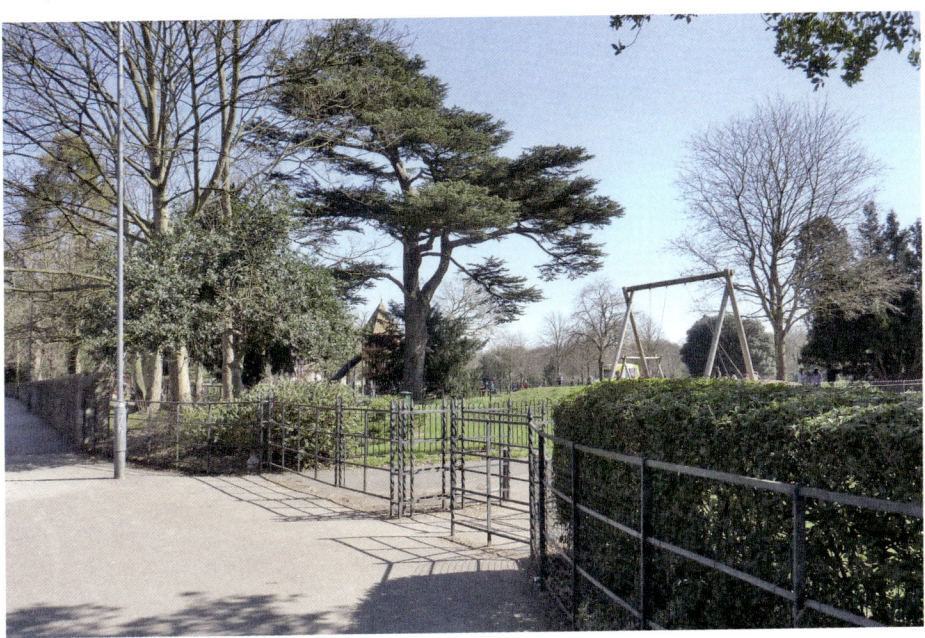

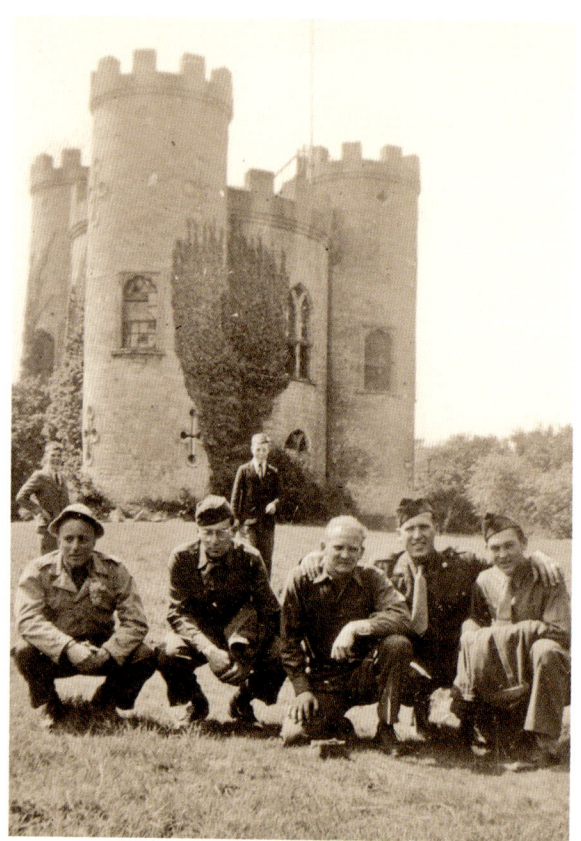

Over There ... at Blaise Castle, May 1944

Cortland Hopkins' photograph of colleagues in the 304th Port Company of the 519th Port Battalion, US Army, and admirers. They were stationed at the permanent US Army Transportation Unit Camp established in huts on Shirehampton Golf Course and King's Weston Park during the war. The 304th were in Bristol from 11 April to 30 May 1944. The 1936 photograph below shows the castle in perfect condition, but by 1944 it was already seriously vandalised – a result, no doubt, of the military occupation and its use in exercises. Ground-floor windows are smashed and bricked up and much damage is evident above. Post-war, nothing was done to repair the now roofless building, and by 1980 it was ruinous and fenced off. Rescue came in the form of the admirable Friends of Blaise, a dedicated band of locals who financed restoration to the point that access to the roof may once more be attained.

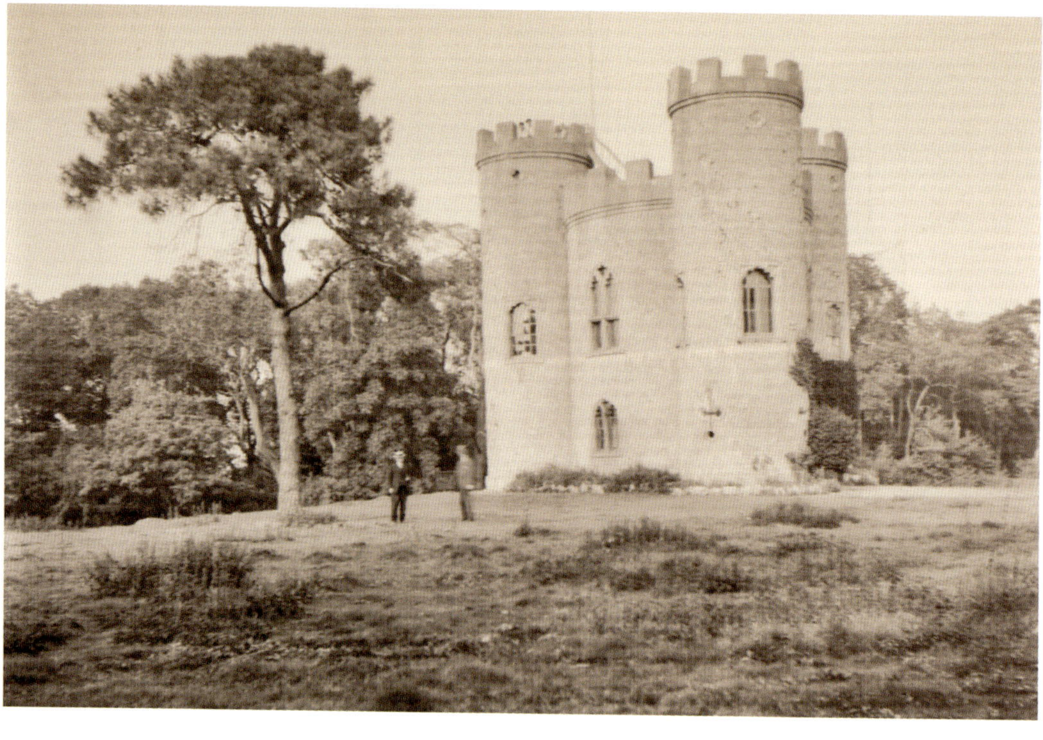

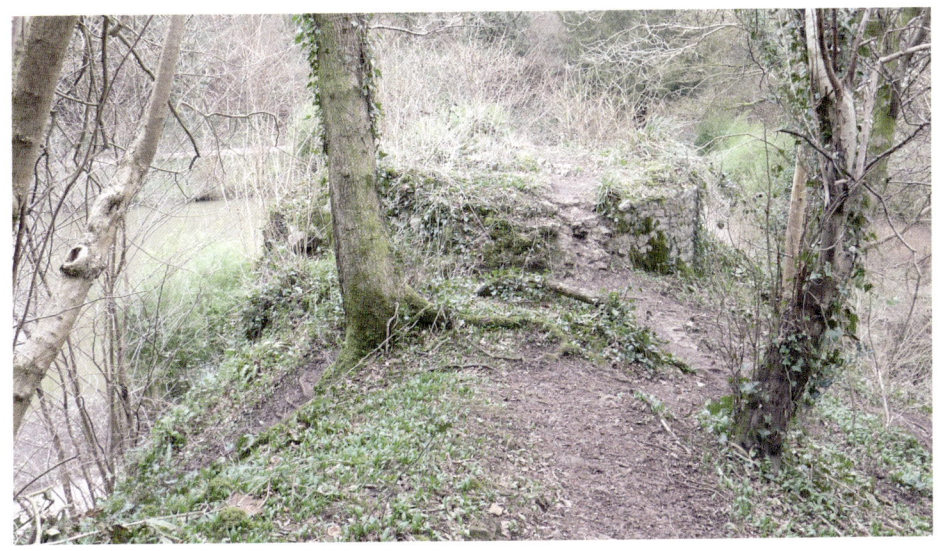

Here a Cold Bath Invites the Weak to Lave

'Above the Bath an airy room we find, To fresco in, when Sirius reigns, design'd.' Edward Davies's 1783 poem 'Blaise Castle' informs us that either Dr Denham Skeet (sometimes Skeate) or the earlier owner, Farr, had built a cold bath with a summer picnic room above it. The bath survives as the tarn below Lovers' Leap. Perched above it, adjacent to its access bridge, are the unexcavated foundations of the dining room now known as 'The Giant's Soap Dish', where the bathers could relax. The poem also tells us that Skeet cooled wine in the cold bath. Nowadays, even with the landscape less managed, the views from the room are still delightful. The airy building features together with its ornamental bridge (here photographed in 1981) in Grimm's 1788 watercolour. It was a domed, hexagonal structure, with large windows positioned to catch the best views. A circular slab stair wound around its exterior.

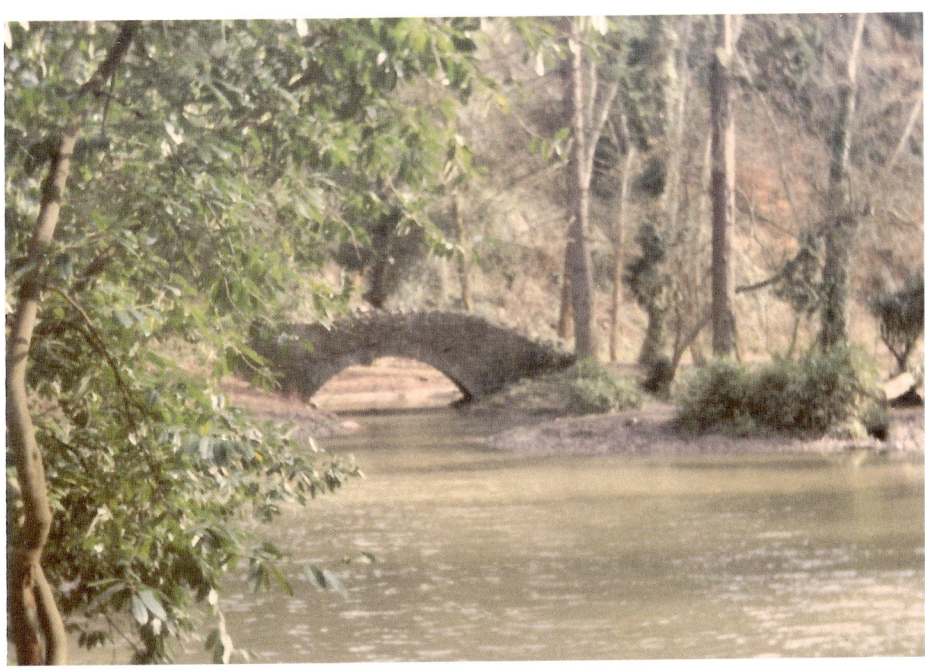

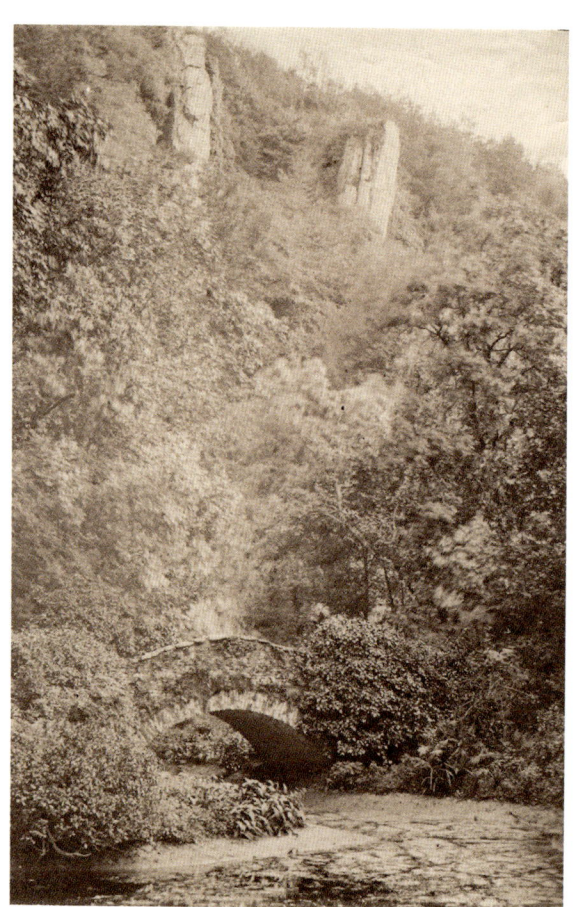

'Here Sat in State the Giant of the Dale'

Local legend named the singular rock projections from the side of Coombe Hill as 'The Giant's Armchair', claiming it as the place where the indolent giant Goram slept while his brother Vincent laboured cutting the Avon Gorge to bring the River Severn to the Bristol area. Goram also decided to cut a gorge, sharing Vincent's pickaxe, but too often dozed in his chair with his feet in the Hazel Brook. Thus employed, he did not hear Vincent's warning shout as he threw the pickaxe from Clifton that subsequently killed him. Other legends claimed Goram was a local cave-dwelling anchorite. The photograph dates from the 1890s. The viewpoint above Goram's Chair afforded one of the most romantic views of Castle Hill and was a favourite with artists such as Charlotte L. May, who sketched it in 1826. A visitor's account of 1807 reported smoke from a limekiln rising from this valley.

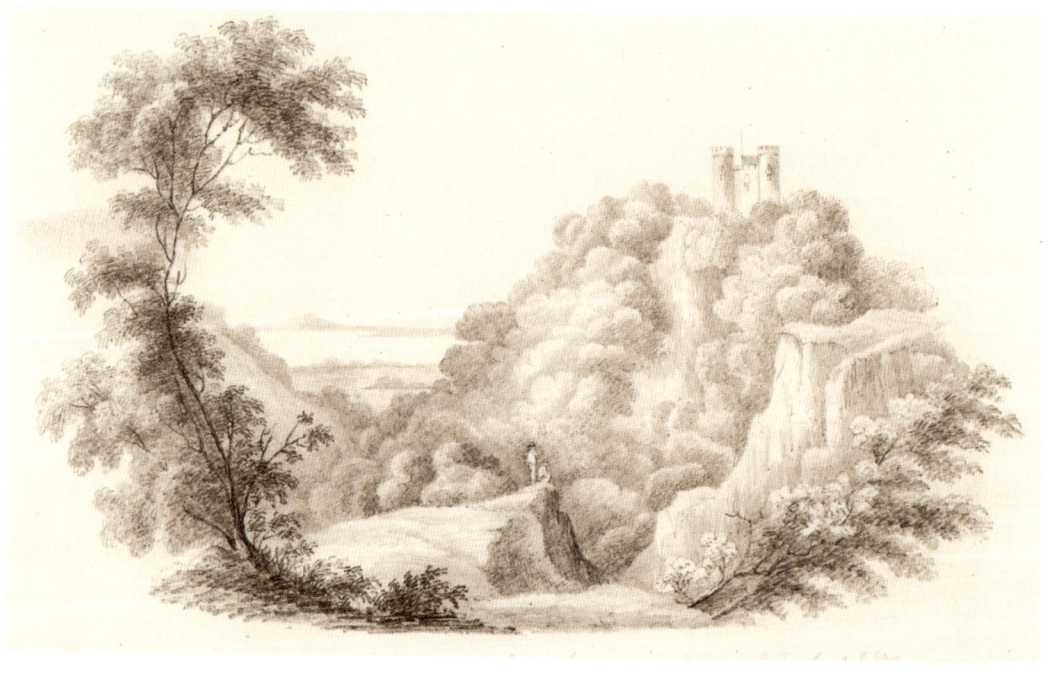

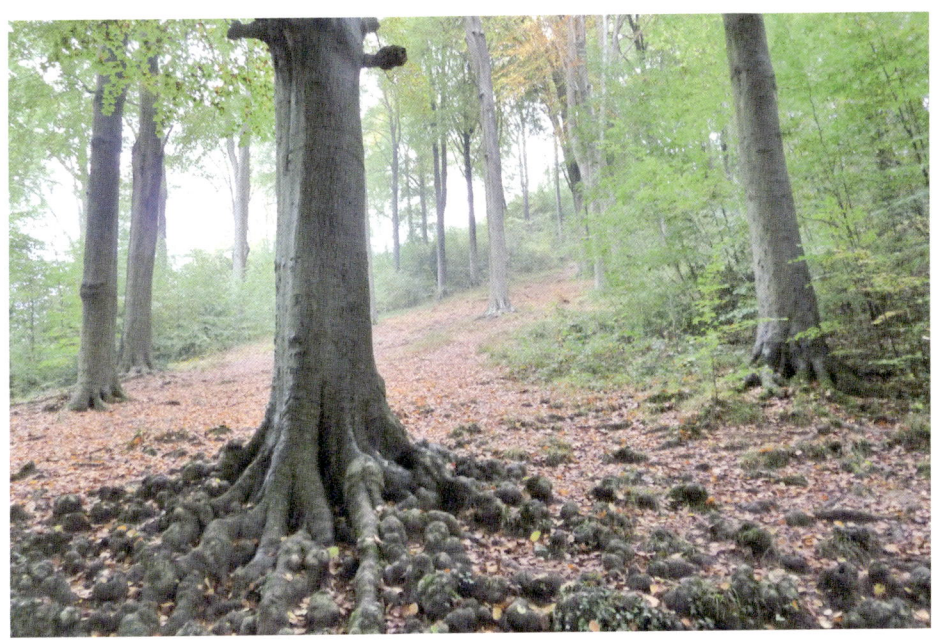

'Here Hanging Woods Afford a Cooling Shade'

Somewhere in the vicinity of Blaise's ancient beech hanger, or southerly, on the western slopes above and beyond the southern lily pond, were the Fairy Steps. These were naturally occurring woodland circles, probably of mushrooms, running down the hillside where, according to local tradition, enshrined in Edward Davies' 1783 poem 'Blaise Castle', fairies nightly danced. Frederick Jones, in *The Bristol Times and Mirror* of 5 June 1928, bemoaned the fact that commercial wood-felling in 1926 had devastated that area of the woodland (seen below) and that the Fairy Steps had disappeared. *The Mercury* in 1900, deploring the poor observance of Oak Apple Day in Bristol, reassured its readers that woodsmen still traditionally gathered boughs and oak apples in the Dingle to sell as, no doubt, they did with Christmas greenery. In 1893, two labourers were sentenced to ten days' hard labour for damaging Mr Harford's ivy in the Dingle to make rustic furniture.

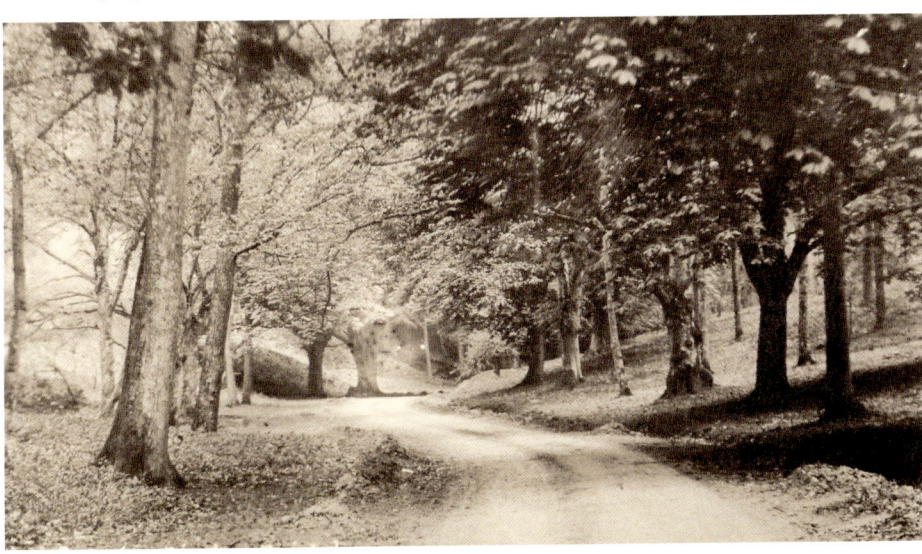

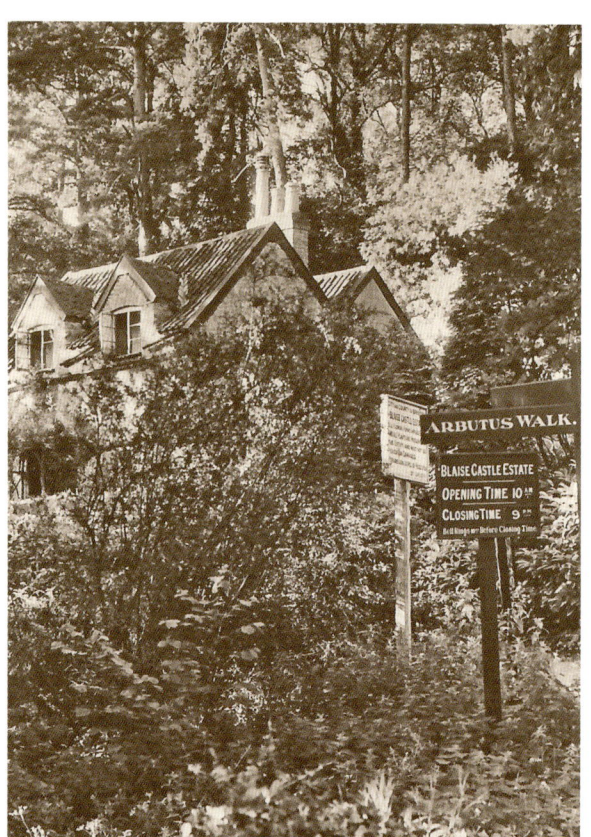

A Forgotten Lodge House

A long-forgotten and rarely photographed building on the Blaise estate stood by the southern lily pond in a cutting in the side of Coombe Hill. It first appears on maps at the same time as the lily pond, and it is labelled 'Pump House'. Given the number of weirs and sluices marked for this lower pond, one can only assume that its purpose was to enhance the water feature by possibly powering a fountain or waterfall from the millpond beyond. It was a substantial cottage with a rear extension perhaps housing the pump. By the 1900s it housed a woodman and became the South Lodge, where visitors entering the Blaise estate from Coombe Dingle paid their sixpences on open days. Whether it was prone to flooding and demolished by the council like the other valley buildings, or was another casualty of Blaise's military occupation, it had disappeared by the late 1940s.

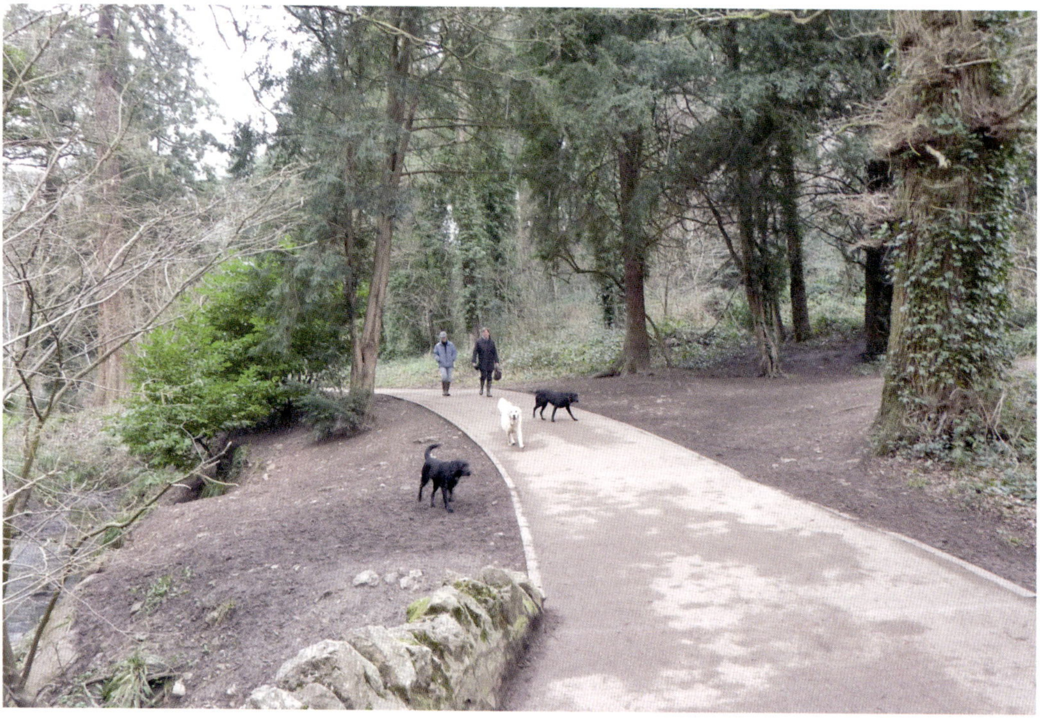

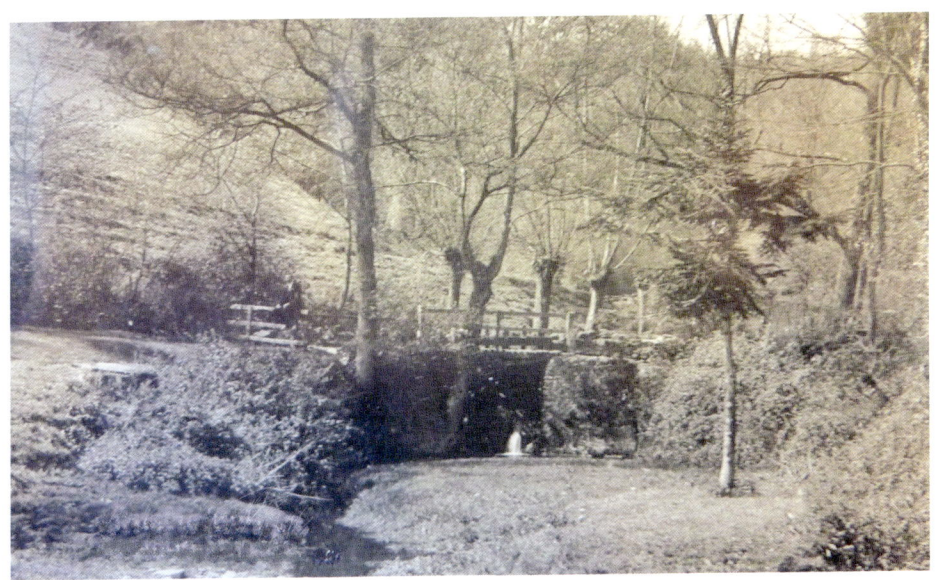

By a Waterfall ... Coombe Dingle, 1911

The Hazel Brook weir near the confluence (in the foreground) with the Trym. A man sits on a fence marking the leat (now filled by the Henbury sewer) that led off from the left of the photograph to power the undershot wheel of Coombe Mill. Behind him stretches the millpond in the form of the dammed Hazel Brook, fringed with pollarded trees. Off picture, to the right, the Trym was similarly dammed and tree-lined. A leat running by the side of the footpath connected both millponds. Although both watercourses are often low in water, and developments in the last century have diverted more, each has a tendency to become torrential and to flood after heavy rain. The Hazel weir appears below after a torrential rainstorm on 21 November 2012. Water finds the course of the old connecting leat on the right. Such flooding ultimately caused the abandonment of all habitations in the Dingle.

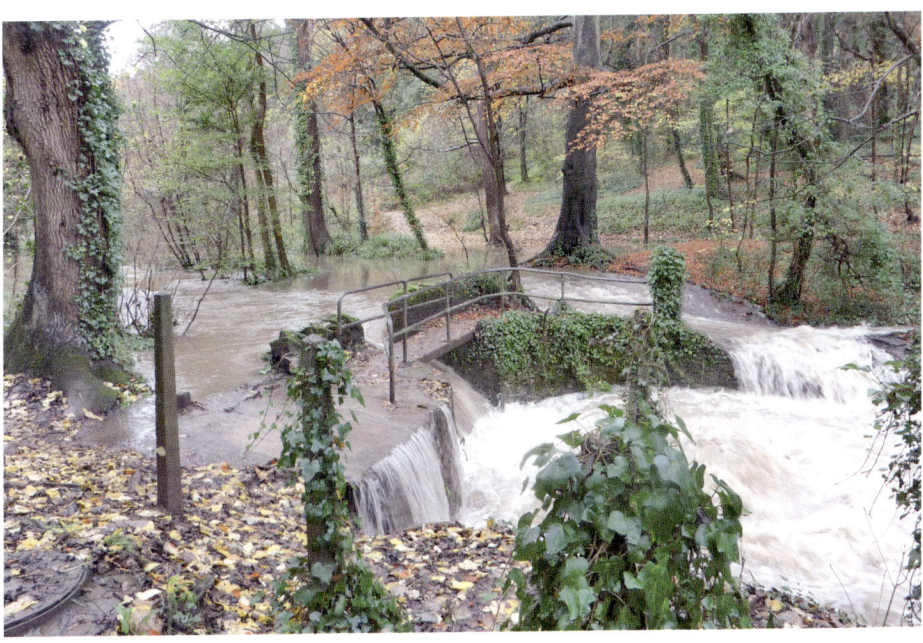

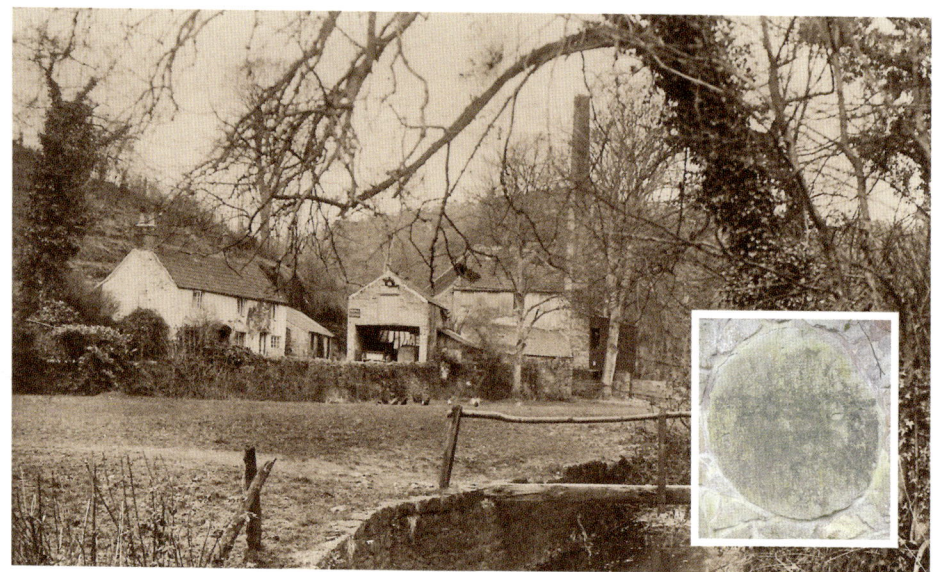

Coombe Mill

There were once three mills in the lower Trym valley, and Coombe Mill was the furthest upstream and probably dated from the eighteenth century, although it may have replaced an earlier establishment. An ingenious system of linked weirs and sluices on both waterways stored water to feed the undershot wheel. This was often inadequate in dry periods, and in 1868 a steam engine, later replaced by oil, was installed to supplement the water supply. Coombe Mill produced flour until the Avonmouth mills made this uneconomic, and its owners, the Ball family, changed to rolling oats for pig meal. This was delivered by wagon with an extra horse schooled to return home after assisting its fellow to achieve the top of Dangerous Hill. By the 1920s, the venture proved uneconomic and the mill closed and was unfortunately completely demolished. Millstones remain, rebuilt into a retaining wall on site.

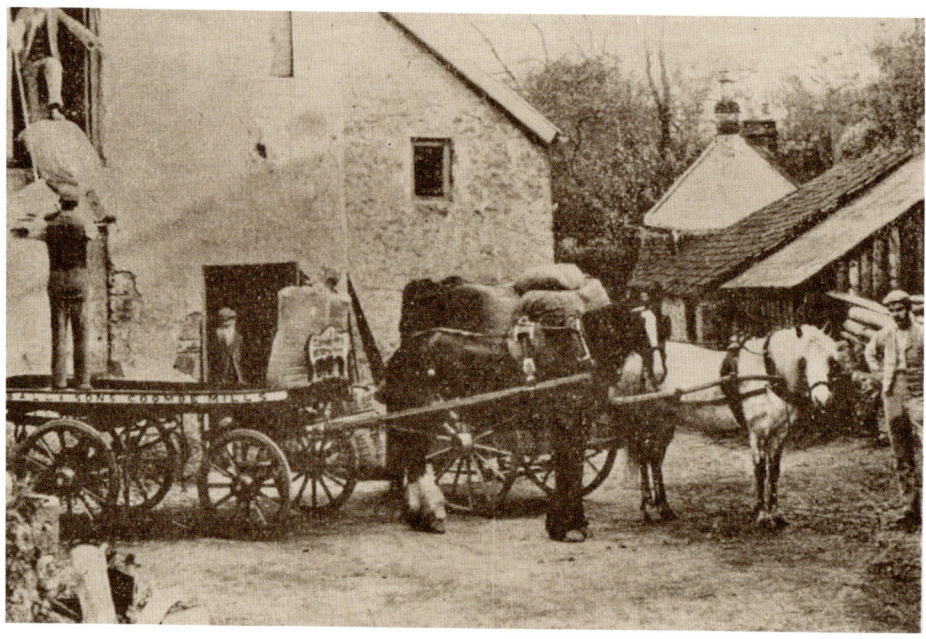

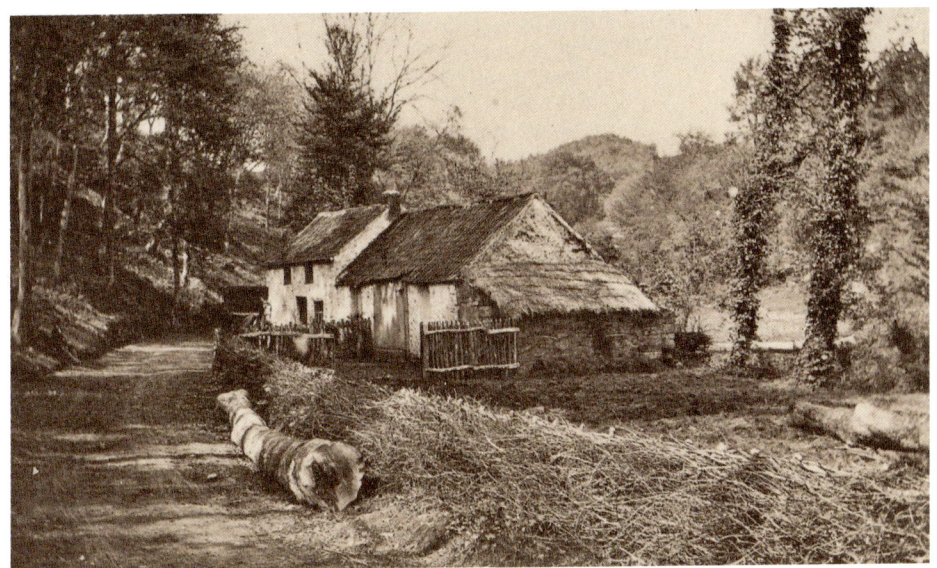

Picturesque Living

A carriage stands outside a whitewashed, riverside cottage in the Dingle in the 1860s just beyond the site of the present car park. In the middle distance is Coombe Mill. Compared with today, the tree cover was far less intense, allowing sunlight and views to be better enjoyed. The thatched byre is attractively weather-boarded with elliptically shaped planks. The rear view shows a trunk utilised as a bridge, and looks to the ridge above where a famous Bronze Age axe hoard was discovered in 1899, and where Hygrove and other villas would stand. The Trym occasionally flooded disastrously, eventually condemning all of the picturesque properties of its valley, including this one by the 1890s. Rosa Ball's Dingley Dell stood beyond this spot. Run as a tea garden and then a café until the 1960s, it was later simply an attractive bungalow, which was again demolished following flooding in the 1980s. Its garden wall remains.

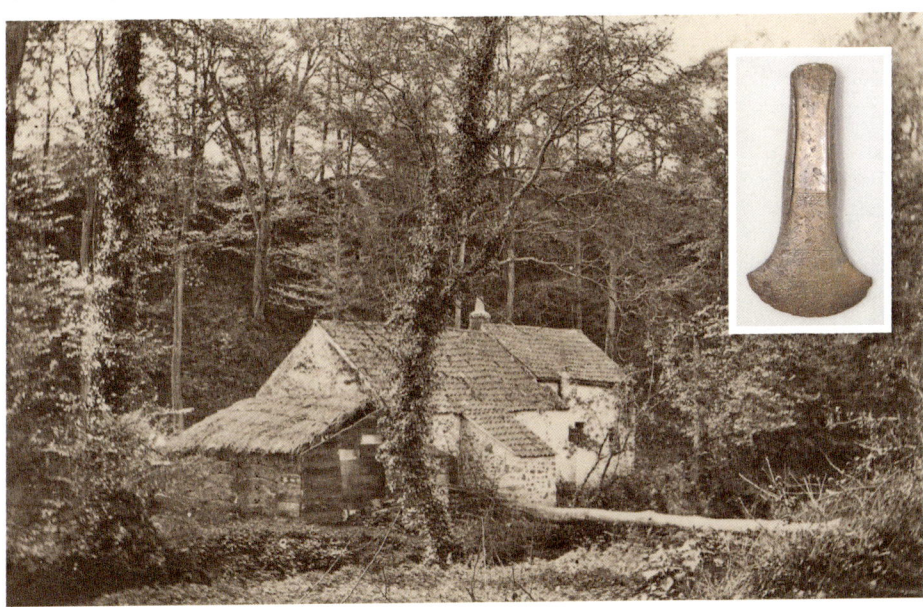

Walk 5

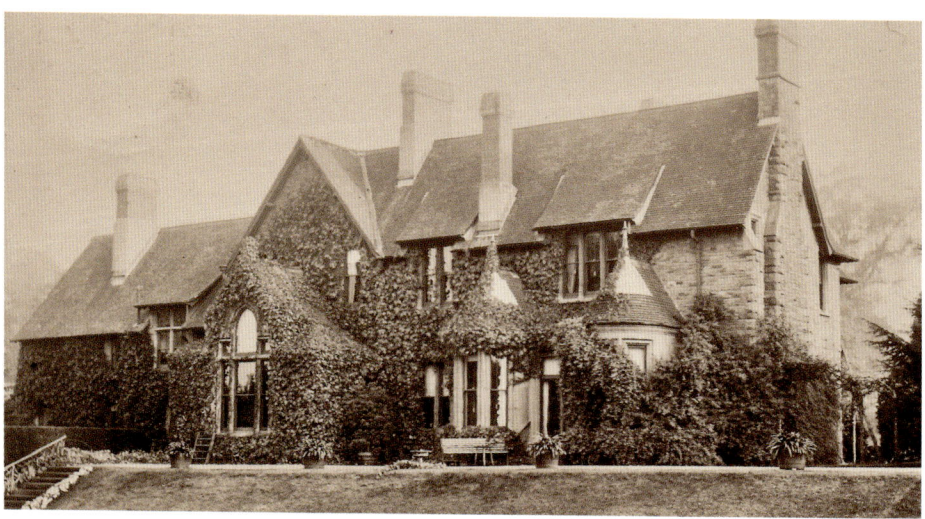

'I Think it a Pretty Little Place'

This was Rockwell, Lawrence Weston, in 1906, when lived in by Mrs William Harford. Situated just north of King's Weston Road, its considerable grounds were comfortably sandwiched between the Greenhill Plantation and Fernhill. It sat high above the village with its lawns and gardens terraced down the hillside and enjoyed stunning panoramic views of the Severn. The photograph shows the handsome northern, garden façade. Built in the 1870s for the wealthy ironmonger Alderman Reginald Butterworth, it housed his considerable young family and a large indoor staff of eight. Rockwell was well placed and within easy reach of both Henbury and Shirehampton. Grove Road ran over the down and its northern branch emerged near Rockwell, giving access to Bowden's Fields and the Dingle. The lodge – once occupied by the gardener – and coach house still survive in Rockwell Avenue but Bellhouse Walk, alas, now covers the site of the demolished house.

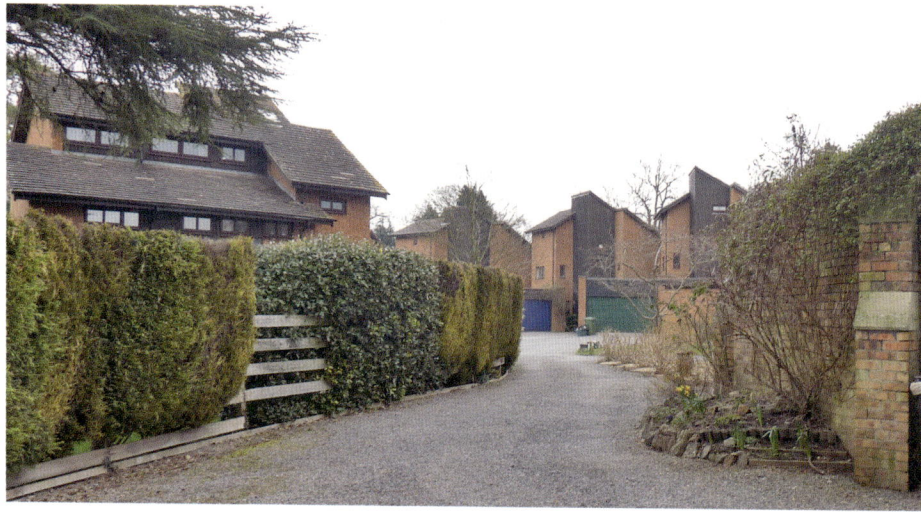

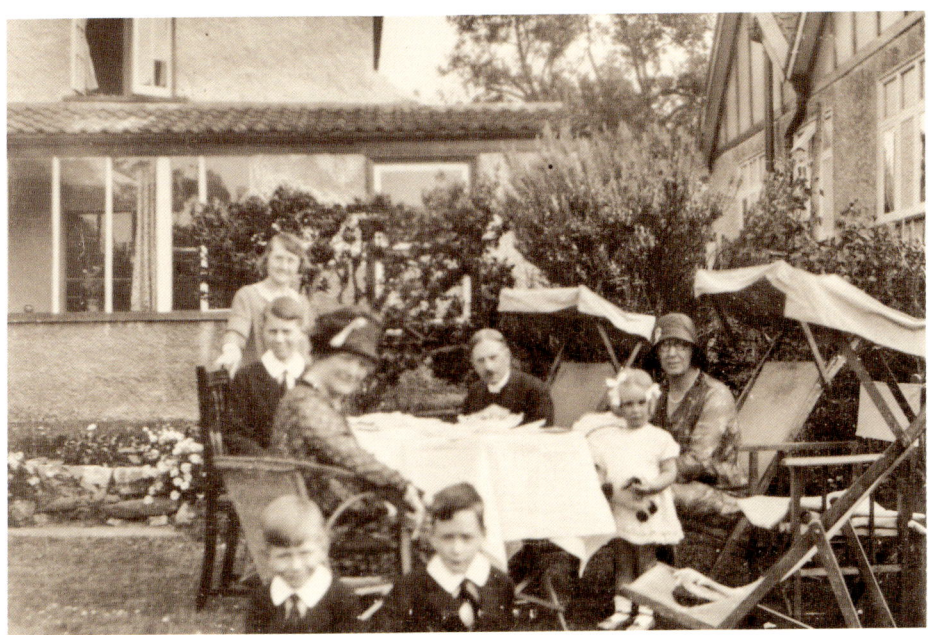

Alfresco Dining in Lawrence Weston

The Revd Frank and Norma Walters (*née* Sargent) with friends at Hillsley, Chapel Lane, Lawrence Weston on 8 June 1930. The sidewall of Lorna Doone, the neighbouring half-timbered and double-gabled bungalow, appears to the right. The old village of Lawrence Weston centred about the single access Chapel Lane and reached to King's Weston Lane. The Methodist chapel stood in the former, and nearby the Mason's Arms and some cottages. Sadly, The Mason's Arms closed and the attractive building was demolished in 2010 after repeated vandalism. It had been converted around 1860 from two houses in a terrace of six that were built in an orchard after 1772. Apart from agriculture, hessian and rope-making for the docks was a local industry. Although now swamped by the council estate, a few original buildings still survive. The cottage, Hillsley, survives in good condition, but neighbouring Lorna Doone is now sadly gutted and overgrown.

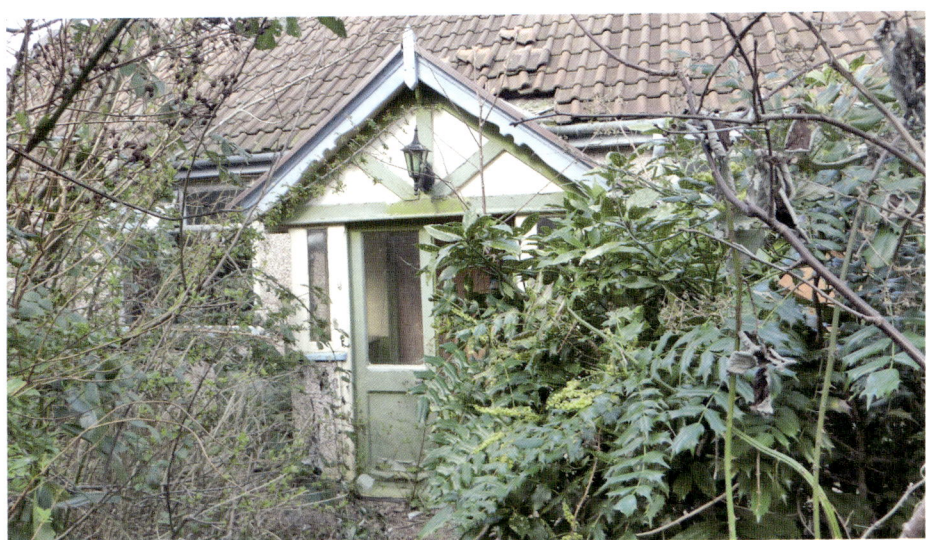

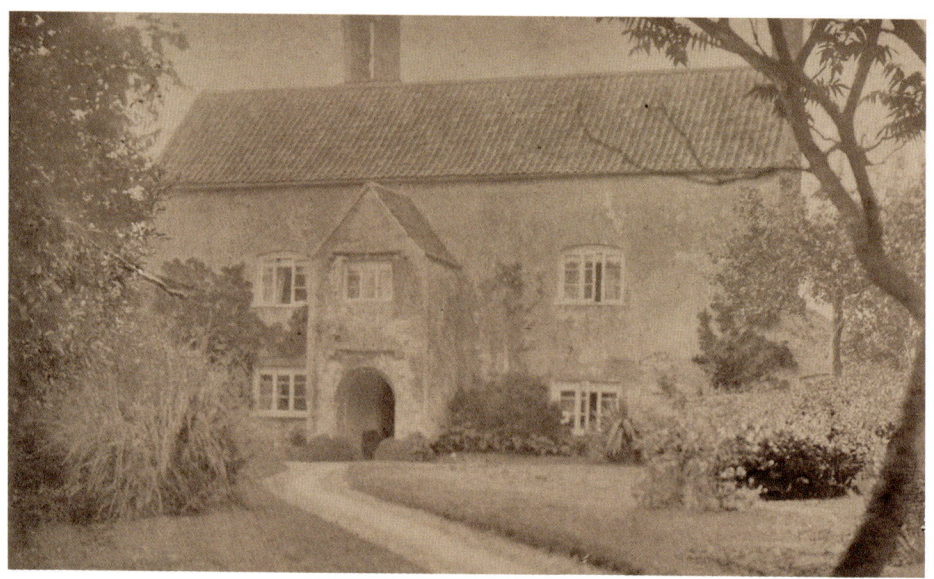

'Take Tea with Me on My Birthday ... 15th September'

In 1910, little Alice Hannah Hignell sent this view of her home, Lawrence Weston farmhouse, as an invitation to her Aunt and Uncle Squire of Shirehampton. A Gloucestershire farming family, the Hignells had farmed on and off at Lawrence Weston Farm since the 1860s, and Alice's father, Clement, had been there since 1908. In 1917 the family moved to Norton Farmhouse, Henbury, where they remained until 1951. The seventeenth-century Lawrence Weston farmhouse stood near the corner of Long Cross and Lawrence Weston Road where the present Youth Centre now stands. In 1946 Lawrence Weston's inhabitants were among the first to be served with compulsory purchase orders for the building of new estates. The original plan praised this 'charming' building, intending to preserve it and other houses, together with the area's rural character. The farmhouse's needless demolition in the 1950s robbed the estate of yet another link with its past.

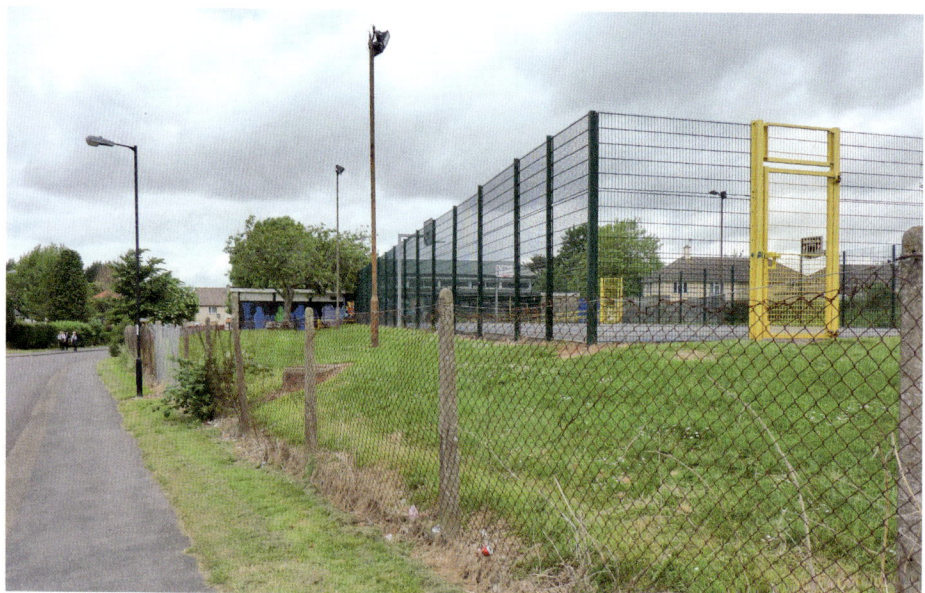

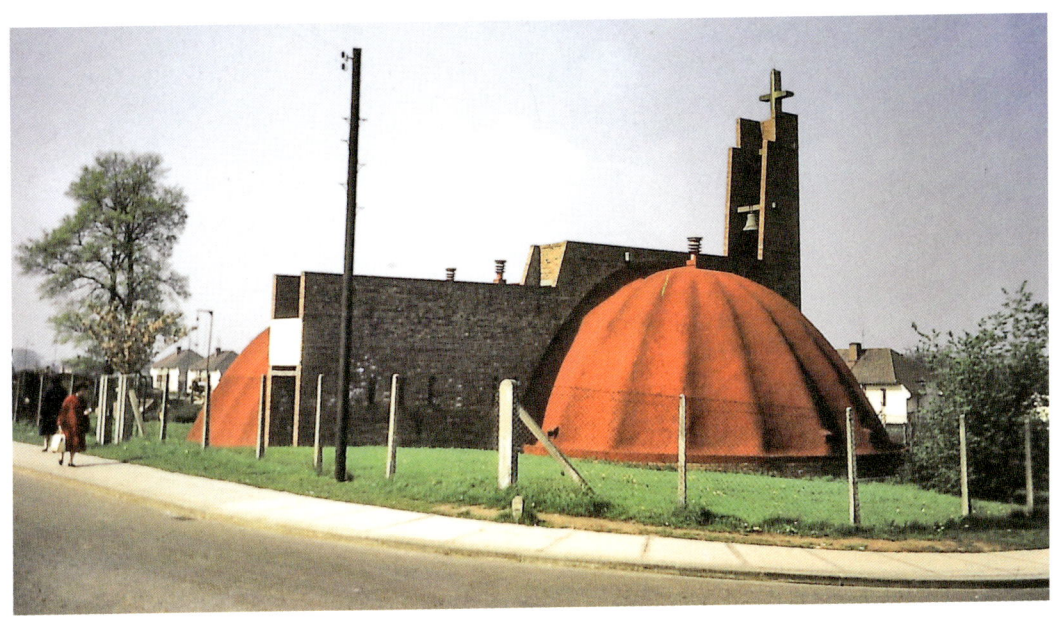

God, Community and 'The Jelly Mould'

The lack of a spiritual centre on the new Lawrence Weston estate led to the building of the church of Christ the King with St Peter, a remarkable temporary structure (seen here from Stile Acres) that was consecrated by the Bishop of Bristol on 16 September 1950. As the first communal building built on the estate, it became the focal point of the new community, with all of its associated activities. Designed by Burrough & Hannam, it cost only £6,000, being constructed by the Ctesiphon technique, whereby a timber form, covered with hessian, had layers of concrete poured over it resulting in self-supporting arches similar in appearance to the Arch of Khosrau in ancient Ctesiphon. A nave and side-aisle completed the building. Known locally as 'The Jelly Mould', bus conductors also referred to it as 'Westminster Abbey'. It was replaced in 1962 by J. Ralph Edwards' less verbosely dedicated St Peter's church.

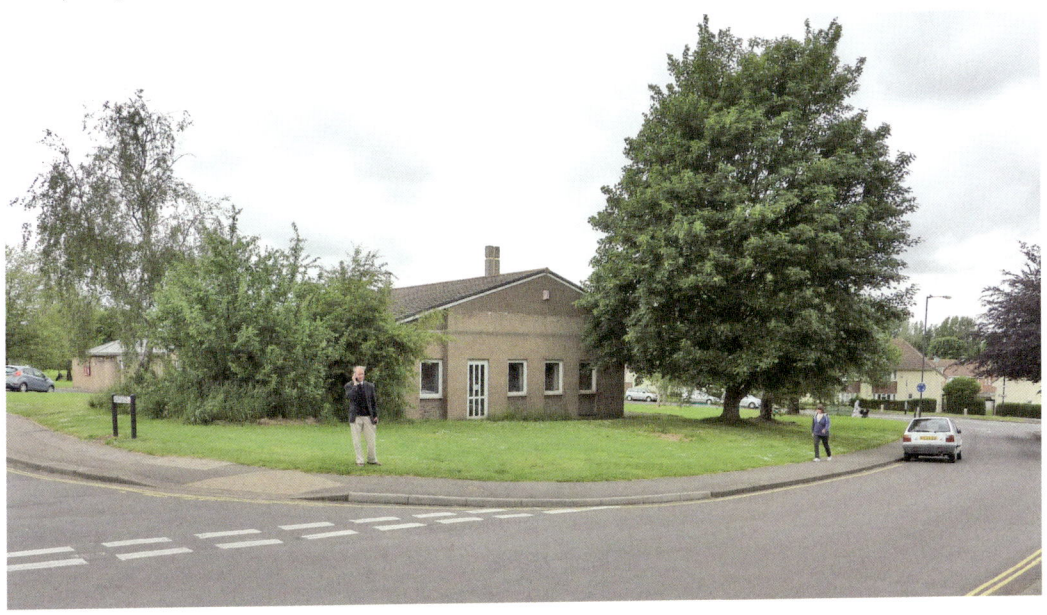

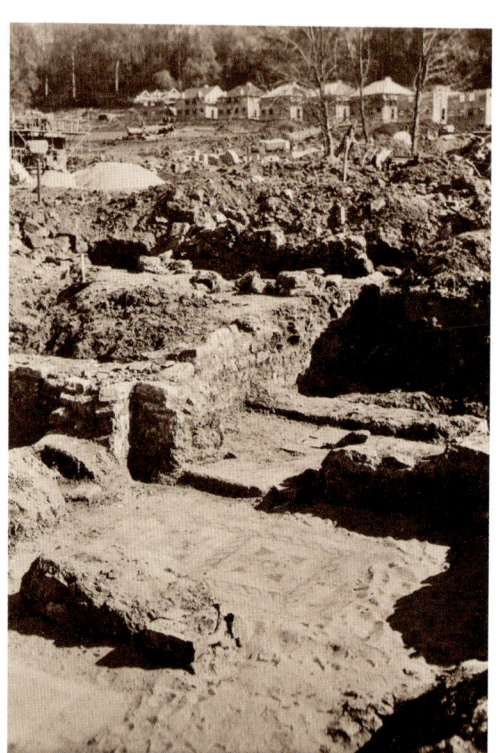

New Homes for Old

Building Lawrence Weston's housing estate at King's Weston in 1947 uncovered two important Roman buildings. Road building unfortunately destroyed part of the complex and obfuscated the complete plans of the excavated eastern building and its earlier unexcavated western neighbour. The excavated house boasted high-quality mosaics, such as appear in the 1948 photograph of its baths. Another pavement, shown in colour, has unique designs suggesting a rare third-century date when few mosaics are known from Britannia. The villa probably had two storeys and remains of stone sideboards and large columns suggest architectural pretensions. Romano-British settlements occurred on both sides of the King's Weston Down, especially in the Lawrence Weston area. Cribbs Causeway is possibly a survival of the Roman road from Gloucester to Seamills. Probably the earliest printed record of 'Cribs Causey' (i.e. Crib's stoney way) was located by the author in *The Oracle* newspaper of 21 May 1748.

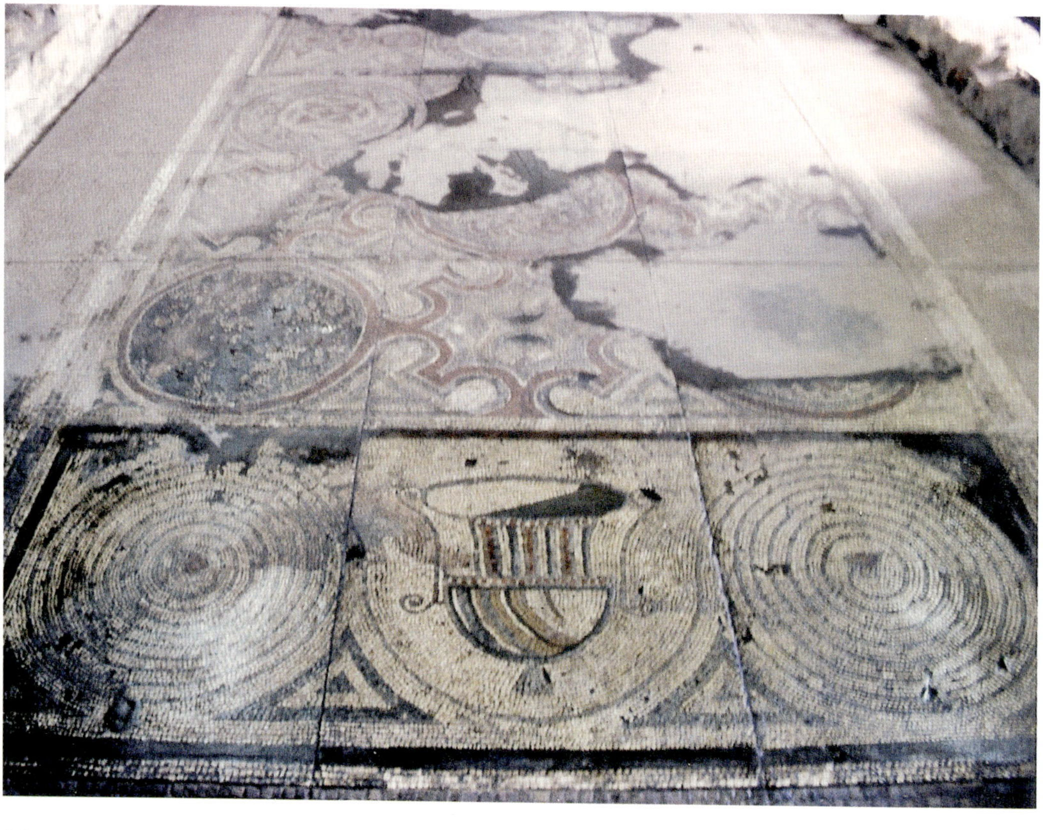

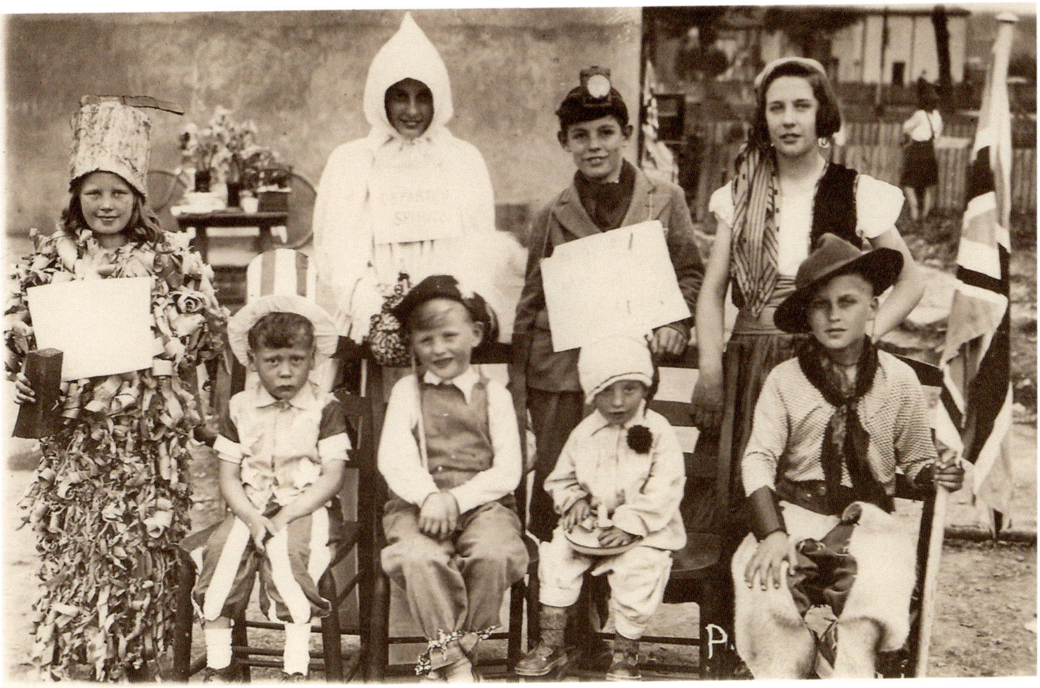

Victory in Europe and in Avonmouth Road, 1945

Children of Avonmouth Road at the VE celebratory party held by that neighbourhood in a small field that is now part of the Portway roundabout. Behind the group stand 148–106 Avonmouth Road, also fated to disappear for the roundabout. Beyond are the last houses on the south side of the road at the junction with The Portway. Four-year-old Alan Anstee impersonates Uncle Sam, and is joined by A Chip off the old Block, Departed Spirits, Dick Whittington, Wee Willie Winkie, a Bevan Boy and two unknowns. These houses, and many others in Avonmouth's St Andrews Road, Poole and Marsh Streets, were built by W. H. Martin between 1934 and 1937. In 1963, Marjory Anstee and her son Robert from 130 Avonmouth Road pose in their garden, which was then backed by allotments and Shirehampton Farm's fields. The house was compulsorily purchased in 1964 and demolished for the motorway approach road.

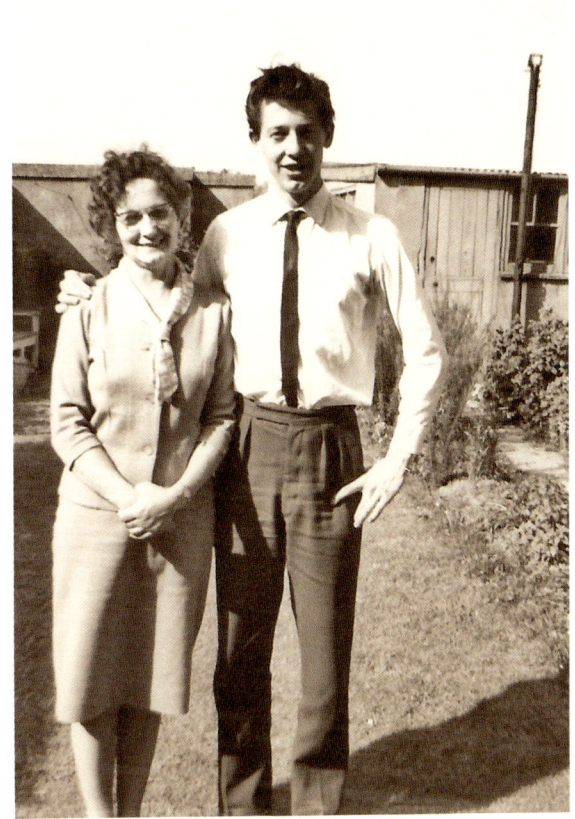

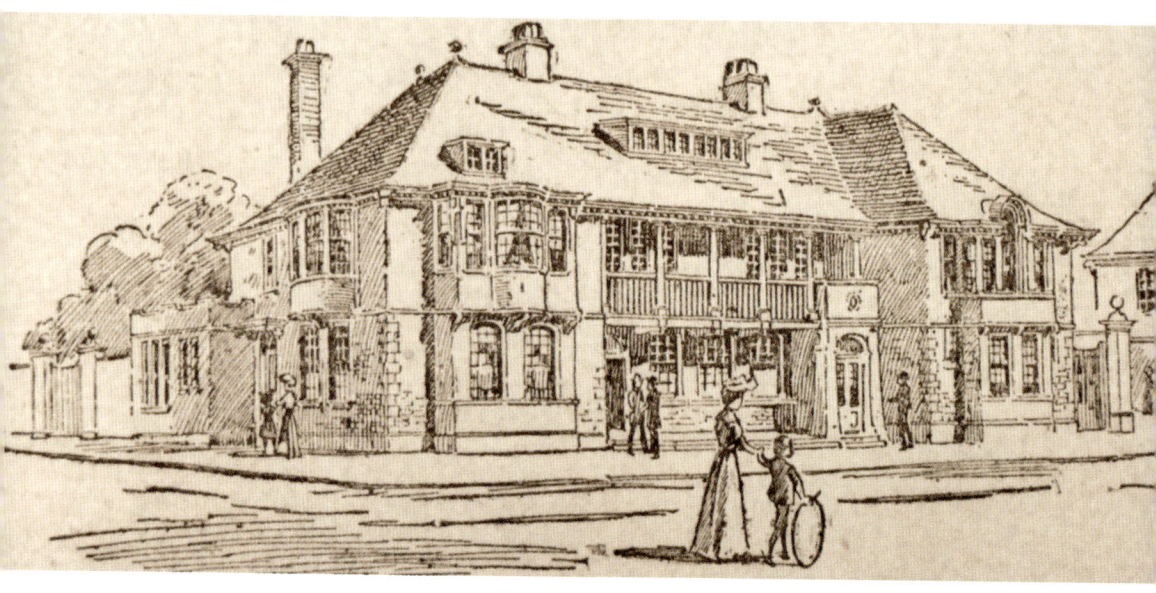

'The Miles Arms ... Suggestive of the Estate Office'

The *Bristol Observer* of 17 October 1903 mentions the imminent construction of the Miles Arms in Shirehampton Road. Bligh Bond had already designed the Avonmouth Hotel in 1899, but now he approached the new hostelry's exterior in the spirit of his Estate Office. The interior plans were by Messrs Paul & James, architects to the instigators, the Gloucestershire Public House Company. The materials were intended to be much the same as those used for the Estate Office but, possibly for economy, brick was substituted for stone during the construction of the ground floor. The striking inset and columned loggia seen in Samuel Loxton's drawing of the projected building was much admired. The hotel offered 'private sitting rooms' to its discerning guests. The building happily survives, although with unfortunate 'conservatorial' additions to its façade. The loggia unfortunately lost two columns to rot before the 1980s and its balusters have been restored upside down.

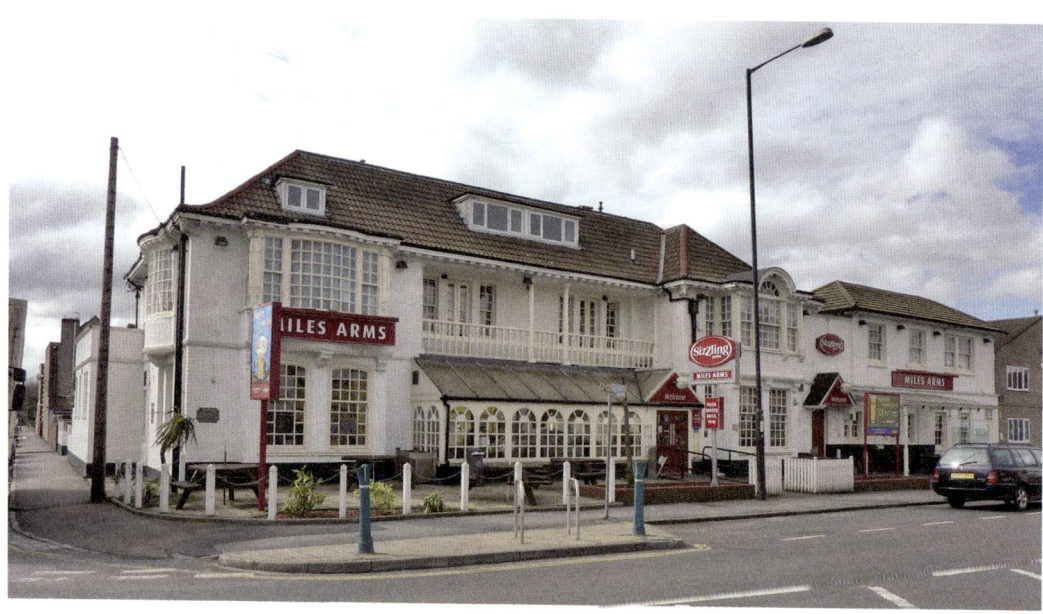

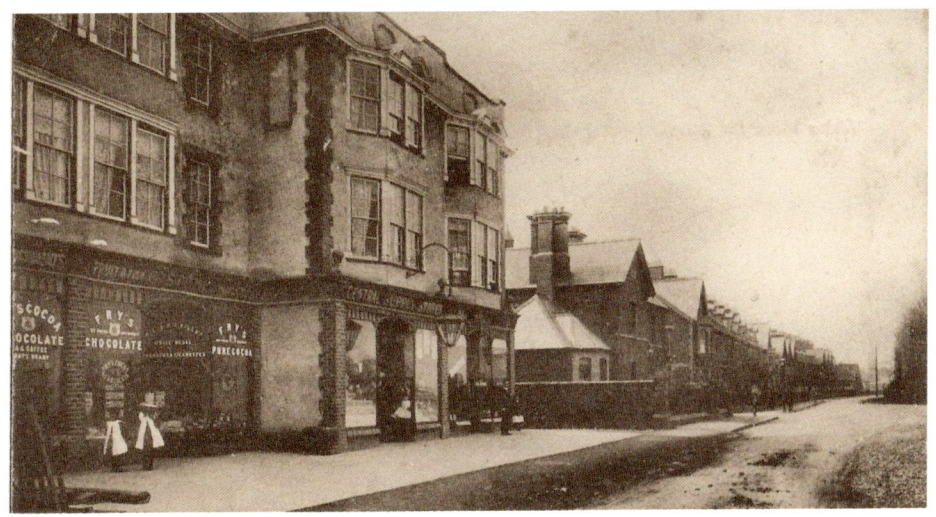

Arts and Crafts in the Avonmouth Road

Richmond Buildings, another of Frederick Bligh Bond's shopping terraces. Earlier than the eclectic and pompous one, at the corner of Gloucester Road, that was soon complemented in materials and rooftop urns by the grand houses in St Andrews Road. Bligh Bond's work riddles Avonmouth, and much of it goes unrecognised and catalogued under the builder rather than architect. Examples may be seen in Green Lane, Farr, Davis and Cook Streets, Portview Road as well as Avonmouth Road. Richmond Buildings once housed the Central Supply Stores. Buff roughcast stucco contrasted with red brick and white paintwork on its façade. Broken pediments topped the canted bay windows, with their Georgian-style glazing. The modern photograph is taken from Smyths Close between the entrance tower of the 1915 bus depot on the left and the Neo-Georgian police station on the right. It shows the central part of the terrace with its surprising pyramid roof.

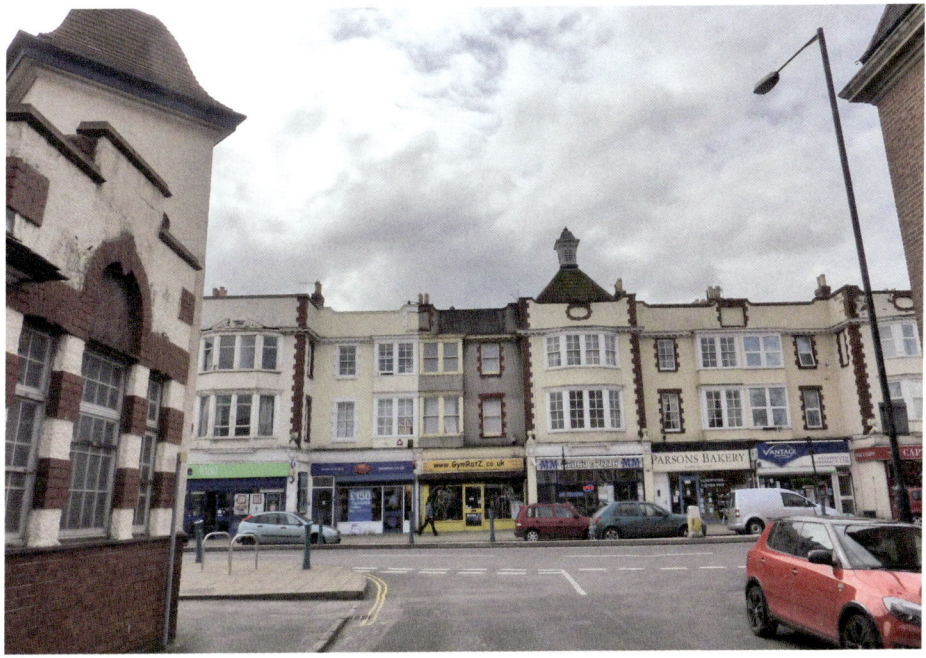

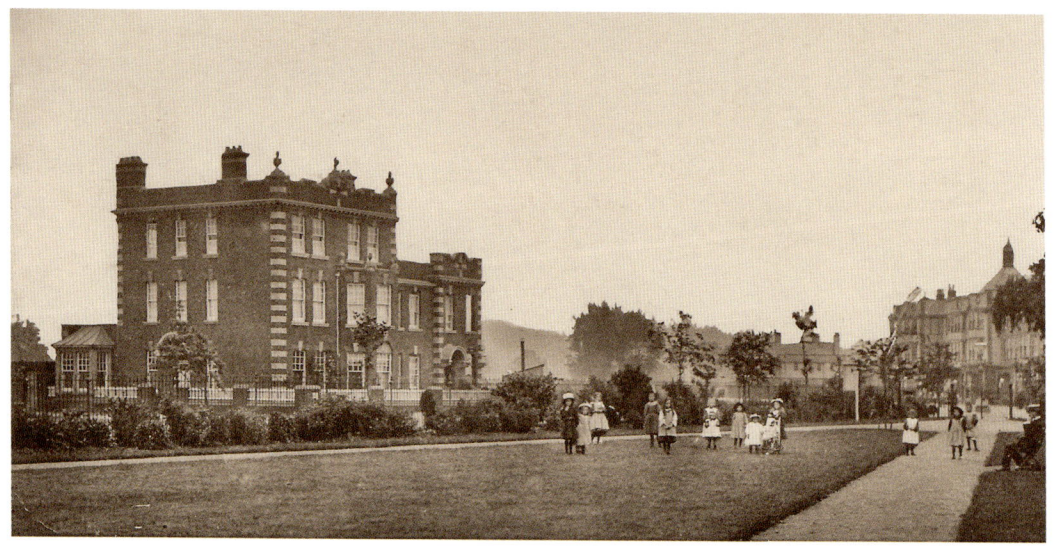

'Girls Come Out to play', Avonmouth Park, 1912

In 1905, Philip Napier Miles donated 2½ acres of Avonmouth land for 'a public pleasure ground'. Bristol Corporation duly enclosed the roughly triangular space with railings and expended £1,000 on layout and planting. A circular bandstand dominated the central walkway. Frederick Bligh Bond's impressive Neo-Georgian houses overlooked the park, hinting at Napier Miles's unfulfilled ambitions of attracting a grander class of resident to his village. Here they are still under construction but the final large block was never built. A special effort was made in Avonmouth to provide 'spick and span, light and bright dwellings' for workers. Orange brick with white joints and gardens with white palings were *de rigueur*. In Davis Street, Bligh Bond experimented with flat vulcanite roofs on his 'cottages'. Christopher Penn's 1993 photograph shows the late 1890s Stride and Davis middle-class villas on Avonmouth Road with the M5 Avonmouth Bridge in the distance.

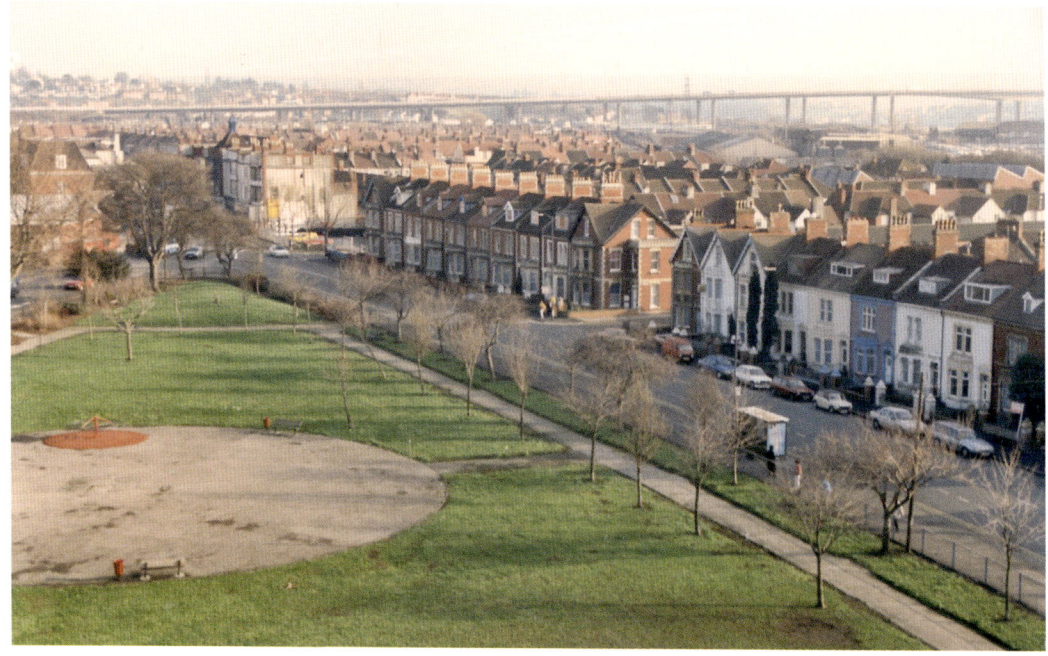

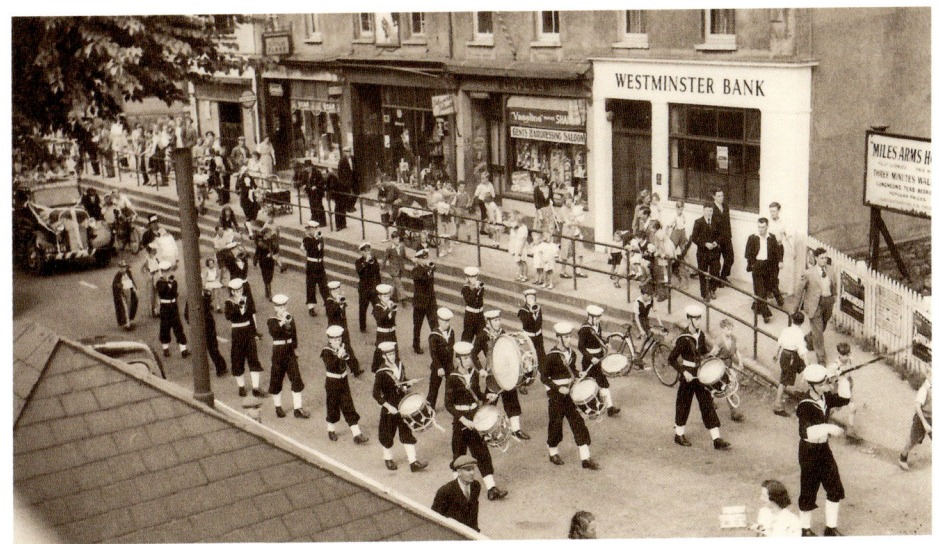

Bustling Gloucester Road

The Boys' Brigade Band leads a carnival procession down Gloucester Road and over the level crossing in the 1940s. Children in fancy dress follow behind or ride in a lorry with its bonnet beribboned like the Union Jack. In a sad contrast with today, the road, leading to the docks entrance, is thronged and the shops busy. The Westminster Bank later expanded its premises before finally closing. The reduction in manpower at the docks, together with changing shopping patterns, adversely affected this road, which dates from the 1870s and was one of the earliest in the village. The raised walkway was reputedly to protect against flooding, but may actually have been intended for a promenade. The Royal Hotel and matching shops seen mid-distance in Christopher Penn's photograph of 1993 were designed by the Shirehampton builder George Heard between 1880 and 1892. Bligh Bond's flamboyant, vulcanite-roofed, corner shopping terrace appears left foreground.

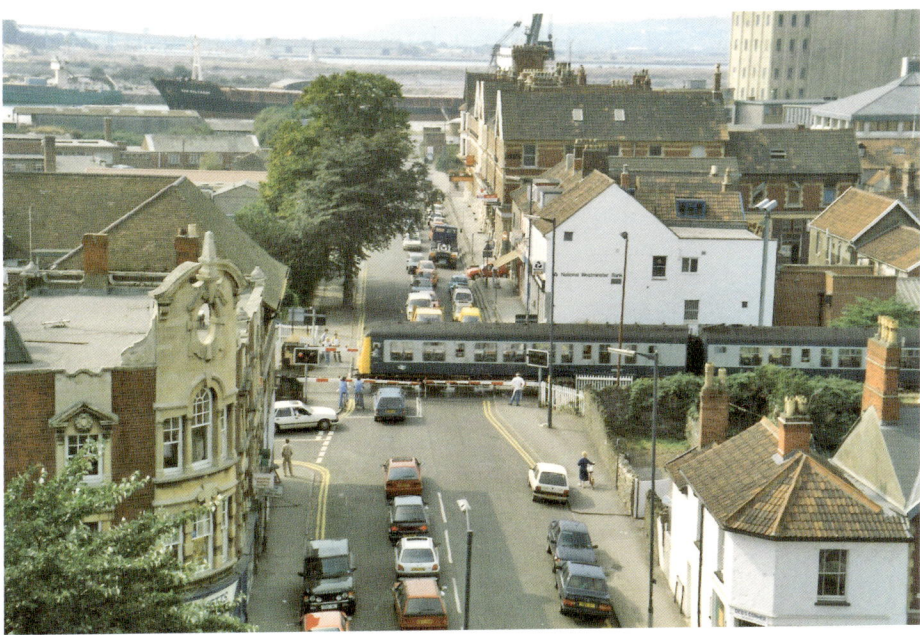

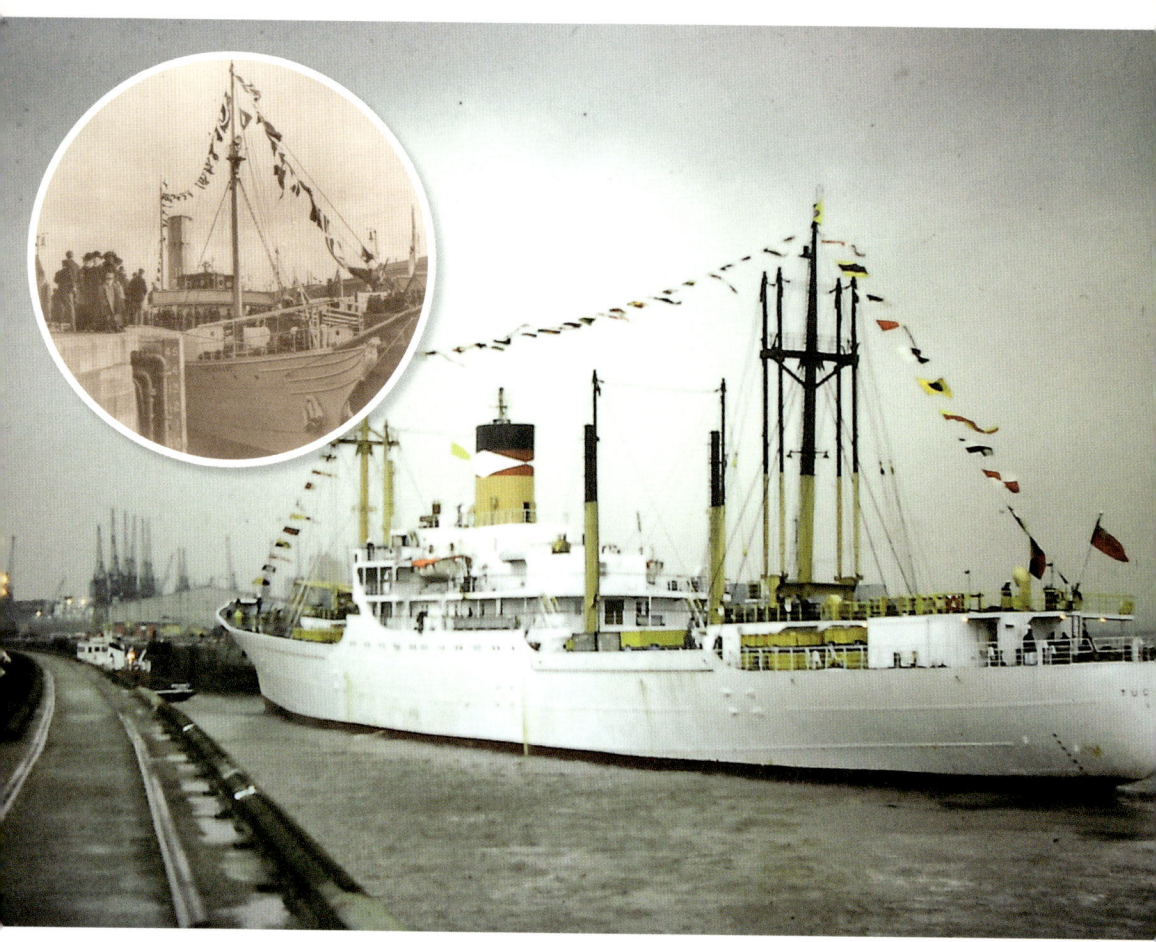

Yes, We Have Some Bananas!

On 19 March 1901, the SS *Port Morant*, the first of a specially built fleet of banana boats owned by the Elder Dempster Company, returned to Avonmouth bearing a cargo of 20,000 bananas and 14,000 boxes of oranges. The firm had won a new subsidised contract to establish a weekly mail and passenger service and to develop the economy of Jamaica by returning with fruit. This was the start of the banana trade in Britain, and for the first time the fruit became popularly available and the subject of comic songs. The significance of the event meant that the children of Avonmouth School were taken to the docks to greet the arrival. The banana boat arrivals became a popular attraction. Elder Dempster eventually became Fyffes, and Avonmouth prospered through the hugely prestigious and profitable trade. On 15 February 1976 the *Tucurinca* arrived to celebrate the seventy-fifth anniversary of the trade.

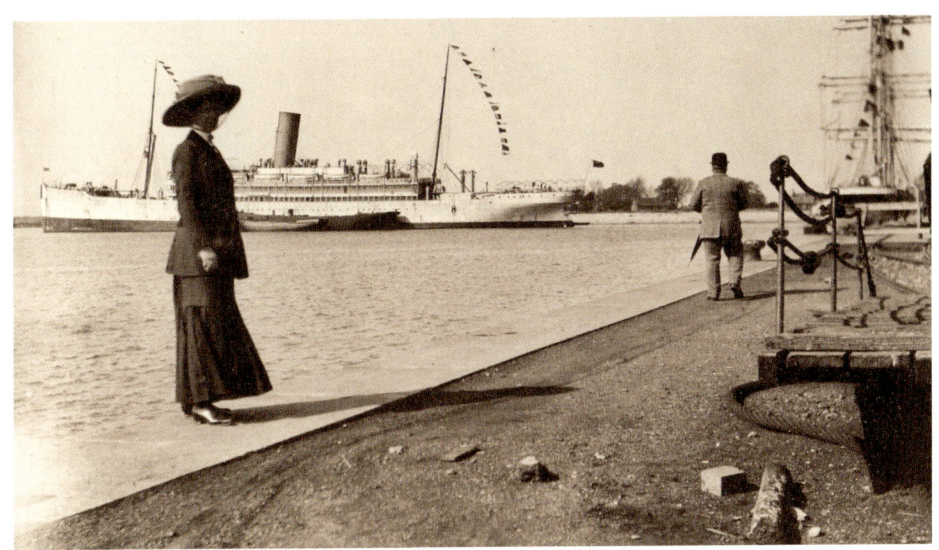

Ruby in a Breeze, Avonmouth, 4 May 1911

Ruth 'Ruby' Sargent at Royal Edward Dock, Avonmouth, one breezy Thursday afternoon in 1911. One of the fleet of beautiful liners of the West India Imperial Mail Service Company is moored at the north-eastern side of the dock behind her standing figure, having previously unloaded its cargo elsewhere. The weekly service from Kingston, Jamaica, brought passengers, mail and bananas to Avonmouth's East Pier for distribution. The Avonmouth Hotel and a couple of navvies' huts appear distantly to the liner's right. The lower photograph shows HMS *Bristol*, a town-class light cruiser that was commissioned in 1910, visiting Avonmouth in 1911. The ship is open to visitors and they flocked to such events in their thousands over a weekend. The nation was inordinately proud of the Royal Navy's 'Rule of the Waves'. HMS *Bristol* was the first British ship to see action in the First World War. She was scrapped in 1921.

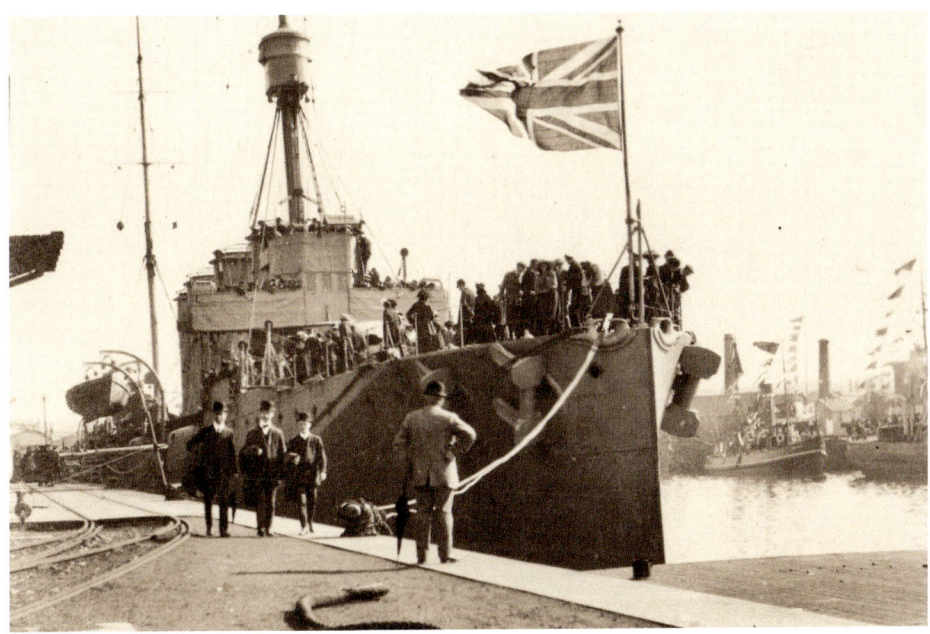

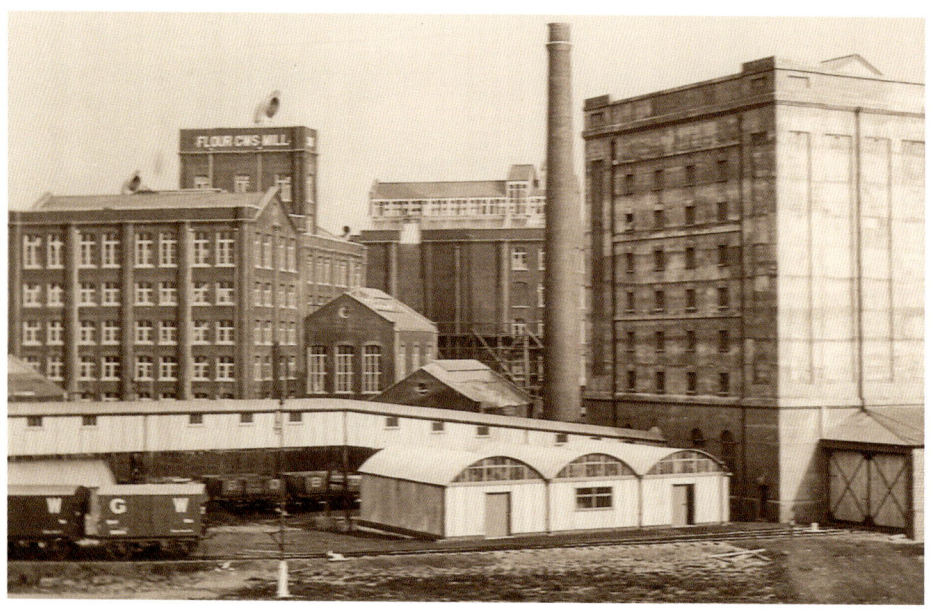

C. W. S. Flour Mills, Avonmouth, 1920

The Cooperative Wholesale Society flour mills were founded at Avonmouth after 1885 and converted imported and home-grown grain into flour. The handsome mill building on the right opened in 1910 and was built of reinforced concrete using the system employed by Francois Hennebique and promoted by his British agent L. G. Mouchel. The year 1897 had seen the first fully reinforced concrete building in Britain in the form of Weaver's Mill at Swansea. By 1911, over 1,070 structures had been erected in Britain using Hennebique's system. Later owned by Spillers, part of the Avonmouth mill complex was demolished in 1976 as redundant. The fine, severely Neo-Classical, concrete building, with its glazed lettering, added much that was striking to the Avonmouth skyline and might have been converted to new uses. Unfortunately, concrete cancer made it unsafe and it was demolished together with its companion in 2013.

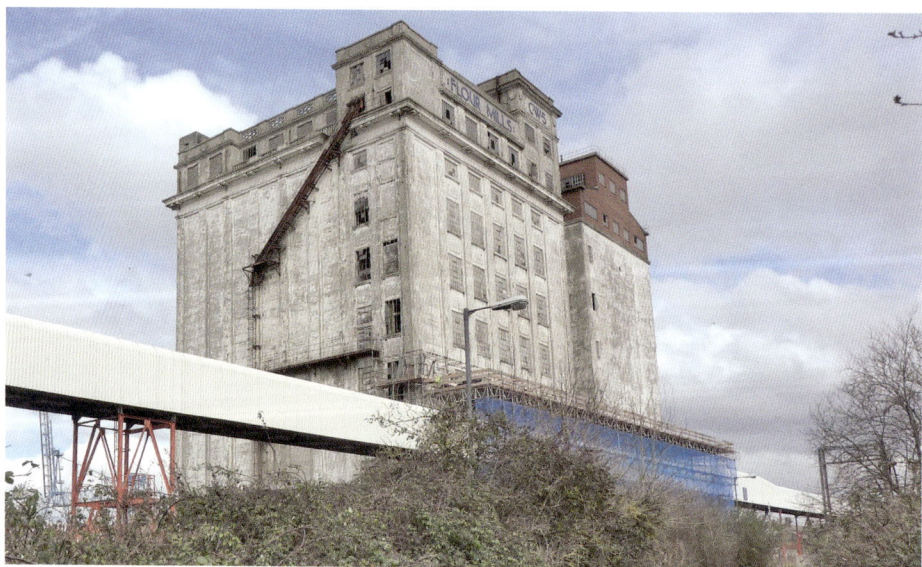